AF352662

and the Reflecting Realities reports generated by the Centre for Literacy in Primary Education in the United Kingdom. I focus here on the CCBC statistics, as these are more indicative of Disney's own cultural and national context, though there is a conversation to be had more widely about diversity in the larger Anglophone world and the legacies of cultural imperialism and colonialism.

Looking at the 2018 infographic, we find that 50 percent of children's books published in 2018 feature white protagonists, 27 percent feature animals or nonhumans, and 10 percent feature African or African American protagonists, with Asian Pacific Islander/Asian Pacific American, Latinx, and American Indian/First Nation protagonists coming in at 7, 5, and 1 percent, respectively (Huykc and Dahlen). Although the data here concerns picture books in general and not Disney films in particular, these numbers reflect trends that are also applicable to Disney's retellings of fairy-tale and folkloresque narratives, especially those that were produced as feature-length animated films.[4] But even though there is a body of scholarship that problematizes the shortcomings of ethnic and racialized depictions across the Disney oeuvre at large, two things remain both true and challenging about trying to problematize attempts at equitable representation. The first is that, though it is becoming easier to identify poor examples of where the attempt to provide a better narrative does not live up to best or stated intentions, it is impossible to provide a singular definition of what it would mean to achieve true pluralistic and multivocal representation on a variety of axes. Second, and similarly, in essence a study like this or the others mentioned needs to make absence visible and, on some level, quantifiable. It must ask about who and what is not seen even in fictional and fantasy spaces and draw deliberate connections to the historical and cultural contexts of production rather than looking at the text or film as a closed system. It holds at its center the idea of the single voice, or the single story, and questions constantly how representation might be yet improved instead of settling for someone else's "good enough."

---

4   I presented these numbers in terms of Disney in more specific detail in a plenary lecture at the conference "Picturing Otherness: A Historical Perspective on Diversity in Children's Literature (20th–21st Century)," held at the University of Hamburg in 2023.

Even, or perhaps especially, when dealing with works that are quintessentially fantasies, racialized depictions reflect truths about the systems within which they are produced, and after all, as Maria Sachiko Cecire has observed, "The Walt Disney Company has literally invested in the idea that fantasy, including pseudo-medieval fantasy, is an important aspect of contemporary adult self-making that enables encounters with the therapeutic child for emotional growth" (Cecire, 242). This self-making is intertwined with, among other things, the availability of accurate reflections of culture and identity, including racialized and ethnic diversity on screen. As Helen Young notes in her work on race and popular fantasy literature, these stories are "never *just* stories but are always connect[ed] to people—bodies—through writing, and reading" (Young, 10), or, in the case of Disney, viewing. This observation is as equally true regarding the "habits of Whiteness" (10–12) at play in fantasy literature, such as that penned by Tolkien and his contemporaries, as it is of the works created by Disney, both during Walt's lifetime and long after he no longer wielded direct influence over the company's creative processes. Such "habits of Whiteness," Young observes, "simultaneously influence who can be present, and what is seen, thought, and done, . . . creating patterns of bodies and spaces alike" (11). Criticism that has focused on problematizing Disney's approaches to diversity in both Renaissance productions and earlier productions has often taken the form of case studies that address a single film or a handful of films rather than presenting a holistic approach to the patterns that can be seen by examining decades at a time.[5] The long view I use here is what I believe will make patterns in both representation and misrepresentation more visible.

5   These case studies have been collated into edited collections, including E. Bell et al.'s *From Mouse to Mermaid: The Politics of Film, Gender, and Culture* (1995); Budd and Kirsch's *Rethinking Disney: Private Control, Public Dimensions* (2005); Ayres's *The Emperor's Old Groove: Decolonizing Disney's Magic Kingdom* (2013 [2003]); Cheu's *Diversity in Disney Films: Critical Essays on Race, Ethnicity, Gender, Sexuality, and Disability* (2013); and Roberts's *Recasting the Disney Princess in an Era of New Media and Social Movements* (2020).

Disney's Imaging: Is It All in the Eyes of the Beholder?

In the 1991 *Beauty and the Beast*, the animated fairy tale that followed on from and surpassed the success of the 1989 *Little Mermaid*, the opening frame tale explains the Beast's transformation. The film's gaze then shifts to introduce Belle, as seen through the eyes of her neighbors in the provincial town she lives near and through the opening song, "Belle." If one pays close attention to the animated world building, there is something interesting at play with language and presumed knowledge. If we consider the different vendors' street signs, all of them are in French (e.g., Boulangerie, Au Petit Chapeau, L'Argent), except for the Bookseller's. The Bookseller is the one person in this sequence who, amid the townsfolk's own (more practically minded) work, takes an earnest interest in Belle's own interests beyond the courtesy of asking how she is. This creates an interesting situation of knowledge formation and even constructs belonging; the language is othering, even though the language of image helps to provide context clues to the setting. But the primarily American audience will recognize "Bookseller" as something that stands out from the unfamiliar; it catches the gaze. Similarly, the lyrics of the song, including the conversational interludes between Belle and, first, the Baker and then the Bookseller, are meant to also help catch the eye, or the ear, of the audience, for they invoke a certain narrative familiarity. Belle starts to tell the Baker about the book she is reading, which has a "beanstalk and an ogre" before she is cut off; a knowing audience recognizes this story as "Jack in the Beanstalk," another point of familiarity built between Belle and the audience. Similar familiarity is invoked when Belle is telling both the Bookseller and the sheep at the fountain about her favorite book: "Far off places, daring swordfights, magic spells, a prince in disguise." Even if we do not know the details of this fairy tale in progress, a knowing audience will recognize these as invocations of fairy tale at large. The familiarity of the stories is the point; we know, on rewatching especially, that the story that is her favorite, the one that she tells the sheep about at the fountain, is the one that she herself is about to live. The familiarity and reiteration become the point, a constant priming of the audience for a story that they just might think they know; they set an expectation for wonder and magic that this ordinary but different girl is about to be swept up in, and therefore so too will the audience. There is much more to be considered about text, books, and narrative transmission with regard to this particular narrative and this character, but, for the sake of this book, I want to focus on narrative as institution and how representation itself becomes institutionalized within the Disney context. In this scene, first released in 1991, Disney is telling audiences in no small way what its "normal" is, despite the potential, later realized, for wider storytelling and more global expansion in the works created within a decade of *Beauty and the Beast* being released.

Considered alongside the long history of predominantly white representation in painting and theatrical, operatic, and illustrated productions of fairy-tale and folkloresque narratives, such data points to the much wider problem of institutionalized whiteness as normative across Europe and the Anglophone world; it has persisted for centuries, despite a history of interactions with and explorations of African, Asian, and Indigenous peoples and the rise of multicultural societies since at least the early twentieth century. This does not excuse Disney, however. The prevailing discourse at the time of the Disney Renaissance about problems concerning diversity positioned the problem overall as a lack of *image*, which is what Nancy Larrick's and Rudine Sims Bishop's works focused on in their critiques of children's media. In this context it becomes easier to understand Disney's efforts in the 1990s in terms of slightly more diverse representation at the level of the image only, without deconstruction of the surrounding issues of hegemonic culture. One key example of this involves how characters were racialized and gendered as heroes and villains in the 1992 animated *Aladdin*. Although Aladdin and Jasmine are darker skinned than previous prince and princess pairs, they are notably lighter skinned than other characters, such as the palace guards or Jafar. Then-president of feature animation Peter Schneider noted that Tom Cruise was the inspiration for Aladdin's features and mannerisms (qtd. in Macleod, 182); the studio also deployed accent-based type casting so that the "good" or "bad" characters could be distinguished through their speech patterns, "by giving the former American accents and the latter clipped British or vaguely foreign intonations" (Macleod, 182). The guards also notably have exaggerated features, especially noses, and wear turbans, and Jafar's effeminate villainy includes a healthy dose of guy-liner, a long flowing robe, and an overall silhouette reminiscent of Maleficent from the 1959 *Sleeping Beauty*.

These aspects lean into an orientalism that cannot be separated from the Gulf War context at the time of production, but they also received significant pushback from the American-Arab Anti-Discrimination Committee (Wise, 105).

The orientalism at play in *Aladdin* also reared its head in 1998's *Mulan*. Specifically, the Huns were noticeably darker skinned than Mulan and the other heroic Chinese characters, and Chi-Fu was cast as a stereotypical effeminate Asian man, whose masculinity is in direct contrast with the defining of masculine values that underpin the narrative progression.[6] And yet both *Aladdin* and *Mulan* were lauded as steps forward into a brave new world for Disney, with Mulan's production also going out of its way to highlight all the research that went into the intention of portraying an "accurate" and "authentic" ancient China. But at their heart, both films highlight the core problem in the approach to diversification taken during the Disney Renaissance: Culture and cultural reproduction cannot happen in a vacuum, and there is so much more to accurate or authentic or believable representation than just changing the landscapes or source material or even the color of the animated characters' skin. To move past that surface-level attempt at imagining a more diverse world, the right stakeholders have to be in the room at the time of creation or hold enough power to speak back to the overall production machine.

Looking back at the Disney Renaissance with several decades' hindsight, the "diverse" narratives presented in this period were in fact normative narrative schema dressed in the trappings of otherness. Especially looking at the characterizations of Mulan, Pocahontas, and Jasmine—the three "diverse" Disney princesses of this era—what we see are three "rebellious teenagers" refusing to conform to the social norms of their othered cultures. Ancient China, the quasi–Middle East of Agrabah, and Colonial North America's Jamestown become pastiches of places where the preferences of US-centric ideals—independence, individualism, and freedom—can become enacted in de facto "other" spaces set up as oppositional to the world that Disney's target audience knows. It would not be in the company's interests to deconstruct hegemonic power dynamics in its narratives, as those very same dynamics are intertwined with the

---

6 For a more in-depth discussion of this, see Anjirbag, "Mulan."

corporation's own power. Nor did Disney need to in order to believably present the idea of a more diverse Magic Kingdom to its audiences. In effect, because the discourse surrounding diversity in media was centered on the concept of physical appearance alone, the solution could simply be a matter of adjusting the images projected rather than addressing the problems more deeply or understanding that they even needed a deeper fix.

The commodification of multiculturalism, beyond commodification of culture alone, does not happen in a vacuum. Disney's productions are oriented within various contexts, including both the corporation's own shaping of its context and the wider cultural and media spheres that surround the dissemination of its intellectual products. In addition, viewers are oriented around the space(s) that Disney occupies in its various iterations. As Sara Ahmed explores in *Queer Phenomenology*:

> The word "occupy" allows us to link the question of inhabiting or residing within space; to work, or even to having an identity through work (an occupation); to time (to be occupied with); to holding something; and to taking possession of something as a thing. How are we occupied with objects? How does an occupation orientate us toward some objects and, in that towardness, to some ways of living over others? How does this orientation take up time as well as space? (Ahmed, 44)

In this case, we might think about occupation from a colonizing sense: How does Disney occupy perception and rewrite space and place to fit its own narratives? How does it rewrite our perceptions and direct us toward certain interpretations or understandings through the net sum of its productions, and what retains perceptual dominance as a "Disney" product and for whom? Who then speaks Disney, sees their self extended by the corporation, or reflects an extension of the intent of the object created by the corporation? Thus understanding how the relationship between transmission of Disney narratives across generations parallels transmission of fairy-tale and folklore narratives makes clearer the impact of Disney's multicultural adaptations beyond the corporation's stated intents. Understanding this parallel also allows for the fact that, like retellings by Perrault, the Grimms, and Angela Carter, Disney versions of fairy-tale narratives are here to stay. Truly, the vast field of criticism and the many fields from which it is conducted affirm this. Even when we criticize Disney, the House of Mouse has our attention, in part because of how well the studio deploys recognizable narrative patterns in which to root perceptions of the brand and its products. As Jessica Tiffin notes regarding her theory of recognition and the fairy tale in relation to Disney:

> Disney fairy-tale films have developed their own, distinctive and instantly recognizable formula, which works in deliberate concord or, at times, dissonance, with the structures of the fairy tale. . . . The Disney formula intersects with and overwrites any kind of narrative its films use, whether popular children's literature (*101 Dalmatians*, *Peter Pan*), folklore (*Robin Hood*), history (*Pocahontas*), or fairy tale. . . . The familiar Disney format is reassuring to children as well as to their parents, who can send children to see Disney films secure in the knowledge that sex and realistic violence will not be on the menu. (Tiffin, 211–12)

That "Disney formula," a term coined by Janet Wasko to describe the formulaic, aesthetic, thematic, and narrative components that constitute what is perceived of as the classic Disney aesthetic (Wasko, 110–19), is in part what could be thought of as the Disney fairy-tale chronotope. The Disney fairy-tale space-time construction can be identified as one that has become its own chronotope, its own kind of fairy-tale narrative. We recognize Disney fairy-tale adaptations as distinct from other fairy tales in terms of the kind of story we know will be related and how it will—uniformly—be different from other, non-Disney adaptations of similar narratives. In his analysis of Disney's place within the wider field of American animation, Paul Wells writes that

> Disney has evolved a production paradigm that in effect renders contemporary ideological and political "specificity" subordinate to the assumptions of Disney's own moral, ethical, cultural and, most importantly, *aesthetic* archetypes. The dominant aspects of this paradigm are encoded caricatural "norms" . . . which undermine, dilute and resist readings of characters and events at a *significantly*

> *specific* politicised and ideological level. Disney has also created
> a mode of "fairytale," which echoes and uses, but does not nec-
> essarily draw on, a literary fairytale tradition, which significantly
> re-locates "contemporary" agendas in a less explicitly certifiable
> social space and time, but nevertheless speaks to contemporary
> idioms. (Wells, 105)

To extend this, understanding Disney narratives as specifically unique in formulaic composition and thus uniquely positioned in their depictions of multiculturalism is further supported by the range of Disney-specific academic criticism that attempts from various angles to deconstruct the intersection of society and culture with the increasing repetition, generation, and prevalence of that formulaic worldview. Furthermore, the ability to identify a particular Disney type of narrative within the broader spectrum of fairy-tale and folkloresque narratives also points to the amount of narrative power concentrated in the corporation and its global reach. This power, combined with the global reach and the impo-sition of a certain type of narrative on whatever it incorporates into the Disney universe, results in a pattern in which the corporation swallows and erases diverse particulars across incorporated narratives and pro-motes "a single story" across various intersections of global societies. In doing so, "making race" or making identity in global context becomes a flattening, a reinterpretation and reorientation of that which Disney's central positioning considers "other."

Intentionally or not, when Disney adapts narratives from other cultures and incorporates representations of Black people, Indigenous people, and other people of color into the Disney universe, the corpora-tion's power and position perpetuate a colonialist and imperialist pattern of "the West," constructing an orientalized or exoticized image of the Other in its depictions of other cultures and ethnicities. Attempts at diverse representation, no matter how much they might be marketed as authentic, need to be rigorously examined from multiple perspectives, primarily the multivocal perspectives of the communities that the corpo-ration claims to depict in specific works of media. This is not just about orientation within Disney space but about how these othered positions are then made to "speak Disney." Clare Bradford's work on language as both a function of narrative construction and a colonizing construct can provide a necessary insight into Disney's deployment of particular narrative constructions. In this case, the language in question is the visual language of images and narrative forms signaled by the auspices of the Disney animation brand and the microsignaling of the greater Disney fairy-tale landscape. Bradford emphasizes this dual nature of language by exploring how Indigenous creators navigate creation in the language of colonizers and how that constructs "Indigenous subjectivities and also thematize[s] the struggles over identity formation that are central to the experience of colonized peoples and their descendants" (Bradford, 43). In making such an argument, Bradford acknowledges that a particular colonizing structure is involved in the creation of a narrative shaped by the language in which it is told, written, or presented. If we translate that concept of language as a colonizing structure into the construct of the transnational media conglomerate that is Disney, we can understand that when it comes to shaping narratives, the structure of the works that Disney produces and distributes globally functions similarly to the linguistic structure of a colonizing language. It subsumes both interactions between peoples and the very shape of daily life into patterns of accepted norms while also assuming and/or conferring authority to the colonizing group by means of command of language. As I have written about elsewhere, by retelling othered stories and incorporating nonwhite people into Disney worlds without deconstructing the external societal factors that led to their prior exclusion, the corporation actively incorporates and assumes authority of these stories under its ever-expanding umbrella.[7] Despite the various aesthetics that signpost the interpretation of certain films as "different" or "exotic" or otherwise signaling cultural authenticity and authority, the producers of all these films are essentially speaking Disney first, and otherness then becomes a secondary consideration to support the construction of a Disney narrative. The "multicultural" films of the Disney Renaissance and those that followed deliberately signal their difference from the larger Disney canon in different ways, and that sense of difference is heightened because of how these films are in fact similar to the rest of the corpus. Their recognizable sameness—as princess films, Disney films, or in some way being understood as "a fairy tale"—subsumes their difference into

---

7 See Anjirbag, "Mulan" and "Reforming Borders."

the larger corporate structure[8] and thus shapes audience interpretation by adhering to various narrative schemata.

The inherent biases that become embedded in such a cultural transaction can be understood through coloniality—the conceptual and ideological matrix of power that arose in the Atlantic world in the sixteenth century and unified imperialism and capitalism; the legacy of colonialism is embedded in global sociocultural and economic institutions and practices (Bacchilega, *Fairy Tales Transformed*, 22). For my purposes here, when I use the term *coloniality*, I am focusing on and describing the idea of the matrix of power that exists in the glocal space (Gutierrez)—the space where the global (in this case, Disney the corporation as defined through both its real economic power and the stories it tells about itself as a universalizing narrator of cultural narrative) meets various local spaces to various effects and impacts. It is in this way that we can better understand how Disney's global hegemonic WENA-centric view interacts with, rewrites, and subsumes particular localities to make them "universal" or "global" and what happens to the locality being represented as a result of that interaction or interference. Or, to put it another way, how does the force exerted by Disney, its coloniality, through its representative choices rewrite how the rest of the world might view or understand a particular locality?

For example, when Disney centers a Western, orientalizing view of a constructed image of China or Polynesia and then projects that depiction outward to a globalized entertainment market, it participates in and perpetuates that coloniality and sets up its own version of the narrative as authoritative and authentic, usually through an ambiguous nod in the credits to cultural experts and consultants. A convenient lay definition of *authenticity* is the quality of being "traditionally produced or presented" (*OED Online*), and cultural authenticity, more specifically, can be represented as work having the quality of reflecting "culturally specific realities experienced by ethnic groups" (Cai, 38). This notion becomes more complicated by Disney's "ambiguous nods," which generate a situation where "acknowledging real ownership is here transformed into self-created authority" (Parasher, 44). This notion of self-created authority, inheritor, new owner, and distributor of "classics" or of "canon" is

---

8 See Elliott.

as much a part of Disney's modus operandi as is adapting fairy-tale and folkloresque narratives and other children's classics for the screen.

Snow White and the Seven Dwarfs is an adaptation of a Grimms fairy tale, just as the next fairy-tale adaptations, *Cinderella* and *Sleeping Beauty*, were adapted from Charles Perrault's versions of these stories. Other feature animated films now considered Disney classics that were directly adapted from a literary, fairy-tale, or folkloric source include *Peter Pan, Bambi, Pinocchio, Song of the South, The Sword in the Stone, Alice in Wonderland, Robin Hood*, and *The Many Adventures of Winnie the Pooh*. Such titles reflect a much needed deeper conversation than can be had here regarding the construction of the Disney classic narrative designation and how it is tied to, reinforced by, and reinforces ideas about canon and Anglophone literature and how that should be critiqued. The idea of what makes a classic, here, is connected to both what makes an "authentic" Disney narrative and what narratives Disney is the natural inheritor of and thereby has the implicit authority to retell. The connection between literary sources and canon is also implicitly connected to the colonizing construction of literary canon in the first place: the works that will spread the ideological matrices of the colonizing power or the works that will deploy the invasive power matrix. As such, the connections between authenticity and authority—in particular, the pull between the performance of cultural authenticity and actual authority—are relevant to how these patterns continue to be perpetuated throughout the Renaissance period.

Multicultural Fractures and the Disney Fairy-Tale Mode: Making Visible Difference and Norms

Books can be—and have been—written already on the Renaissance period of Disney's animated productions, so one might ask, What would even be the point of reinvestigating this period? However, since the Renaissance films' initial appearance in 1989, it is more possible to see how this period in Disney history marked a simultaneous shift from and reinforcement of canon and classics. Canon is in many ways as much about rule making and boundaries of aesthetics and narratives as it is about authorized or authoritative narratives—not only the generation of the "real" story but the maintenance of the set narrative boundaries and how far they might be pushed as storyworlds expand. In the case of Disney, this means analyzing how the expansion beyond the European fairy tales and folktales and the adaptations of largely British children's classics not discussed in this work redefined the boundaries of what it meant to be Disney and who was expected to be welcome in its storyworld. In the 1990s this was achieved by turning to international legend, myth, and folklore in more global settings. Essentially, Disney *becomes* in its most recognizable output *international*; that becoming is not separate from what came before but rather builds on that earlier foundation and the biases, tending toward a central construction built around a presumption of whiteness, encoded in the company from earlier eras. Films of the Renaissance era and afterward are marked or transformed by a surface-level play to difference, which then becomes hypervisible compared with the already established norms of the broader Disney aesthetic.

Canon in the case of Disney becomes in part about aesthetic, in the sense of who or what is plausibly imagined in its particular brand of fabulist or fantastic or wonderous space, and how those spaces should be composed in the first place. In deploying what Richard Schickel termed the "politics of nostalgia" (Schickel, 168), the company relies on multigenerational audience nostalgia, which it actively generates, to help solidify how recognizable the brand's particular aesthetic is. Tiffin's characterization of fairy tales as definable through the quality of recognizing them as "fairy tales" (Tiffin, 3) also has some parallels to how Disney films are identified. Audiences can recognize the visual and narrative language of Disney films through what is familiar or similar from film to film, which is a product of both the marketing language of "fairy tale" used by the company and the enforcement of a certain level of uniformity in narrative patterns. Difference, by default, becomes more visible through comparison with more true-to-brand properties—things that have been around longer and reiterated across more generations. On the one hand, the visibility of difference is heightened. To make certain narratives come across as more authentic to their origins (such as *Mulan* or *Brother Bear*) or to their settings (such as *The Lion King* and *The Emperor's New Groove*), the visual production is presented differently from, say, that of 1950's *Cinderella*. Artistic style shifts and different framing devices are used, and maybe there are a few unexpected twists in how the narrative eventually resolves. However, the sense of difference remains notable even as these films themselves become "classics" or are received as part of the Disney canon or are otherwise absorbed into simultaneous franchises, such as Mulan and Pocahontas joining the Disney Princess brand cohort.

The Renaissance era marks the point where Disney solidifies its treatment of difference as *different*. After 1989, adaptations of fairy-tale or folkloresque narratives that do not come from European sources are included, but they are implicitly set in different spaces—whether invented Middle Eastern kingdoms, ancient China, post-antebellum Louisiana bayous, humanless African savannahs, or prehistoric North America. To date, despite the 1997 primetime television broadcast live-action *Cinderella* starring Brandy, the 2019 primetime television broadcast 30th-anniversary hybrid musical and film production of *The Little Mermaid* starring Auli'i Cravalho, the 2022 primetime television broadcast 30th-anniversary production of *Beauty and the Beast* starring H.E.R., and the 2023 live-action feature film *The Little Mermaid* starring Halle Bailey, Disney fairy-tale adaptations have not put nonwhite bodies in the white spaces of the so-called classic fairy tales, thus maintaining the hegemonic whiteness of its fairy-tale mode. As such, people who might identify with the conservative, middle-class, white American construction of Disney's implied intended audience do not have to then grapple with something that would challenge their own constructs of normalcy through an example of equitable and just hybridity. By making the "multicultural" films different, even just in terms of surface-level glossing of difference, the corporation does not risk alienating a significant portion of its audience (a concern discussed regarding the marketing of the *Cinderella* adaptation featuring Brandy and Whitney Houston; see Chapter 3), and it is also able to expand its appeal to a broader, more global audience. And still, these surface-level, almost self-reflective differences are obviously seen and recognized as different from some construct of a more normal, "classic" Disney, and that visibility of difference thereby makes these properties somehow still not equivalent properties, despite the status they gain with time. In essence, the Disney Renaissance and the following decade marked a course correction from earlier problematic representation, but it still traffics in a more couched, tacit form of racism through erasure and misrepresentation. This method leaves its own impact on later attempts at more nonracist methods of representation.

These moments of difference and how and where they fit, or are or are not made to fit, within the idea of a Disney classic matters on several points. They raise questions about what is "safe" to retell; what gets edited as a sign of accountability and through editing erased from the company's public history; who can be represented without being too different, too Other, or too much of a risk. The particular avoidance of declared historical periods in this multicultural construction, especially with regard to representing Blackness, feeds into a sense of the eternal Disney, which can be laden with proto-European historicity—what Martha Bayless describes as a "history-flavored Otherworld" (40)—versus otherness that needs to be located somewhere else, or sometime else. The Disney Renaissance in some ways, then, cements a trend of using specific times and locations as a way to avoid engaging with the contemporary; it is less complicated and less risky to tell stories of "then" or "there" or to just allude to difference in recognizable but decontextualized ways that keep the target white conservative audience from being alienated from "their" fantasy spaces. The kinds of stories retold thus need to be marked or transformed by visual, surface-level difference, perhaps to market them as authentic, but with the result of them always being able to be distinguished as different from the productions derived fully from WENA heritage. Even for marketing purposes, the idea of an "African" Disney film was tempered by allusions to *Hamlet* in promotional materials and the script itself (see Buhler), a move in line with the Disney mode of adapting canonical WENA-centric literary material. The result of films marked or transformed by surface-level differences is then that none of those choices thereby force an engagement on deeper levels with contemporary society for viewers, who can experience the film worlds with distance and plausible deniability, with Disney innocence. Not every viewing of a film needs to be a political act, and the ability of some to just elide the differences and take Disney's stated intentions at face value is not inherently a bad thing, but it does require noticing that the longer these products stay in the public consciousness, the more they are further reiterated.

Disney also cannot escape its ties to fairy tale and its aesthetic, history, and baggage in terms of the kinds of worlds that it constructs, because of both past works and the fairy-tale aesthetic that Disney has developed across the brand. Returning to Zipes's concept of the "Disney Spell" beyond Walt's death and his personal interference in the Disneyfication of European fairy tales, we see that as the Disney universe continually expands, the stories that it retells, remakes, and replaces solidify its cultural primacy. Its ability to do so strongly, if not seamlessly, to impress itself into different spaces and pull myriad forms of otherness into its own narrative constructions and definitions with more than a patina of authority, is affected through a construction I think of as the Disney fairy-tale mode. It is this pattern of narrative manipulation and storytelling that I see as solidifying in the Renaissance period (1989–1999) and rerooting the brand's aesthetic in the contemporary.

Whether drawing from identifiable European fairy-tale narratives or otherwise invoking the folkloresque, Disney imposed more than just a visual or aural aesthetic or particular narrative patterning. The Disney fairy-tale mode is the particular sum of narrative patterns, texture, visuals, audio, marketing, and so on that work together to distinguish the Disney film from others and that also work on audiences as part of a greater intertext to guide interpretation of the narrative proffered. Stories told in the Disney fairy-tale mode are in a constant dialogic with the greater construction of what the company is—and what it is not. In essence, what I attempt here in part is a study of Disney adaptations and original films that draw on the fairy tale or folklore, especially those under the Walt Disney Pictures or Walt Disney Animation Studios banners, to deconstruct how the shallow, safe fairy-tale narrative pattern established in *Snow White and the Seven Dwarfs*, *Cinderella*, and *Sleeping Beauty* is something that Disney narratives are shunted into emulating—whether they fit that mold or not. Nevertheless, between the opening—and closing—use of the castle title card, there is an implication of a completeness of viewer experience. That completeness is what the Disney fairy-tale mode moves to describe and define. Even when discussing these films in terms of differences, we have orphans, dead or injured or missing parents, or foundlings. We have calls to heroism, to greatness, to family, to a higher calling, to love, and to finding oneself. We have narrative patterns that evoke Shakespearean tragedy or Joseph Campbell's monomyth or disambiguations of the hero's journey—but made safe. And most important, we have happy endings and some source of, if not magic proper, then wonder or enchantment. It is the so-called Disney magic: the ideology, the rhetoric, the taking of and remaking of old stories and proffering them to a culture, a nation, a globe, as somehow a new form of cultural capital, laden with a new kind of power. The

Disney fairy-tale mode does not just describe an expression of magic, it carries a spellbinding force of its own and describes the mechanism behind which the corporation became both "metonym" for America and "monolith" (E. Bell et al., 4–5) of Euro-Anglo-American late-stage capitalism and then stepped so much further beyond that.

Of course, the fairy tales proper are much more straightforwardly told in this mode; they come from the European narrative cultural scope that served as a precursor to Disney—mothers are dead, fathers are dead or absent, step- or surrogate parents are evil or otherwise terrible. The child must make their way in the wide world or prove worthy of being rescued. But even when ostensibly moving away from the "fairy-tale *qua* fairy-tale," to paraphrase Bayless's idea of the "castle-flavored entertainment of the Disney world . . . not set in the Middle Ages qua Middle Ages, but in a fairy tale that is set in the 'Middle Ages'" (39), the construct is hard for Disney to escape, because on some level, the corporation is reading and adapting these things to fit its patterns, its modes of storytelling. When the corporation reaches outside its particular familiar original narrative scopes—European fairy-tale and classic, usually Anglophone children's literature—the Disney fairy-tale mode attempts to smooth over the cracks, gloss the differences, and make them pretty.

But such an action has an almost opposite effect; in Disney's attempts at multicultural hybridity, the cracks and fractures between cultures, time periods, histories, and so on only become more visible to viewers. The Disney fairy-tale mode as a narrative strategy causes the differences to be incorporated—not seamlessly but visibly—into the greater whole of the corporation. By naming, seeing, and drawing attention to the breaks that become apparent as Disney tries and fails to seamlessly incorporate difference into the corporation's ethos, we can better visualize and understand the history of the films across the context of the history of the company and the societies and cultures it operates in and exerts power on. We have a better construction of the films as living artifacts in a continuum, not as static points of past eras. The Disney fairy-tale mode explains in some ways why it seems difficult for Disney to get out of its own way in terms of mediating the space between its fairy-tale wheelhouse of Eurocentric narratives for a primarily US audience and what it could be as a truly international, multicultural brand focused on a more multivocal, pluralistic representation that is truly inclusive.

2

BLACKNESS IN ABSENTIA

Implicit Equivalences, Erasures, and Impacts

The 1994 *Lion King* starts in a striking way. The red lettering of "Walt Disney Pictures Presents" appears on a black background with bird and animal chatter filtering in for a brief moment before Lebo M's voice calls the sunrise into being. A red-yellow curve rises from the dark-black horizon, pushing red light up from the bottom of the screen, illuminating the landscape in silhouette—a vast open space with a single tree rising in the distance. As the sun continues to rise and the chant prologue of the song "Circle of Life" continues, the landscape becomes populated: Rhinoceroses, gazelles, a cheetah, a variety of birds, elephants, and other animals dot the screen, brief interruptions to vast naturescapes as Disney builds its Serengeti world. All these animals move toward Pride Rock as the chants give way to English lyrics and the presentation of the new lion cub. But one mammal is distinctly absent: humans. In a move reminiscent of but not disconnected from US frontier landscape painting traditions that imagined the American West as an untouched, pristine, unpopulated place waiting to be "civilized" or colonized, Disney's Africa is a dark continent waiting to be populated with the images of its shaping, even as chants, drum patterns, and instrumentation aurally point to existing cultures and imply local human populations.

If the Disney fairy-tale mode is a method of incorporation, of extending membership as it were, it becomes equally necessary to look at who is not incorporated or who is not extended that membership. We can extrapolate from the whiteness at the core of the Disney fairy-tale mode and understand that this whiteness is constructed in relation to the unnamed but ever-present and ever-othered Blackness that is by default excluded from holistic representation by the corporation. Kheli R. Willetts writes about Disney's animations as continuing a "legacy of caricatured Blackness" (Willetts, 10), where the "images continued to highlight the differences between Africans and Europeans and create[d] a dichotomous relationship that presented Europeans as good, pretty, intellectual, refined and driven, commonly articulated as *whiteness*, juxtaposed against bad, ugly, emotional, savage and lazy Africans, representing *blackness*" (10–11), a "racialization of humanity that served as the foundation for many theories related to the validity of inherent *inhumanness* of black people" (11; emphasis in original). That "racialization" and validation of a perception of an "inherent inhumanness" feeds into and contributes later to what Ebony Elizabeth Thomas identifies as a perception that speculative fiction was not and is not for Black readers and viewers (Thomas, 2). Thomas writes that "when people of color seek passageways into the fantastic, we have often discovered that the doors are barred. Even the very act of dreaming of worlds-that-never-were can be challenging when the known world does not provide many liberating spaces" (2). In her book *The Dark Fantastic: Race and the Imagination from "Harry Potter" to the "Hunger Games,"* she continues to explore how even in the networked social media and media environment that exists today, which "affords more scope for the imaginations of young people" (3), access to imaginary space is still far from universal. Disney's tacit, structural, historical anti-Blackness needs to be explored through this vein of criticism and as part of a wider landscape of barred access to the fantastic through aesthetic production legacies. Thomas describes the disparities in representation in children's and young adult media spaces as an "imagination gap" (4–7): "caused in part by the lack of diversity in childhood and teen life depicted in books, television and films. When youth grow up without seeing diverse images in the mirrors, windows, and doors of children's and young adult literature, they are confined to single stories about the world around them and, ultimately, the development of their imaginations is affected" (6). Thomas's construction of the imagination gap and how it makes visible the failure of adults to recognize the ways that young people are being mis- or underserved sets up her discussion of what she terms "the dark fantastic," or "the role that racial difference plays in our fantastically storied imaginations" (7). Although her work focuses on more contemporary, mainstream fantastic works by primarily white creators, the problems that she identifies have also been taken up in relation to other fantasy spaces by scholars such as Helen Young and Maria Sachiko Cecire.

In her 2016 *Race in Popular Fantasy Literature* Young addresses the perception of fantasy as a genre with "a reputation for being a Eurocentric genre, that is, one which is by, for, and about White people" (Young, 1), and she investigates how the genre can help readers and viewers consider "Whiteness as race and racial habit" through the ways it both "does and does not overtly engage with discourses around race and difference" (2). The "habits of Whiteness" (10) that Young describes as being rooted in the founding of the modern fantasy genre in the nineteenth and twentieth centuries are also traced in the legacy of early fantasy writers by Cecire. In her 2019 *Re-Enchanted* Cecire explores the specific legacies of fantasy and their connections to the construction of national identity, including the further positioning of Disney in relation to these ideas of belonging in fantasy spaces. This is all just to say, in effect, that the problems I identify with exclusion from fantastic spaces are not limited to Disney; Disney's works and overall corpus share many issues that plague many other areas of artistic and cultural creation for mass audiences. But once again, the corporate structure and reach of Disney make the continued deployment of an aesthetic whose structural whiteness is as much rooted in a sense of dealing with the corporation's legacy of anti-Blackness as it is a general aesthetic pattern particularly insidious. Disney's fairy-tale and folkloric adaptations have also been marked in their own ways by this aestheticization, and so that same anti-Blackness has already inflected the Disney fairy-tale mode and needs to be made visible.

Even though much attention is paid to expanded representation and to who was "included" during the multicultural push of the Disney Renaissance, it cannot go unstated that there was also a tacit exclusion of Blackness and Black storytelling in meaningful ways in that period, something that has barely begun to improve since then. We might indeed call out that in the Disney transmedia landscape, Black bodies on screen are a conspicuous absence and are often siloed or separated out or otherwise differentiated from "standard" franchise fare. Disney animation's history when it comes to depicting race and ethnicity is fraught with stereotype, especially when depicting Blackness. The most notable examples that seem to be brought up when discussing classic Disney animation involve the original *Fantasia*, the crows in *Dumbo*, and, of course, *Song of the South*. These films feature the reproduction of racial stereotypes, from the Amos and Andy–esque characterization of the crows to the distortion of Joel Chandler Harris's Uncle Remus stories, and the further distorting of Uncle Remus from a storyteller with dignity to a racist stereotype built for white sensibilities—an Uncle Tom—in *Song of the South* (Wasko, 140). The "Pastoral Symphony" sequence of the original *Fantasia* features two servant or potentially slave centaurs, Atika and Sunflower, who unlike the tall, graceful, white, and European-coded centaurettes, are caricatures of little African American girls, with stereotypical hairstyles, buck teeth, big lips, and the bodies of donkeys. Atika and Sunflower wait on both the centaurettes and Bacchus. Following the Civil Rights Movement in the United States, Atika and Sunflower were erased from subsequent re-releases of *Fantasia* (Korkis), including on Disney+, despite the description caption that reads "This program is presented as originally created. It may contain outdated cultural depictions."[1]

The Disney Renaissance films, with their colorful and multiculturally accented undersea world, their foray into the "Middle East," their "African" adventure, and even their gospel treatment of the chorus from classical dramas, all seemed to announce a step firmly away from these outdated, problematic stereotypes. However, even *The Lion King*, which, compared with the similarly timed *Pocahontas* and *Aladdin*, seems "unproblematic in terms of racial representation" (Wasko, 141), has its fair share of problems. Along with the obvious disparity of exploring one of the world's largest continents through an animal story and calling it diversity, the "portrayal of the three 'hooligan hyenas'" has been called into question, as they are obviously coded to be "definitely recognizable

---

1   It should be noted, though, that the "exotic, brown-skinned zebra-girl servants" of Bacchus (Wade) remain in the iteration available to stream on Disney+. It should also be noted that as of early 2025, the practice of providing warnings about outdated, insensitive depictions ahead of certain films on Disney+ is in flux, in line with the current political climate and context, including the backlash rising in the wake of social changes realized through the 2020 Black Lives Matter movement and protests.

as Black and Hispanic characters lurking about in a jungle version of a ghetto" (Wasko, 141; see also: C. R. King et al., 57–61). All in all, these depictions serve to limit, if not fully remove, the issue of the caricaturized and stereotyped Black body on screen and thereby, through erasure of the potentially problematic image, to erase the potential problems and demonstrate "Disney's major strategy for negotiating the tricky issue of representing race: exclusive anthropomorphism" (Byrne and McQuillan, 96). Through this conceptualization it is no accident that Black-coded characters, unlike other nonwhite-coded characters who exist in their own specific spaces, spend most of their time visualized as animals or nonhumans (see *Treasure Planet*), providing a presumably easy out from the problems of fully realized multicultural character development. Even Tiana is more frog than princess in the 2009 *Princess and the Frog*, despite this film being heralded as both a return to a traditional mode of animation and narrative and the first-ever Black animated Disney fairy-tale princess. Disney production magic ultimately means that if the problem cannot be solved or skirted, it can eventually be disappeared, like Sunflower, Atika, and Uncle Remus. The overall result of all these absences is that

> when the texts eliminate children of color entirely, the message of the relative unimportance of these children is clear. . . . While the absence of people of color in fairy tales may not be intentional or sinister in either the source text illustrations or the dominant Disney versions, the damaging effects of the preponderance of the almost all-White world of the fairy tales, and in particular of the fairy tale princess, should not be underestimated. (Hurley, 228)

Disney has handled tacit Black representation since 1989 through what might be described as the idea of Blackness in absentia. The "white space" (Anderson) of the Disney mediascape is solidified by making humane, positive Black human bodies and experiences unpicturable—not because there was an attempt to do so but because absence implies that such things are not even imaginable in the whole new world of post-1990s Disney. This imagination gap, to borrow Thomas's term again (Thomas, 4–7), is not incidental but deliberate, and we can identify this particular constructed gap by looking at how and where Black culture and the implication of Black representation become incorporated into films largely divorced from Black bodies through accent, music, and geographic implications—a Blackness instead of cogent representation. Looking back on Disney's most deliberately multicultural era, representation of Black people is conspicuously absent from the animated film offerings and remained so until 2009. Other than the Muses in the 1997 *Hercules*, Black human bodies are largely absent from any of the Disney Renaissance films. Other than Doc Sweet in the *Atlantis* films and Frozone in *The Incredibles* (2004), Black human beings are not seen in or incorporated into the Disney universe as more than a sidekick or narrative device until *The Princess and the Frog* in 2009. After this fairy tale, there would not be Black bodies on screen in a theatrically released film until Nonso Anozie's casting in the 2015 *Cinderella*.

As such, it is almost as though on some level Disney is cognizant of the particular minefield it would enter by trying to use the same techniques to "fix" its representations of African Americans or of Blackness generally, based on how fraught not only its own history of caricatures of Blackness is but also the history of animation. Erasing and obscuring past mistakes, avoiding depicting Black bodies, or depicting Blackness primarily through spoken accent in animal or other nonhuman bodies is an erasure of a certain depiction of positive humanity. If we accept that Disney's primary understanding of storytelling is at the image level without engaging with deeper hegemonic constructions of race and institutionalized biases, the steps of avoidance and erasure of past mistakes almost make sense. Yet the refusal to engage with Black bodies on screen while still trying to present the company as becoming more diverse arguably has had the effect that, thirty years or so onward, Disney still has no idea how to incorporate Blackness into its productions ethically or equitably. Willetts writes:

> Mickey is the unofficial *wishmaster*. He and his animated entourage are interwoven into the fabric of this nation and the lives of many families who pass their love for Disney and its magic from one generation to the next. Yet for all its allure, Disney's world is not magic for everyone. Although many may cite *The Princess and the Frog* (2009) as evidence to the contrary, the arrival of a

Disney-born black princess—more than 70 years after the appearance of their first effort to create an animated fairytale with *Snow White*—offers little consolation to people like me who spent their childhood on a quest for a reflection of myself in the world of Disney.

Growing up I searched for characters who mirrored the people in my community and reflected the values and aesthetics of the Other, in this case, African, Latino, Asian and First Nations Diasporas. Instead, Disney gave me caricatured representations of the diversity of my world. Disney's diversity was often channeled not with cartoon characters but through animals whose speech and mannerisms reflected animated minstrelsy. . . . These characters were the rule instead of the exception. The portrayals were presented during the ascent of America's favorite mouse with images that dashed my girlhood wishes for Disney magic that looked, and felt, familiar and beautiful. (Willetts, 9–10)

In this passage Willetts describes her own experience with what Maria Sachiko Cecire later terms in her work "the moment" (Cecire, vii), the feeling of realizing one might not actually belong in one's beloved fantasy spaces. Although, as Willets notes, Disney pre-Renaissance was even worse, erasure and the half-measure presented in *The Princess and the Frog* were not the right fix when one has spent one's childhood searching for a reflection of oneself in Disney, only to find betrayal instead. These things are certainly not limited to Disney, but Disney's particular penchant for excluding "familiar and beautiful" depictions of otherness, especially Blackness, in the contemporary era demands further consideration than simply the historical context for the open caricatures.

Part of this problem is Disney's fixation on image and a seeming lack of realization that accent, dialogue, dialect, and even music have as much an effect on the perception of race as the drawn image itself. Willetts notes that Disney "continues their utilization of caricaturized representations" and that "over time their portrayals have become even subtler," citing King Louis from *The Jungle Book* and Sebastian from the 1989 *Little Mermaid* among others (Willets, 20). Sebastian, like King Louis, is an anthropomorphized animal, but his race is constructed through his Caribbean accent rather than through the eugenics-inflected conflation of Blackness with a "jive-talking" (Willets, 20) ape body, a conceptualization that in itself folds the voices and accents of many island nations into an othered stereotype crafted for the white gaze, or in this case, ear. So too are the voices of the hyenas in *The Lion King*, where accent and stereotype are meant to convey an inherent evilness, compared with the uninflected "American" accent of the literally golden lion-child, Simba. Eleanor Byrne and Martin McQuillan in particular identify in Disney a "strategy of using well-known black actors to voice cartoon animals" (Byrne and McQuillan, 104). They identify Whoopi Goldberg as Shenzi, James Earl Jones as Mufasa, and Eddie Murphy as Mushu in *Mulan* and Sebastian in *The Little Mermaid* as representing the "classic Disney formula for racial representations in 'Disney Classics,'" and they specifically cite Mushu and Sebastian's creation for and insertion into a Chinese and European tale, respectively, as evidence of "the specific interest Disney has in introducing them to its source stories and disarming the destabilising potential of America's racial fantasies and fears" (105). Even in 2009's *The Princess and the Frog*, accents play a role in character construction, particularly that of Ray the firefly, whose Cajun inflections are meant to be comedic but have the multiplicitous effect of encoding race and class as well as historical period. The use of specific music such as jazz and swing in that film serves a similar purpose,[2] as does the partnership between Hans Zimmer and Lebo M on the score for *The Lion King*—an effect that becomes even more pronounced in the stage show and the score and soundtrack for *The Lion King II: Simba's Pride*. The soundscapes of *The Lion King*, like the infusion of gospel music sung by the Black female Muses in *Hercules*, therefore code different signifiers of Blackness into the films, even though Blackness remains unseen for most of the time in the films in terms of the lack of Black bodies featured taking up space and given visual attention on-screen.

Whichever way otherness or difference or culture becomes constructed in films such as *The Little Mermaid*, *The Jungle Book*, *Mulan*, *The Lion King* films, and *Hercules*, it is always done in opposition to the whiteness that underscores Disney's "normal" or classic aesthetic. Films such as *Beauty and the Beast* and *The Little Mermaid* exemplify this tacit

---

2 The use of swing in *The Jungle Book*'s "I Wanna Be Like You" also
   serves a similar purpose, albeit with a different intent and tone.

rooting of not only their internal aesthetic but also the Disney aesthetic in whiteness (see Lacroix), with the notable fact that this is done even though Disney does not actually make films about race or racialized identity. Race is meant to be incidental to other constructions of identity in the films (this is also done with disability, something that can and should be discussed further in relation to *The Hunchback of Notre Dame* and *Snow White and the Seven Dwarfs*). The princess-driven fairy-tale films of the Disney Renaissance are constructed in a dialogic with the early fairy-tale films of Disney's heyday. This dialogic relationship in turn contributed to both the construction of the Disney Princess franchise and the continued perpetuation of the overall contemporary Disney brand, which is undergirded by the threads of classic Disney and its aesthetic. That sense of a constant compass pointing toward Disney's internalized construction of normal is continually reinforced through the reiteration of Disney classic canon, which is in some ways built on an absence of visualized, raced difference that is never set as equal to whiteness. Even after the Renaissance era, when Disney as a company might have felt that it had somehow pushed the boundaries too much, the corporation could walk that boundary back a bit through a return to the canon, or something that reiterates the hallmarks of the canon, to pacify and placate its core audience. The tacit racialization of a return to canon or the idea of a more normative aesthetic can be seen in particular after the Disney Renaissance period and the release of *The Princess and the Frog* later in 2009 through three "new" fairy-tale narratives that center whiteness and are extremely lacking in terms of ethnic or racialized diversity—*Tangled* (2010), *Brave* (2012), and *Frozen* (2013)—and the live-action remakes of Disney classic films. These three films together reiterate a sense of Disney's normal, a normal that solidified especially as Disney continued to remake the othered films such as *Aladdin* and *The Lion King* in live-action and CGI versions in the 2010s.[3] Through the various cycles of reiteration since 1999 especially, a loose rotating pattern seems to have emerged. As

---

3 The effects of this return to Disney's traditional aesthetic and narrative patterning are something that I considered in more depth in a plenary lecture at the conference "Picturing Otherness: A Historical Perspective on Diversity in Children's Literature (20th–21st Century)," held at the University of Hamburg in 2023.

Disney tries new things, it also reminds the public of who they had been before through the rerelease of the classic films or through remaking a film that viewers remember as quintessential Disney. Such patterns of reiteration make differences between the films hypervisible. The absence of Blackness also becomes hypervisible in this context, as something that begins to feel like either pointed inclusion when it does emerge or otherwise something the company can excuse as a natural omission from this brand of storytelling.

The Unpopulated Continent: *The Lion King*'s Inherent Anti-Blackness

The question remains: If there is an inherent play toward normative whiteness in the very fabric of Disney culture, then where does the (forced and constructed) oppositional position of a sense of Blackness fit? There is one film from the Disney Renaissance set in Africa, *The Lion King* (1994), but it is devoid of human representation, instead populating its narrative spaces with various animals. Except for the casting of James Earl Jones as Mufasa, the overtly race-coded characters are representing villains in the form of the hyenas. *The Lion King* is a complicated, multifaceted text, considering its wider footprint and how it has persisted in many forms outside the animated film itself, including two sequels, several spin-off television shows, and various stage shows. It is not a fairy-tale adaptation but rather the presentation of a thematic talking animal story where nonhuman entities reflect human social and political structures and relationships in dialogue with understandings of the folkloresque, compounded by Rafiki's shamanic presence and supernatural elements. Although I will not be doing a full deconstructive reading of the musical production of *The Lion King* here and only consider it more briefly than it probably deserves, I acknowledge that there is a quite different conversation to be had about the centering of Black bodies in theater, especially given that the human body cannot be fully obscured by the puppetry used in that production (see Wickstrom, 109–21). However, given the expense of tickets to attend that stage show (unlike *Hamilton*, there has been no move to provide access to a recording of the stage show through the streaming service Disney+), the accessibility of the experience of that production and the work that went into it is relatively limited compared with the wider accessibility of the animated feature. I will, however, be discussing the 2019 reiteration here. The CGI photo-realistic remediation was an almost scene-by-scene reproduction of the Disney Renaissance-era animation, and so it is worth examining what such a decision implies beyond being another example of Disney's pattern of nostalgic reiteration.

The story of a young lion who loses his father in an accident, runs away, and then is called home to save his kingdom is uniquely original fare compared with the other films considered in this book, and it is distinct in its literary-mythic quality. David Whitley writes that, rather than *The Lion King* being a retelling of a folkloric or mythic narrative from somewhere in Africa, "the film's literary roots lie in the contest of ideas about 'kingship' that animate Elizabethan drama—especially *Hamlet* and *Henry IV*" (Whitley, 128–29). Stephen Buhler notes that "over the decades, Disney has followed the strategy, initiated in the early twentieth century, of promoting English literature as a preserve for 'Anglo-Saxon' culture in the United States" (Buhler, 127). *The Lion King* is a part of that construction with its distinct Shakespearean appropriations, such as the similarities between Scar and *Hamlet*'s Claudius as well as Richard III, in terms of his "disfigurement" and his use of "hired assassins" in the hyenas (Buhler, 122). As Buhler observes:

> *The Lion King* offers a comic trio of hyenas, who are gleefully immoral. . . . The very recognizable voices for these "dark" and shadowy clowns have provoked considerable comment: Whoopi Goldberg and Cheech Marin provide decidedly urban versions of African American and Hispanic American speech for Shenzai and Banzai respectively, while Disney stalwart Jim Cummings jabbers maniacally as the dim Ed. Many listeners have taken offense at the stereotypical nature of these voices, especially given Disney's sometimes appalling depiction of nonwhites and long-standing ideas of Africa as a "dark" continent. (Buhler, 123)

Patrick D. Murphy asserts that the combination of anthropocentrism and sexism combine uniquely in Disney so that "it is not simply that humans are conceptualized as the center of the universe but rather that men are the universal center" (Murphy, 127–28). I would extend this assertion to say that the inherent whiteness in Disney, exacerbated by how much the paratexts of films such as *The Lion King* mobilize exoticism signaling as part of their marketing, means that for Disney white men are the universal center, with nonwhite "men" only placed to serve this center.

Though perhaps somewhat obvious, this racialized point of view needs to be named openly in order to be better deconstructed, to identify how race is mobilized to signal either normative or nonnormative incorporation in the Disney transmedia universe. Especially when dealing with the elision between anthropomorphizing the construction of the Other and the deployment of colorism and anti-Blackness and how that is reflected in the construction of Africa in this film, it becomes more important to name the effects of the pattern in animation where "Africa may be the only place pictured in animated films that has no human occupants" (C. R. King et al., 58). As David Whitley notes:

> The palette of *The Lion King* [is] carefully chosen to suggest the colours and light of Africa, and so on—the ultimate aim is not to create the impression of a realistic landscape. The exotic distancing effect created by tropical settings instead creates a kind of dreamscape where, to an even greater extent than in other kinds of Disney animation, fantasies and deep-seated cultural longings can be projected and worked through. (Whitley, 16)

But this space for deep-seated cultural longings is already occupied by colonizing fantasies, and to so blatantly create a realism-inflected "dreamscape" out of a very real and under- or misrepresented landscape reflects those fantasies implicitly through its construction of what C. R. King and colleagues refer to as a "heterotopia" (C. R. King et al., 57), where the "homogeneity of the continent is confirmed through the timeless and/or ahistorical elements of the narratives" (58). They further note that *The Lion King*, like other films such as the *Madagascar* franchise by Dreamworks and *Tarzan*, "all take audiences to an imagined Africa—a vacant, timeless, malleable setting to restate facts in a natural register" (58). As Byrne and McQuillan observe regarding the 1994 animation, "*The Lion King* is set in a part of Africa that both is and is not locatable. The opening scene pans from the Victoria Falls to Mount Kilimanjaro, to what may be the Niger Delta. These dispersed landmarks offer a shorthand for 'Africa the continent' whilst deferring any realization of an actual place" (Byrne and McQuillan, 102). Despite the accuracy of specific landmarks and the detailed attention given to connoting difference in environment through color palette, there remains the problem of simply equating a continent with implied Blackness, as *The Lion King* has through the decades become recognized as "Disney's 'black' film," "operating in an exclusively animal kingdom" and "significantly preoccupied with race but . . . also in a keen state of denial about the politics of representation" (101). And yet there remains a disjuncture between the proclaimed too-vastness of Africa represented in the opening lyrics of the film and "this self-confessed inability to represent Africa mask[ing] the less loudly proclaimed reluctance to represent black people as people at all, African or otherwise" (101).

But *The Lion King* is even more complicated. Simba's coming of age is facilitated by two surrogate father figures in Timon and Pumbaa, whose co-parenting trumpets a progressive view of family, but their Swahili catch-phrase "Hakuna Matata" is deployed in such a way that it both "conjures up notions of suitably Falstaffian irresponsibility" and "echoes colonialist stereotypes of native 'laziness'" (Buhler, 124). Stephen Buhler further describes the complication of the raced villainy of the hyenas as juxtaposed between casting James Earl Jones and Robert Guillame as Mufasa and Rafiki and casting Matthew Broderick as adult Simba and having a songbook by Elton John and Tim Rice (123). An auxiliary issue was the problem of royalties for the use of the 1960s pop song "The Lion Sleeps Tonight" in the film and the stage show. "The Lion Sleeps Tonight" is rooted in a song from the 1930s, "Mbube," by South African singer Solomon Linda, who was neither credited nor compensated by Disney until the settlement of a lawsuit in 2006 (Browne). For a company so meticulous about image and narrative construction, when deconstructing the choices made for this film at the intersections of geography and race, what emerges instead is a hodgepodge of mixed intentionality with an uncharacteristic lack of direction. The film set in "Africa" merely reflects a WENA construction of an unmanned continent rather than a meaningful local engagement with the many real cultures, people, artists, and storytellers who live there.

More than twenty years later, that lack of direction persists. The photorealistic CGI version of *The Lion King* directed by Jon Favreau is a fairly faithful if not 100 percent one-to-one recreation rather than a reimagining of the animated film—with a degree of course correction, such as the omission of the racialized hyenas and a predominantly Black cast. As with other remediations, "the cyclical re-release strategy for key Disney animations is based on the claim that these timeless 'classics' will appeal to, and should be seen by, each new generation" (Murphy, 125–26). The 2019 version repeats the pattern of reaffirming the primary positioning of the original animation as *the* Disney classic by proffering something slightly different but very much in dialogue with and conscious of its difference from the animation. In addition to the changes in characterization of the hyenas, Beyoncé and Donald Glover play the adult Nala and Simba, respectively. There are some alterations to the soundtrack, notably, the insertion of the Beyoncé song "Spirit" to accompany Simba's return to the Pride Lands (and the companion album, "The Gift," for which Beyoncé is the executive producer [Giorgis]), an extended iteration of "The Lion Sleeps Tonight" that caused further controversy with the Linda estate (Browne), and a truncated iteration of "Be Prepared." Despite centering Blackness through casting and the film's music, there is still no human representation of Black bodies on the Disney screen, and the "Black film," as termed by Byrne and McQuillan, in terms of Disney classics reiterated, remains situated elsewhere than the fairy-tale narratives otherwise chosen for this kind of reimagining. One wonders why in 2019 the choice for a photorealistic CGI rendering of the animated film was needed, in lieu of perhaps a staging of the original musical for distribution in movie theaters or putting the same kind of budget and star power behind a new narrative that might have depicted humans, in either live-action or CGI.

Although the 2019 reiteration of *The Lion King* included more diverse voice actors and cast primarily well-known Black stars to voice the iconic characters, continuing the pattern identified by Byrne and McQuillan (104), it remains that none of these actors are seen on-screen. Therefore the aural effect of Blackness as a culture that informs mass media cultures remains divorced from the image of Black bodies. The photorealistic CGI is an impressive leap in technological advancement for the studio, but, in a media landscape where naturalists and documentarians such as David Attenborough have already produced programming that takes readers into the real spaces of animal habitats across the African continent, it is curious to decide to re-create a real space in such a veneer of reality over the "believability" that guides the animation ethos of the corporation. We can potentially view the casting of Black voice actors while simultaneously disappearing them from fully populating the screen through the lens of "plastic representation," as outlined by Kristen Warner. Plastic representation "uses the wonder that comes from seeing characters on screen who serve as visual identifiers for specific demographics in order to flatten the expectation to desire anything more. In this instance, then, progress is merely the increase of black actors on screen in both leading and supporting roles" (K. Warner, 35). In this instance, the 2019 *Lion King* remediation uses not bodies but recognizable voices with significant celebrity attached, and these hold commercial weight and become a quantifiable asset to the goals of the capitalist corporation: to extract revenue from old and new audiences. Such casting thus becomes arguably part of a

> system that reifies blackness into an empirical system of "box checking." It is a mode of representation that offers the feel of progress but that actually cedes more ground than it gains for audiences of color. When audiences, cultural critics, and even industry professionals buy into the subtle but popular belief that social progress occurs when the focus of representation is placed solely on the racially visible difference of above-and-below-the-line talent, it means that for industry gatekeepers and executives, less time has to be devoted to developing and appreciating the meaningful cultural and historical differences of those bodies. (K. Warner, 36)

If the goal was to revisit the intellectual property for a new generation of fans, why not, at minimum, stage the musical in its purpose-built New York City or other globally located stage, record it, and release it to theaters and then stream it in a recognition that the stage musical prices skew access away from traditionally minoritized groups?

Briefly, the musical production of *The Lion King*, as conceived by Julie Taymor, remains, at the time of this writing, one of the most popular stage musical productions in the world, one that "established Disney as a formidable presence on Broadway and global stages" (Grossman, 117).

Although there is much to be explored in this production, I would like to highlight a few things that it does particularly well. First, it is deliberately not a literal adaptation, such as the method used to recreate *Beauty and the Beast* on stage several years earlier (122), but rather what director Taymor referred to as a "theatricalization" (qtd. in Grossman, 122) to create a "double event" that ensured that "human and animal—live actors and the characters they played—be visible simultaneously" (124). Second, the musical pulls out and makes prominent the cultural specificity from the animated film's compositions, particularly the South African influences that were provided through Lebo M and his chorus, who sing in Zulu throughout the film (119). As Barbara Wallace Grossman outlines in more detail, the music for the stage musical was influenced by a sequel soundtrack album to the animated film, called *Rhythm of the Pride Lands*. The songs drawn from this source include a "strong South African chorus and lyrics in African languages including Xhosa, Zulu, and Tswana" (Grossman, 123). Lebo M also returned as a collaborator and contributed additional compositions and even attempted to demand that at least half the chorus be South African, though this was in conflict with the policies of Actor's Equity (128). After the opening at the New Amsterdam Theatre in 1997, Taymor recognized how the double event she envisioned regarding the staging begat a second occurrence of doubling: "White theatergoers saw it as a primal fable; black audience members as a story about race" (129). As the show has persisted and traveled the world, it has become standard practice to incorporate "culturally specific changes and localized references to make the show more appealing to theatergoers in a particular country" (130). All of this leads to the simple conclusion that processes and understandings for culturally specific retelling and nonliteral adaptation exist within the Disney mediascape and its production legacy.

Nevertheless, the pattern for what could have been a better revisiting of the narrative was not followed. Nor could the producers get away from what seems to be an ingrained reflex to highlight Blackness for marketing without being troubled by Black bodies or having to grapple with the construct of an ahistorical, "no place" utopic construction of a nonspecific Africa that does not acknowledge how extractive colonialism and genocide and their ongoing legacies have affected the people and cultures who actually occupy that space outside the "dark continent" of the white imagination. Thus the white imagination continues to occupy and colonize the continent, and the end result is the building of a highly realistic version of a real environment, a preference for the simulacrum over the real, as the simulacrum becomes a controllable version of the African continent to be manipulated per the needs of the creators. In fact, we could consider the photorealistic CGI construction of African savannah through Jean Baudrillard's concept of the hyperreal, where

> it is no longer a question of imitation, nor duplication, nor even parody. It is a question of substituting the signs of the real for the real, that is to say of an operation of deterring every real process via its operational double, a programmatic, metastable, perfectly descriptive machine that offers all signs of the real and short-circuits all its vicissitudes. . . . A hyperreal henceforth sheltered from the imaginary, and from any distinction between the real and the imaginary, leaving room only for the orbital recurrence of models and for the simulated generation of differences. (Baudrillard, 2–3)

Baudrillard has famously used Disney, specifically Disneyland, to illustrate the connections between the hyperreal and the imaginary, calling the theme park "a perfect model of all the entangled orders of simulacra" where "everywhere in Disneyland the objective profile of America, down to the morphology of individuals and of the crowd, is drawn. . . . Disneyland exists in order to hide that it is the 'real' country, all of 'real' America that *is* Disneyland. . . . Disneyland is presented as imaginary in order to make us believe that the rest is real" (Baudrillard, 12). The photorealistic CGI builds on this reading of how Disney constructions of realism affect the intersection of the real and the imaginary, freeing the corporation from the limits of cultural, geographic, or national boundaries. There is no need to involve the real, to reach into real spaces or collaborate with real people and cultures. If it is too complicated to balance ethical connections and boundaries, then a controllable, perfectible, malleable version can just be incorporated into the future. Although this is not a step that has been taken yet, the potentials facilitated by the technology are not too much of a leap and have to be recognized. As cultural tensions heighten on various axes and as conversations about the alleged potentials for AI in media productions are coming to the fore, it will remain to be seen whether Disney as a corporation can resist the temptation and instead commit to moving in more ethical directions on the matter of representation, despite choosing to attempt a literal adaptation of the 1994 *Lion King* in CGI instead of following other possible models.

As stated, primarily well-known Black actors were cast as the voice-over talent, but there remains a skirting of "Africa" by the US-based corporation. Because the 2019 production is a closer recreation and reproduction, it repeats the erasure of Africans in the animation that C. R. King and colleagues call "a violent act, a symbolic clearing" (C. R. King et al., 59). Through the lack of any represented indigenous community or local person, the corporation created a scenario in which "no one has a claim to this locality; there is no need to mention the legacies of colonialism or the imprint of underdevelopment" (58). Even steps in a direction that might act as a corrective to the earlier failure are still complex and still end up framing a version of quasi-pan-Africanism through a WENA-led lens. As part of the marketing and release strategy, an album produced by Beyoncé called *The Lion King: The Gift* was released as an accompanying album with songs from and inspired by *The Lion King*. This production was made in addition to the album of the film's songs and score and also had its own accompanying musical film or visual album released in 2020, titled *Black Is King*. This visual album interprets both *The Lion King* film and the album *The Gift* but features Black bodies on screen as it tells the story of a young prince who was exiled in his youth and then reclaims his throne as an adult. Criticism of the productions largely centered in-group perspectives from across the African continent that called into question how Disney and Beyoncé constructed this presentation of pan-Africanism, what and where and who was represented, and how (see Paquette; Nsofor and Ngumbi). Essentially, in these productions the continent remains framed by an implicitly colonizing or imperialist view, in that it is still US-centric outsiders projecting a narrative onto a crafted image of a place that is filled with embodied real cultures and people. To take after Sara Ahmed's reading of orientalism and orientation, "Africa" to a WENA- or even just US-based audience still is encountered and mediated through the construction of a US-based interlocutor, the Other mediated through and incorporated into the familiar so that it can be oriented toward or "tend toward" the gaze of a WENA audience, reshaping the oriented cultural object in the process (Ahmed, *Queer Phenomenology*, 129–32). This is therefore a construction that raises the question, How does this production impact the counter-image of the corporation that is opening up a mass-market global creative space? Nevertheless, *Black Is King* still reimagines the story of *The Lion King* in a not dissimilar way to how the stage production recreated the narrative on stage, and it puts a lot of effort into putting Black bodies on screen in positions of unfettered beauty, power, and potential.

Another interesting dynamic to consider is that *Black Is King* is very much a *Beyoncé* production rather than a *Disney* production. There are many practical and creative reasons for this framing and the space between the two creative "brands" and how the production becomes executed. However, I think there is also a valid cynical point to be made regarding the corporation not going out of its way to claim authoritative ownership of the creative product. Similar to the circumstances I will discuss around the production and framing of *The Wonderful World of Disney Presents Rodgers and Hammerstein's Cinderella* featuring Whitney Houston and Brandy Norland, the corporation almost carves out a space of plausible deniability regarding its involvement in a production that was potentially quite polarizing for its traditional viewership during a politically fraught cultural moment. What I mean by plausible deniability is that if conservative audiences created a backlash to its production, Disney could presumably wash its hands of direct involvement and make the excuse that as a corporation it was just streaming the film; if it was more well accepted by other audiences, well, look at how far they have come and how diverse and accepting the corporation is now. This is of course highly cynical speculation of corporate intent, but I do think that Disney's years of political lobbying in various directions and patterns of quite deliberately courting specific audiences in different directions for different aims and effects create a necessary paratext to fully exploring how Disney enters and is involved in various conversations surrounding different kinds of representation. As of 2023 the corporation itself still seems marked by an attitude of what can only be presumed to be fear of unapologetically putting Black voices and, particularly, geographically and culturally specific Black voices and productions center stage without having some sort of mitigation, interpretation, or buffer in place.

Again, my reading of the situation here is marked by a degree of cynicism and a knowledge of wider social contexts and networks, but Disney trades on perception above everything else. To still either separate narratives from the "classic" Disney label or minimize or replace Black characters and actors with animal or object bodies midnarrative, despite so many claims and campaigns to purportedly celebrate minoritized identities, is incredibly telling regarding the distance the corporation still needs to travel to reach a state of equitable representation. This context will always undercut and underwrite any positive changes or more positive moments until the negative patterns stop being reproduced.

The Gospel Truth: Sidelined Blackness

Several years after the success of the animated *Lion King*, Disney released *Hercules*, a gospel-infused re-visioning of Greek mythology made palatable to a family audience. The 1997 production starred talent such as Roger Bart and Danny De Vito, and, though not fairy tale proper, made some interesting choices with regard to its framing that makes it worth considering here. As various scholars have discussed, the storybook opening frame is a recognizable trope in Disney films, especially those drawing from fairy tales or what is considered classic literature, such as *The Jungle Book* or *Peter Pan*. This even appears in later films that parody fairy-tale narratives, such as *Enchanted* or *Godmothered*. In *Hercules*, instead of the book conceit, the animators drew from the idea of stories being pictured on Greek pottery and also from the idea of the chorus in Greek drama. The narration at the beginning of the film, voiced by Charlton Heston of *Ben-Hur*, *The Ten Commandments*, and *El Cid* fame, first takes viewers to a museum with classical artifacts, talking about the "Golden Age of powerful gods and extraordinary heroes." The animation moves as though it is a camera panning through the gallery, before snapping into focus on an amphora as the narrator introduces the figure of "the mighty Hercules." As the frame zooms in on the vase, which ostensibly depicts Hercules' fight with the Nemean Lion, the first of his twelve labors of myth, the camera's gaze shifts slightly upward to above the main image on the vase, to where five Black female figures are standing. They interrupt the narrator, criticizing the boring way in which he is starting to relate the story of Hercules, "making it sound like some sort of Greek tragedy." Heston's narrator turns over the framing of the story to them. As a recognizably gospel-inspired baseline begins to frame an opening song, the women introduce themselves as the Muses, "goddesses of the arts, and proclaimers of heroes." They then, in song, introduce the parts of Greek mythology that viewers will need to know in order to navigate this reimagining of Greek myth, particularly the war between the Greek gods and the Titans. The storytelling is a combination of art on vases coming to life and the muses singing to convey what they call "the Gospel truth"—in this case how the world was formed and became a good place to live. As the music progresses through changing keys, the framed storytelling ends with a vase depiction of Mount Olympus, which is zoomed in on to become the "real" (yes, still animated) Mount Olympus where the story that viewers came to see is about to begin. The Hercules fanfare plays as the film's title stretches across the screen, and as the film enters the narrative space of Olympus, viewers see the colorful portrayals of various gods and goddesses on-screen. The frame story has been left behind, and the narrative is about to begin properly.

This opening serves several purposes. First, it culturally locates the coming narrative through a Disney lens—not a fairy tale or a literary classic this time—and so instead of a storybook frame, we have the deployment of where ancient myths appear today, on pottery and other artifacts that have survived from the so-called classical period. This ties into a particularly Disney visual language while also creating a visual connection to the legitimacy of the narrative—it is possible to see an amphora depicting Hercules slaying the Nemean Lion while Athena looks on in the British Museum as well as images of the artifact in various other digital photo archives.[4] But this connection could have been made without the figure of the Muses being invoked, especially given that the first image of the vase or amphora is situated in what looks like a museum space. So, then, what purposes does invoking the Muses serve for Disney?

In and of itself, their presentation becomes a connection to a culture of relating epic tales of heroes and, arguably, of deliberately

---

4 See, for example, the Theoi project archive galleries, specifically entry M19.5 in the gallery Greek Vase Paintings 4: www.theoi.com/Gallery/M19.5.html.

tying into the Homeric trope of the invocation of the Muses. Although in *Hercules* this is not a matter of retelling European fairy-tale narratives through an Americanized lens, the Disney pattern of connecting its version to more authoritative versions or modes of storytelling is a deliberate way of constructing the idea of implicit inherited cultural authority. By doing this, the corporation shifts the window of this cultural authority to a wider frame, one that not only encompasses French, German, and British literary fairy tales or classic literature but also includes a view of the Mediterranean, itself a portal to a wider world that might become incorporated into Disney's scope. The Muses literally embody not only the idea but also the role and function of the chorus from Greek drama. In both narration and song, they help to move the story along within its own frame, but, given the scope of myth drawn from to create the Disney *Hercules* narrative—in just the core storyline, the labors of the hero himself, the relationships between the gods (such as Hades' resentment of those on Mount Olympus), the origin of the world through the battle between the Olympians and the Titans—they also provide necessary background and framing throughout the film. The Muses become the musical core of the film, singing four of the six songs: "The Gospel Truth," "Zero to Hero," accompanying Susan Egan's Megara in "I Won't Say (I'm in Love)," and "A Star Is Born." The remaining two songs, "Go the Distance" and "One Last Hope," are an earnest rendition and a comedic parody, respectively, of the "I want" song that became part of the musical core of films during the Disney Renaissance. But the songs featuring the Muses are heavily gospel inflected, a step away from the more Broadway-inflected feel of Disney albums from the same period (Wells, 138–39).

In an entertainment feature for *Nylon* magazine marking the twentieth anniversary of the film, Taylor Bryant highlights the musical and cultural importance of the Muses as drivers of the film and as positive representations of Black women in animated film. She writes about how *Hercules* was different from other films of its era and how it might have actually opened the door for the potentials of Tiana in *The Princess and the Frog* twelve years later:

> Another departure: seeing five black women in an animated film.
> Not just that, but these five black women were portrayed as beautiful, smart, if not slightly silly, goddesses. The actual characters

were made to look like the singers voicing them, down to their
gestures, hair, and bodies (there were cameras in the studio to
record the ladies). . . . Which means we got curls on some and
straight styles on other. Short and curvy body types as well as tall
and skinny. A muse with a penchant for drama and another with a
passion for dance. We got real, nuanced women. (Bryant)

Not only do these five animated women, Calliope, Clio, Melpomene,
Terpsichore, and Thalia, have actual names, but they also prove that the
company has long been capable of representing Black women in authentic ways, at least when it feels it has a niche where they can fit, even in a
mythical space. That niche comes from the cultural associations of the
gospel-driven music that accompanies the film. Directors Ron Clements and John Musker deliberately drew the God–Greek gods connection
with gospel music; and composer Alan Menken recalled countering his
instinct to do "something very classic and Greek" with the idea that gospel fit because "that's what you sing when you're singing about God—or
in this case, the gods" (qtd. in Snetiker; see also Bryant).

But gospel has a particular cultural positioning and association in
the United States. Thus, although we can all follow the logic in casting
these voices, there is also an implicit connection to this genre of music
as music of narration, emotion, and storytelling, and it is very much
related to oral cultures of the US South, specifically Black culture in the
US South and the legacies of surviving chattel slavery. Racialized identity, history, and music become intertwined here and embodied in the
drawn images of these five Black women who give voice to the story of
the gods, whose role as Muses is to be in the service of the gods, without narrative agency for themselves. So although the Muses are the only
depictions of animated Black women in a Disney feature film until 2009
and *The Princess and the Frog*—and the only ones in any fully mythical or
fairy-tale animated space—they are relegated to being kept apart from
any actual action or having any agency or stories of their own. We also
have an odd connection that warrants further exploration: Historically,
WENA culture has legitimized its primacy through drawing connections
to the legacy of classical Hellenistic cultures and the Roman Empire,
and there is a simultaneous pattern of appropriating Black culture and
arts in especially US cultures. In both cases, the originators rarely if ever

have control over how the things they create are then appropriated, used, and reshaped, usually without any degree of acknowledgment or credit. There is future work to be done on the construction of canon through the appropriation of various kinds of perceived legitimacy, but for now, I will leave us with that thought to mull, as I turn instead to the other ways that Blackness appears in Disney productions, with or without Black people attached.

Problematizing Accent and Appropriated "Blaccent"

Disney's animation itself does a lot to shape the characters, but the connection between voice and image is especially important, and how an actor performs the script has long had a direct impact on how the animators might shape the scenes, down to the recording sessions being taped for the artists' reference, which are often later redeployed as paratextual "making of" or "behind the scenes" featurettes. In this light I want to especially focus on how voice shapes perception of racialized identities in animated productions, drawing predominantly from C. R. King, Lugo-Lugo, and Bloodsworth-Lugo's exploration of the topic in *Animating Difference*.

If we return to the 1994 *Lion King* for a moment, we can see through King and colleagues' analysis that voice acting becomes deliberately racialized to specific effects that affect interpretation of the characters and their social hierarchies, and this effect does not rely solely on how the characters are cast. The racialization, especially deliberately racializing villainous characters to connote certain interpretations or readings by audiences, is shaped by the time and place in which the story takes place. By setting the film "in a world outside the flow of time" and also without reference to local or indigenous populations or cultures (C. R. King et al., 58), the chosen geography becomes not a specific setting but rather a backdrop on which to play out WENA fantasies, as discussed earlier. The animals thus become stand-ins for humans as the "children of nature," where

> the animal protagonists of animated films set in Africa go native or, better said, play at being Africans in a manner recognizable to their audiences. Organized into something resembling "tribes,"

within or across species boundaries, they consult "witch doctors,"
modify their bodies with paint, feathers, and vegetation, engage
in traditional rituals—to affirm manhood and participation in the
community—and have worldviews marked by superstition and
animism. (C. R. King et al., 59–60)

This is, of course, pretty standard fare for WENA exoticization of colonized places, and we could easily draw a connection to other narratives
considered WENA classic literature where animals become surrogate
parents for humans to play out fantasies of exploration and processes
of civilization. But again, *The Lion King* has no human bodies, and thus
social concerns become more deeply projected into the depicted natu-
ralized world. And perhaps even more importantly, the social concerns
are those of a contemporary imperialist United States rather than the
British narratives of empire of several centuries before. Thus, as King
and colleagues observe, in *The Lion King* "those outside of the tribe do
not resemble the stereotypes of Africans" that the other animals who are
part of the Pride Lands community stand in for; "rather they draw upon
the U.S. language of racialized social problems," where "the darkness
beyond the prideland, marked by the elephant graveyard and prowled by
the hyenas, is an allegory for urban America" (60). King and colleagues
draw from the observations of Robert Gooding-Williams to explore how
this allegory is constructed in two steps: First, "it uses Whoopi Goldberg's and Cheech Marin's voices to represent the speech of two of three
prominent hyena characters as black English and Latino slang respectively"; and second, it depicts "the building that is the hyena's abode as
a bleak-looking and over-crowded high-rise, the unambiguous image of a
housing development in the projects" (Gooding-Williams, qtd. in C. R.
King et al., 60). The villainization of the hyenas is directly related to how
Goldberg's and Marin's voices would be interpreted in the context of
the visuals presented on-screen; and these characters are implicitly not
only set up as villains but also othered and presented as on the outside
of and disruptive to the "civilized" and "more ordered" structures of the
utopian construct of Africa that is the Pride Lands ruled by Simba's lion
family, who are set up as the natural leaders and maintainers of natural
order and hierarchy. Thus "the audience is meant to identify with the
animals, who play at being native, and recognize the threat to the natural

order in the form of more familiar and troubling outsiders," echoing Manuel M. Martin-Rodriguez's conclusion that "*The Lion King*, far from being an innocent adaptation of folklore . . . is better read as an effort to engage and work through the competition and conflict associated with Latino migration northward, an allegory that restabilizes the white core through a story about lions and hyenas in an invented Africa" (60). As such, "the social world finds expression through nature" in *The Lion King*, and, through nature, as seen with the hyenas, the "natural hierarchies reflect and reinforce social stratification" (60). This stratification is not divorced from racialization, and such films that use these politics as part of their narrative and setting constructions participate in a "recolonization" of Africa as a continent "by Eurocentric projections and preoccupations" by "carrying the imperial logic of erasure and assimilation at its extreme," "simultaneously reinforc[ing] notions of exotic difference and vanish[ing] Africans" (61). Again, this is accomplished through the intersecting subtexts of how image and sound, specifically accent, work together from a specific social, cultural, and historical context and by assuming a particular primary audience that would have been already trained through other media to interpret these things together in this way, even if not consciously.

One might ask why I am relying so heavily on the delineation of a problem framed and defined in a scholarly work from 2010. Surely such issues and practices would have been addressed and turned away from as an industry standard by now. But industry change is slow, especially when the people with the most power in the industries still come from largely homogeneous backgrounds. It is unfortunate that the reality is that the problems that King and colleagues identified in the 1990s and 2000s productions in their 2010 work have persisted into the 2020s and are perpetrated by the same companies. The connection between problematized, racialized urban identities and problematic or villainous characters might not be quite as pronounced in the 2019 *The Lion King*, but the aesthetics that shaped the animation are so closely held to in the photorealistic CGI that the specter of such connections remains, perhaps even more so because of the deliberately diverse voice actor casting and the dearth of human representation.

But say, hypothetically, that Disney had chosen to do something that constituted more of a wholistically equitable step forward in terms of how it chose to reinterpret the animated *Lion King* or otherwise do something completely new that centered culturally and/or geographically specific Black voices and stories. Such a hypothetical shift would still be potentially undercut by the reality that these productions exist in a network, not a vacuum, and would be understood and interpreted in concert with decisions such as casting Nora Lum (aka Awkwafina) in multiple roles across the wider corporation's productions. Awkwafina has courted controversy across her career as someone who has engaged in cultural appropriation of Black culture, particularly African American Vernacular English, or AAVE, in order to achieve her own fame and success. In particular, she has been criticized for her continued use of a "blaccent," or the use of AAVE and proximity to Blackness to promote her career (Cao; see also Thompson). In essence, cultural markers that have made her an appealing pop culture figure or garnered attention are often seen as detrimental or negative when presented by Black candidates.

The controversy around Awkwafina's blaccent and cultural appropriation came to the fore after her roles in *Ocean's 8* and *Crazy Rich Asians* in 2018 and when the news broke that she would be cast in the Disney productions *Raya and the Last Dragon* and the live-action and CGI production of *The Little Mermaid*. Although there was fan outcry against the casting, or at the very least demands that the actress not use a blaccent in either film, especially given that she did drop the accent and appropriation when beneficial to her career (Shotwell; see also L. M. Jackson; Makalintal), Disney leaned into the idea that *Raya* was a milestone in Southeast Asian representation for the company in terms of influences and casting (Moon). The corporation arguably even doubled down on the idea that the appropriation of AAVE by a non-Black actor was acceptable with the "Scuttlebutt" rap in the 2023 *Little Mermaid*, where Awkwafina voiced Scuttle (Brunner). The glossing of accent and identity in *The Little Mermaid* becomes even odder when we realize that Daveed Diggs, of *Hamilton* fame, who does not have a Caribbean accent, was cast as Sebastian and used a dialect coach to develop his accent work (A. Jackson; Bonomolo). The star power and recognition of both nonwhite actors is certainly understandable, but yet, if the corporation wants to have certain characters played or portrayed in a certain way, why not just cast people who already embody those identities to bring these much-loved characters to life? Until those levels of representation are grappled with by the corporation, steps made toward diversifying the Disney mediascape will be shallow at best and more likely tokenizing.

Impact Versus Intention: The Politics of Anti-Blackness Underlying the Disney Fairy-Tale Mode

Without Black bodies on-screen in multifaceted, pluralistic depictions, the question yet remains: Can Disney successfully incorporate Black identities—not the signaling of Blackness or some gesture at a constructed version of a homogenized Africa—into the core of the Disney transmedia universe, its fairy-tale canon? Insofar as the Disney Renaissance is concerned, *The Lion King* stands in for Africa in terms of landscape and certain musical influences, whereas Asian representation falls under a retelling of a Chinese ballad, the Middle East and South Asia are folded together in *Aladdin*, and several varied if unsuccessful attempts at representing Native Americans or First Nations peoples, or more broadly Indigeneity, followed the *Pocahontas* debacle. Stereotyped Blackness is relegated to accents in anthropomorphized supporting characters—either as comic relief in the case of Sebastian in *The Little Mermaid* or to signal villainy, as is the case with Whoopi Goldberg playing one of the hyenas, Shenzi. Until *The Princess and the Frog* in 2009 there was no attempt to address a large portion of not only the US population but also the global population. I cannot try to decipher whether this was a deliberate turning away from an institutional issue or simply a major foible that balanced the economic value of a "safe," traditionally historically rooted audience against progress and the dismantling of the whiteness at the core of the corporation. If we consider the Disney fairy-tale mode as a process of incorporation, a method by which difference is made to fit a narrative and aesthetic frame, the implication is that, to Disney, Blackness does not fit the mode and even, arguably, breaks it, to the point where even when a film is realized without Black bodies present, the inherent aesthetic whiteness of the Disney core aesthetic is made more visible. As Sarah E. Turner recognized, despite the potential consumer value of more diverse audiences,

> Classic Disney clearly imagined an audience that was white and
> that shared the ideologies of the hegemonic culture; *Jungle Book,*

> *The Lion King, Song of the South*, and *Aladdin*, for example, all illus-
> trate Disney's recognition of the social and racial positioning of its
> audiences, a positioning that would recognize tropes of blackness
> or racial representation but that would not problematize the use
> of those tropes in any way. . . . Disney is not going to seriously
> challenge those tropes of blackness. (Turner, 93)

However, 1 can with hindsight deconstruct the refusal to look at the problem of whiteness and tacit anti-Blackness through avoidance of talking about race in the context of contemporary Disney as contributing to a larger social problem that has never reconciled Black people on-screen as normative, best evidenced through Disney's only animated feature film to star a Black princess.

Even after *The Princess and the Frog* was released and the corporation included Tiana in the Disney Princess brand lineup, audiences were not quite convinced about her being a "real" Disney princess (see Dundes and Streiff). The film garnered a fair amount of criticism both from its first announcement and its surface-level deployment of Black culture without further interrogating what kind of fairy tale was being proffered to Black children in the greater context of the Disney fairy-tale universe. Even as a surface-level fix, this film does not change the company's seeming overall discomfort with depicting Blackness in a way that might challenge the comfort of a conservative white target audience. Symptoms of this discomfort arguably appeared again in 2018 with the production of *Ralph Breaks the Internet*, which features several key scenes starring the Disney princesses. The antiracism charity Color of Change noted that, in early trailers for the film, Tiana's transformation into CGI involved a distinct change in her appearance beyond the two-dimensional to three-dimensional shift. The charity released a statement saying, "In the choice to whitewash an image that represents us, [Disney] totally removed and replaced Princess Tiana's full lips, dark skin and kinky hair. By doing so, they are showing us that they don't care about reflecting the diversity of the Black community" (Horton). Following a petition and internet campaign, the CGI depiction was redone to match the 2009 animation. But it still raises the question, Where does Disney's apparent discomfort with unapologetic Blackness come from, and, furthermore, what has this continued discomfort in turn helped to passively communicate to generations of viewers?

I cannot begin to deconstruct the source of such discomfort and avoidance. But I can assert why, beyond the images themselves, it matters if the realization of the intention is imperfect. I started my path to a doctorate degree by pursuing a master's degree at the University of Edinburgh in 2013, a couple of months after the Black Lives Matter movement was founded on 13 July 2013 following the murder of Trayvon Martin on 26 February 2012. Looking at the protests in response to the death of George Floyd on 25 May 2020, this timeline is significant. In the time I completed two advanced degrees, never mind the time I took to rework the research of the second degree into a book, state-sanctioned violence escalated with more unprosecuted murders and deaths of Black people at the hands of the state, not only in the United States and the Anglophone world but across the world at large. A lack of plurality in representation combined with real-world representation that both adultifies Black children and demarcates them "a threat" (Myers) has real-world effects in terms of the toll it takes on the misrepresented community and how members of it are seen by the wider society. To draw from the oft-bandied refrain of the Black Lives Matter protests, silence is both compliance and violence. If the language of Disney is one of images, then a lack of a particular image is erasure, is silence on the part of the corporation and an act of tacit violence against this community. There is a "responsibility" by those who "make images" to do better, and through the creation of images for children, creators "are affirming a vision of the communities in which we want to live" (Myers). We can see a much wider, much darker impact of bad or no representation by looking more closely at the impact of the lack of positive images of Black people in media for families in the United States.

Looking at the problem of representation in children's books, Kekla Magoon notes that the publishing industry reflects a "modern minstrelsy" where there is an expectation of a certain version of Blackness to be performed in order for something to be deemed acceptable to the industry, and thus

> those of us writing to expand representation of Blackness face certain challenges about authenticity from the largely white audience

of publishing. We are being asked to perform Blackness to the satisfaction of some mythical standard of believability while, at the same time, it has never stopped being okay for white creators to perform Blackness in any way that they choose. (Magoon)

This "pressure to conform to the white gaze" and both its historical use and modern propensity to "reinforce white supremacy" (Magoon) are also present in other media that not only centers the white gaze in its narrative structure but also does not deconstruct the narratives to which Blackness is constricted, thus ignoring the harm that might cause. Even shows that look like they are moving in a progressive direction, such as *Westworld*, based on both their on- and off-screen talent, can remain problematic, as Hope Wabuke asserts:

In [the 2020 murders of Ahmaud Arbery, Breonna Taylor, and George Floyd] we see the lie at the center of *Westworld*. There is no need for the fantasy of the Wild West theme park to allow white men to pantomime the unthinkable in order to find their "true nature," as the game promises. *Westworld* already exists for them in reality. . . .

The diversity is still relegated to stereotypical, and often painful representations. One wonders which is more harmful: absence, or toxic representation? . . . And so, the same way women of all races critique the pornography of violence against the female body that is a driving force of so many cop and action dramas, I ask this: can we not get more imaginative than only imagining black pain as a catalyst in black life—than monetizing very real black pain for white entertainment and white profit? (Wabuke)

In both the minstrelsy of the children's book industry and the drive to capitalize on the pain and dehumanization of Black people, what is not visible in the mainstream are more pathways for imagined futures for Black people. Disney is a small piece of the overall problem, but nonetheless a significant one.

As already established, Disney's works, especially the fairy-tale narratives, have become synonymous with "safe" family entertainment. That idea of "safe" very much is determined by the hegemonic constructions of the particularly US society that Disney *safeguards*. That is achieved in part by not straying too far from the expected norms of the target audience with what Disney presents to its white, middle-class, conservative, Christian base. Whereas other cultures became incorporated into the Disney universe post-1989 on some level—poorly but as visually represented as *humans*—Black people were not afforded even the same level of poor representation, were not extended that meager humanity in the same way. If Disney—based on the worlds it draws—cannot see a large sector of the human population *as human*, treat that sector as multidimensional humans with the same level of possibilities as its "normal" (read: unraced/white) characters, how will anyone else? It is not enough to just not traffic in stereotype. Antiracist efforts require actively making sure that Black people are seen as people—not animals, not hallmarks of specific accents, not as faceless sources of cultural artifacts to be appropriated—and, not as targets in a broken system of justice that has labeled them as inherently dangerous. Not actively counteracting that narrative of inherent danger in the corporation's most widely distributed product by not including human depictions of the people most harmed by that hegemonic society that Disney props up, is an apathy that we need to understand not as simple inaction but as actively contributing to harm for as long as it continues. It needs to be explicitly named. As much as Disney proffers its narratives as timeless, they exist within specific historical contexts, and their relationship to the historical context of anti-Blackness as it persists in the contemporary is one that must be more closely examined as well. Naming and noticing the construct of Blackness in absentia in the Disney universe, especially from the point of the Disney Renaissance onward against the backdrop of unnamed normative whiteness, is a part of that.

3

WISH UPON A STAR, BUT WORK FOR IT

Disparities in Dreaming

In 1950 Disney released its second animated fairy-tale feature film, *Cinderella*. Together with the release of *Snow White and the Seven Dwarfs* (1937) and *Sleeping Beauty* (1959), these three films would solidify Disney's particular aesthetic of fairy-tale magic in the public imagination. Cinderella's story became one of the Disney keystones, providing a foundational figure and narrative for Disney's brand of storytelling and, later, the Disney Princess franchise and becoming the symbolic presence of the transformation and wonder of the lived experience in Disney's parks. The 2015 remediation further solidified *Cinderella* as a canonical Disney narrative in the contemporary, but Cinderella as a figure has had many afterlives not only in terms of a wider fairy-tale and folklore context outside the Disney remit[1] but also, interestingly, from within the boundaries of the corporation itself.

Through making and remaking the *Cinderella* narrative in different ways, Disney has asserted its consistent authority to define the boundaries of who or what the "Cinderella" story embodies, in the process consistently asserting its authority as a company over the domain of contemporary fairy tales and emphasizing the idea of the Disney princess as "the 'princess of all princesses'" (Do Rozario, 34). Jack Zipes criticized Disney's imprint on the form of the fairy tale as the "Disney Spell," a particular "stranglehold" on the genre of the fairy tale that began in 1937 and was reiterated in the 1990s (Zipes, "Breaking," 21), when Disney as both filmmaker and, later, corporation "changed our way of viewing

---

1 See Hennard Dutheil de la Rochère et al.; and Woltmann.

fairy tales" through "revolutionary technical means" that "capitalized on American innocence and utopianism to reinforce the social and political status quo" (21–22). The assertion that Disney as a corporation has had a significant impact on the fairy-tale form still holds true today. The pluralism of both *Cinderella* narratives and other fairy-tale narratives told repeatedly under the Disney umbrella illustrates the corporation's unique imprint on the texture of not only the fairy-tale narratives it produces but also Disney narratives at large.

In the last chapter I focused on how anti-Blackness remains at the core DNA of the corporation; in this chapter I look at moments in Disney's history that point to a potential for growth and their limitations. If we understand that Disney's core anti-Blackness is shown through the legacy of racist stereotypes in its animated and live-action programming and in the way that representation of Black characters is tacitly avoided through the company's reemergence and borderline rebranding in the 1990s, then we might consider the ways in which Disney did try to diversify its productions in the 1990s as either a kind of tokenism or exercises in colorblindness (see Valdivia). In this chapter I explore how Disney fairy-tale narratives operate palimpsestically in the Disney corporation and how the use or existence of multiple versions ends up solidifying a sense of reiterated reference to an original; I also highlight the shortfalls in how the corporation approaches wider representation, in the context of the habit of anti-Blackness on an aesthetic level.

When considering the multivocality of fairy tales or folklore narratives, one might first think of the plurality of narratives generated across time, culture, languages, and geographies. But, consider the media generation of the Disney corporation across its history and its voice and power as it has taken or been to some effect granted the mantle of the creator of the authorized, Americanized fairy tale (Haase), the inheritor of writers and collectors such as Perrault and the Grimms. There is an interesting discussion to be had regarding power, voice, ownership, and authority as the corporation continues to generate multiple versions of fairy-tale narratives under a single corporate umbrella. The specific intertextual nature of fairy tales as they continue to be adapted across media, cultures, and different times has led to a conceptualization of an intertextual web of narratives (Bacchilega, *Fairy Tales Transformed*; Haase; Tiffin). When examining works from the same corporation, it is important to also consider the effects of what Kamila Elliot terms "tie-intertextuality" in the context of "franchise adaptation" as conceptualized by Clare Parody. Parody notes that "adaptation and adaptations that are situated in a transmedia project are the products of a particular market strategy; they are contributing to and drawing on a particular kind of fictional experience and negotiating particular types of intertextual relation" (Parody, 212), a description that aptly describes Disney's overall adaptation strategy. Disney uses such methods as nostalgia and concepts of inherited cultural lineage in its construction of brand identity. Disney works are inherently intertextual; the aesthetic is deliberately engineered to tie Disney media to a particular cultural identity. These intertextual modes then become part of re-creating and reestablishing the brand. All difference reaffirms the primacy of the "original" (see also Anjirbag and Hunter), making Disney's multiple versions antithetical to the wider conception of versions of fairy tales, despite the fact that they also exist in the greater context of the narrative web. We can describe the many iterations of Disney productions of *Cinderella* narratives as a "corporate palimpsest," paying careful attention to what is kept visible and retained across versions and what is overwritten. Disney's manipulation of "tie-intertextuality" or "corporate intertextual incorporation" (Elliott, 193) allows the corporation to reaffirm the dominance of its "original" narrative while also oversaturating the image of Cinderella in popular imagination through sheer volume of output. By looking at the *Cinderella* films together, I demonstrate how the corporation plays with the idea of multivocality and multiple audiences while simultaneously drawing borders around the definitional idea of what a *Cinderella* narrative is and who might be encapsulated by it.

Putting the Shoe on An-Other Foot: Three *Cinderella* Narratives

At the time of this writing, the Disney corporation has released three theatrically produced *Cinderella* stories as Disney feature films. These are the 1950 animation, the 2015 remediation, and 2009's *The Princess and the Frog*. There are also the made-for-television productions: 1997's *The Wonderful World of Disney Presents Rodgers and Hammerstein's Cinderella* and the 2022 Disney+ production of *Sneakerella*. For the purposes of this chapter I am limiting my discussion to the 1997, 2009, and 2022 productions. To have so many narratives coexisting within one corporation without overwriting each other is an interesting phenomenon that I address elsewhere.[2] For the purposes of this chapter, I focus on the pattern revealed by examining where Blackness collides with the classic Disney *Cinderella* aesthetic and narrative patterns. When it comes to representations that would collide with or disrupt that aesthetic, the paradigm for narrative creation is changed to accommodate that disruption. As previously noted, difference is handled differently in the Disney universe, and surface fixes for diversity do not work to create equitably diverse representations that hold the same weight as the Disney fairy-tale narratives that are considered variations of the classic version. As can be seen by exploring these iterations, which attempt to center either multiculturalism or African American heritage, the studio tries to do better in terms of racially and ethnically diverse representation, with the caveat of not alienating its core base of viewers. But its decisions nevertheless have a negative impact, despite the company's best intentions to step outside its conservatism.

A New Standard of Beauty

In the 2024 *Descendants: The Rise of Red* film, a Disney Channel production set in the world set up by the *Descendants* film trilogy and other transmedia and targeted ostensibly to a contemporary adolescent audience, one of the biggest nostalgic throwbacks to Disney fairy tales seen in this franchise was actually likely aimed not at the films' audience but at an older one. Brandy Norland and Paolo Montalban reprise their roles as Cinderella and the now King Charming from a 1997 made-for-television production of the *Cinderella* musical; their daughter is now one of the protagonists of the new film. It is not just the fact that both Cinderella and the king are present; in a scene where they tell the story of how they fell in love at a school dance, they pay homage to the ballroom scene from their own *Cinderella*; they dance together and sing the iconic "So

2   I spoke on this topic at the 2022 International Society for Folk Narrative Research conference in London, and that work was then expanded and published in the *Journal of American Culture*; see Anjirbag, "Pumpkin-Carriage Palimpsests."

This Is Love" from the 1950 animated feature film (instead of the Rodgers and Hammerstein "Ten Minutes Ago," which is the feature of the ball scene in the 1997 version). Almost three decades later, Disney's first live-action Black princess steps partly into the slippers of her animated predecessor, a role that her own iteration of the role was markedly different from, creating a fascinating moment of plurality in the corporation's fairy-tale productions. In a way, *Descendants: The Rise of Red* provides a glimpse of a "happily ever after" that might have been, after the credits close on the wedding scene that completes Cinderella's realization as royalty, but with nonwhite people front and center, doing what every couple dreams of doing one day: embarrassing their teenager with how much they are still in love—a fairy tale of sorts in its own right.

In 1997 Whitney Houston co-produced a version of Rodgers and Hammerstein's *Cinderella* for Disney's primetime television program, *The Wonderful World of Disney*, which was broadcast on the ABC television network. The telecast debuted on 2 November 1997, forty years after the original CBS television broadcast of *Rodgers and Hammerstein's Cinderella* in 1957. Robert L. Freedman adapted Hammerstein's original book, deliberately updating the musical's themes to fit the contemporary setting. The decision to use colorblind casting resulted in a cast that featured not only Houston as the Fairy Godmother, but Whoopi Goldberg and Victor Garber as the Queen and King, Paolo Montalban as the Prince, and Bernadette Peters as the Stepmother, alongside Jason Alexander, Veanne Cox, and Natalie Desselle-Reid in other roles. African American pop singer and actress Brandy was featured as the first Black Cinderella, a casting decision that would not come close to being repeated until the Disney's animated production of *The Princess and the Frog* in 2009, the 2019 production of *The Wonderful World of Disney*'s presentation of *The Little Mermaid Live!* and the 2023 live-action and CGI remediation of *The Little Mermaid*.

The positioning of the 1997 *Cinderella* within the greater corporate structure of Disney is different from the other films discussed in this book. *The Wonderful World of Disney* programming is a legacy production from Walt Disney's own days, even if it no longer holds a weekly primetime broadcast slot. Paul Wells discusses the debut of *Disneyland* on the ABC network in October 1954 (Wells, 76) and tracks how television became a medium through which the corporation embraced the "politics of nostalgia" (Schickel, 168) identified as integral to Disney's success across generations. But nostalgic for what? There is a deeper and more wide ranging conversation to be had regarding the crossroads between conservative American values and romanticized medievalism,[3] but, nevertheless, Disney has capitalized on nostalgia from generation to generation by first re-releasing films cyclically in theaters and, later, re-releasing the cartoons on television framed by the concept of Disneyland as a fairy-tale land that could be entered—later, literally entered by means of the theme parks.[4] The films, television shows, parks, and other parts of Disney's corporate structure intersect to create a transmedia storyland where people can interact with narratives across media and on their own time, with the interplay between the media, the parks, and the other corporate outputs continuing and retelling different aspects of different stories at different times and in different ways. But the impression remains that it is all part of one overarching, continuous, and revisitable story of Disney fairy-tale magic. Walt Disney's *Disneyland* television programming, hosted and curated by its visionary creator and later branded as *The Wonderful World of Disney* after several other name changes, had lapsed, changed networks several times, and evolved from its original conception by the time that *Rodgers and Hammerstein's Cinderella* was announced. But by releasing this fairy-tale musical on television in a legacy time slot as *The Wonderful World of Disney Presents Rodgers and Hammerstein's Cinderella*, the corporation achieved several things. First, it used that nostalgic draw through the "Wonderful World of Disney" part of the title to signal to viewers that this was a particular kind of family, Disney entertainment, being broadcast to America as an extension of its movies, its parks, and its magic. Also, by including the reference to Rodgers and Hammerstein in the title, beyond citation, the corporation ensured that viewers understood that this would simultaneously be something new, something separate from the *Cinderella* of classic Disney animation.

3 This romanticized medievalism is something I discuss more in-depth in Anjirbag, "Enter the Castle."

4 Sabrina Mittermeier's *A Cultural History of the Disneyland Theme Parks: Middle Class Kingdoms* more cogently addresses the cultural and spatial politics of the parks than I am able to do here.

Marking it as separate served several purposes. First, it protects the Disney *Cinderella* brand, the beloved strawberry-blonde who epitomized "princess" and the notion that "dreams come true" for decades. Second, viewers are prompted to recall the original through the deployment of visual iconography and metonym, such as a blue dress, a glass slipper, evil stepsisters, and a pumpkin carriage. In doing so, they relate the new version to the earlier edition, reestablishing the primacy of Disney animation as the authoritative version that the live-action stands in relation to. The simultaneous proclamation of "ours" (Disney) but "not ours" (Rodgers and Hammerstein) and the marketing campaign that featured Whitney Houston as a producer, thereby sharing authorship in several directions, created space between Disney and the potential pushback against what was at the time a progressive production. Although multiculturalism has been more at home in Disney's television programming than on the silver screen (see Valdivia; Leon-Boys and Valdivia), this production was still a fairy-tale film, more in dialogue with the animated feature fairy-tale film tradition by Disney than its television programming. Thus the corporation carved out a space for experimentation in presentation while also avoiding a promise for more inclusive representation in its fairy-tale films. This was something *different*, not an evolution of the brand or the presentation of a new normal. The only African American or Black princess of the multicultural Disney Renaissance of the 1990s was not to truly be a part of the Disney universe, implicitly othering both this transformative tale and those who might have seen themselves within it.

In remediating a stage show that had its own history, Disney still put in the same attention to detail in creating a sense of magic and wonder to construct its fantasy setting and engage viewers in an intertextual space where the new iteration remained in dialogue with other experiences of the *Cinderella* tale. Before viewers first meet Brandy as Cinderella in the marketplace, the film is framed first by the title screen reading "The Wonderful World of Disney and Whitney Houston Present Rodgers and Hammerstein's Cinderella" and, second, by Whitney Houston as the Fairy Godmother singing snippets of the musical's song "Impossible," cut through with the narration of "a slipper made of glass is just a shoe / and dreamers never made a dream come true" (*The Wonderful World*). With an exuberant wave of her arms and an opening line that encodes the idea of hard work as more important than a belief in dreams, the movie musical moves into its opening credits depicting a cobble-stoned town center with ridiculous, brightly colored pastiches of quasi-period peasant and merchant costumes that are deliberately multicultural—and stated to be as such twenty years later in an interview with the cast, crew, and production team (James). The opening signals a different retelling of an already twice-told classic *Cinderella* story (the legacies of both Disney and Rodgers and Hammerstein) and relegates it to the setting of a storybook fairy-tale village come to life, complete with the castle looming far away on the hill overlooking the town. This is a different approach to take from, say, the throwaway remark that dates the animated *Sleeping Beauty*—Prince Philip exclaims to King Hubert, "Now Father, you're living in the past! This is the fourteenth century!" as he tries to argue that he should be allowed to marry the peasant girl he has met in the forest—or the dating through ephemeral details seen in the costuming and material aesthetics of the feature film live-action remediations of the 2010s. This version of *Cinderella* is produced as an anomaly within the Disney fairy-tale corpus.

Now, let's take as a given that, based on the company's deployment of nostalgic reiteration of its properties, all Disney films and properties coexist at all times as part of a transmedia narrative multiverse. Looking back across the Disney fairy-tale and folkloresque film corpus from the vantage point of the 2020s, not only are there few examples of Blackness being centered in a given narrative, but, when it is centered, it is separated from Disney's core fairy-tale Magic Kingdom aesthetic and brand identity. It exists as negative stereotype (the crows and the faceless workers in *Dumbo*), Afrofuturism (Marvel's *Black Panther*), a construct of Black excellence as being outside the Anglo-American context (Walt Disney Pictures' *Queen of Katwe*), a concept consigned to specific historical contexts (*The Princess and the Frog*), or, as seen in this iteration of *Cinderella*, a storybook aesthetic. Unlike other iterations of fairy-tale narratives that are rooted to some degree in historical details to generate their particular aesthetic, this story is something that will never be and has never been in the real world. Although constructing a fantasyscape that so clearly centered both Blackness and a plurality of diversity in the casting of extras was a revolutionary thing for Disney in 1997, it is also clear that the corporation never fully accepted this version of its fantasy world, as this construction of diverse and multicultural world building has not persisted in a significant way. This is directly juxtaposed against the vastness of possibilities presented for white children in the Disney universe; they are given the tools to imagine that, once upon a time in their histories, they could have access to all the potentials of wonder and magic, and therefore they can still dream that they can become anything. The 2015 Kenneth Branagh–directed film gets to be an iteration of the "normal" Disney *Cinderella*, the direct inheritor of the 1950 animated feature film. The Whitney Houston 1997 production is instead, implicitly and explicitly, othered.

In her *Shondaland* interview with the living cast and crew for the film's twentieth anniversary, Kendra James identifies the production as "one of the most inclusive, expensive (with a $12 million budget), and ultimately beloved TV movies of all time." She adds:

> The casting of this "Cinderella" was historic and not without its detractors—not since "The Wiz" had a production dared to imagine that a story so firmly fixed in the cultural zeitgeist could be seen as anything other than lily white. And for a generation of young children of color, "Cinderella" became an iconic memory of their childhoods, of seeing themselves in a black princess who could lock eyes and fall in love with a Filipino prince. Whitney Houston's persistence had paid off, her dream of a multi-cultural "Cinderella" production was realized, and its effect was achieved. (James)

Called a "Cinderella for the millennium" by executive producer Neil Meron at the time of release (Meron, qtd. in Purdum), the casting project—diversity at every level—represented in some ways a hope for a new vision of what the wonderful world of Disney might look like and who might be welcome within it. Before this 1997 production, the range of multicultural depictions following the 1989 reboot of Disney animation included questionable accents in *The Little Mermaid*, the heavily orientalized *Aladdin*, the use of anthropomorphism instead of people to represent a continent in *The Lion King*, the rewriting of history in *Pocahontas*, the exoticization and oversexualization of Esmerelda in *The Hunchback of Notre Dame* (see Hurley), and the depiction of the Muses in *Hercules* as Black women fulfilling the dramatic role of the chorus by means of gospel music. *Hercules* premiered on 27 June 1997, and *The Wonderful World of Disney and Whitney Houston Present Rodgers and Hammerstein's Cinderella* aired on ABC in November 1997, crowning pop star and actress Brandy Norland as the first Disney Black princess.

The aesthetic of the 1997 *Cinderella* is different from that of other Disney productions. If Disney as a corporation marks its territory through the use of the castle, especially in fairy-tale adaptations, this particular castle is as much an anomaly as the production itself. Whereas other Disney castles are overwhelmingly inflected with quasi-historical, quasi-medieval detail, this castle is inflected with whimsy and oversaturated with color and leans further into a theatrical fairy-tale aesthetic than any other space. The exterior shots were done on the permanent set of the Universal Studios Little Europe lot, and interior shots were filmed on the same MGM stages where *The Wizard of Oz* had been filmed (James). Executive producer Craig Zadan noted that the oversaturation was a deliberate choice, because the production team was incredibly self-conscious about the deliberate decision to create a multicultural *Cinderella* in 1997:

> Conceptually, when we discussed this with Robert [Iscove, the director], we wanted to make sure that our diverse vision wasn't so obvious that it became self-conscious and try-hard. . . . We wanted it to just be what it was, a fairytale. So what we did very purposefully was to demand that this production be thoroughly color saturated. We wanted everything to be hyper colorful and richly vivid. That was the goal. We wanted the image on screen to have so much color in it—primary colors especially—that the skin colors almost dissipated in that you weren't staring at "that person's this or that" because the design dictated that everyone became part of the same story. (Zadan, qtd. in James)

This conception of how color would play a part in the perception of a fairy-tale or fantasy world was an unconscious, or perhaps an openly unstated, response to the world building synonymous with the Disney aesthetic, as well as a conscious response to perceptions about what it meant to do something "multicultural" at the time. The idea that the "skin colors almost dissipated" was a way of subtly erasing the significance of racialized dynamics from this kind of a world, despite being a production that aimed to center Blackness. Such is the erasure at the heart of colorblind productions that are, in this case, attempting to absent or minimize the Blackness that made this musical so significant for so many viewers. Instead of building a space for Black bodies within the space of the Disney fairy-tale chronotope, the setting of this productions becomes visually othered through that color saturation, so different from the castles, forests, and villages of the historicized medievalist fantasy worlds of the other fairy-tale narratives.

The year 1997 is a point from which we can look backward and forward in time, both in terms of what diversity and multiculturalism meant in the context of the corporation and what it meant to be a Disney princess, to be seen and reflected in a Disney fairy-tale narrative, and what it might mean to see oneself in a fairy-tale or fantasy narrative. Ebony Elizabeth Thomas writes, "When people of color seek passageways into the fantastic, we have often discovered that the doors are barred. Even the very act of dreaming of worlds-that-never-were can be challenging when the known world does not provide many liberating spaces" (Thomas, 2). This version of *Cinderella* seemed to be positioned to herald a new swath of "liberating spaces," opening the doors of new iterations of old worlds to nonwhite people generally but especially to Black people. Travis Payne, one of the dancers in the production, observed that "walking onto the set for the first time . . . it was just like fantasy. Everything was larger than life, from the sets to the costumes. And the diversity of the cast was very overwhelming at first. Not in a bad way—it just wasn't something we were privileged enough to see often" (Payne, qtd. in James). Payne's statement is revealing. As a professional dancer who would have been intimately connected with various areas of American performance and production, he was overwhelmed by the thorough representation on a soundstage. He defines this level of saturation of multicultural representation as something "like fantasy" in 1997. From a vantage point of more than twenty years later, it is apparent that truly, for Disney, this was a pinnacle achieved and then not reached for again really until the production of *The Little Mermaid Live!* in 2019. That means that, for more than twenty years, nonwhite people, young and old, have been excluded from a vision of a fairy-tale world that included them as more of a token part and have not benefited from that moment of privileged, multilayered magic.

The multicultural casting, especially of several Black women in leading, iconic roles, was not without its detractors. In the *Shondaland* interview, Zadan noted:

> I'll tell you what was going on behind the scenes: There was an executive at Disney—who will remain nameless—and he was very nervous about a black Cinderella. He loved the idea of Whitney being the black fairy godmother, but he came up to us and said, "Well, if you're coming up with someone like Brandy as Cinderella, why can't you go get Jewel instead, and have a white Cinderella and a black Fairy Godmother. It'll still be multicultural." I think he was saying to himself, "Who's a white version of Brandy?" We said absolutely not. The whole point of this whole thing was to have a black Cinderella. We didn't want to make it with a white Cinderella. We weren't interested in a white Cinderella. Still aren't! We never approached anyone other than Brandy for the role, and Jewel was never approached. (Zadan, qtd. in James)

Meron, in the interview, notes that this unnamed executive was acting independently of the network and Michael Eisner. Zadan continued:

> But it's important to mention because it shows that even at that moment there was still resistance to having a black Cinderella. People were clearly still thinking, "Multicultural is one thing, but do we have to have two black leads?" . . . We even got the dancers we wanted—we cast Latino, Asian, white, and black dancers. We were so consumed with making sure that we didn't let any area of the production fall into an easy casting situation. For each and every detail, we wanted to make sure we were meticulous with how we put these roles together. (Zadan, qtd. in James)

The multiracial casting approach to create a kind of colorblind effect in the world was deliberate and was described as a "checkerboard" that needed balancing. But *colorblind* and *multicultural* or *multiracial* are not terms that erase the concerns and dynamics of racialized identity—if anything, they result in a heightened consciousness of color—something made evident when the role of the Stepmother proved the most difficult to cast. According to executive producer Debra Martin Chase:

> No white actress wanted to be seen as being mean to the black Cinderella. . . . I would write these long letters putting the role in context, explaining the importance of what we were doing with the multicultural cast, and the cultural impact we hoped to have. I wanted them to understand that they wouldn't just be coming on board for a great show; it was also going to be important culturally. (Chase, qtd. in James)

After casting Bernadette Peters in the role, the decision to cast the step-sisters as one Black and one white was made "just to further hit home that color is irrelevant in this fantasy world" (Meron, qtd. in James).

However, color was very much relevant, as seen in the decisions about how to use color across the settings—using both Gustav Klimt and Maxfield Parrish as inspiration (James)—and how Cinderella would be dressed. Costume designer Ellen Mirojnick said:

> I took a lot of care when thinking about how to costume around the Cinderella and Stepmother relationship. We were very conscious of not doing something that reflected a stereotypical way of looking at a poor black girl. You know, the maid sort of thing; the poor girl who is under the thumb of a white woman. She still needed to have a presence. I didn't want to tag any extra baggage onto it. (Mirojnick, qtd. in James)

To have that awareness in the costume designer, about how race and racial-ized identity play out even in fantasy worlds, was important to making sure that Brandy could be believed as Cinderella in a multicultural fairy-tale world, something the actress herself expressed concerns about (James).

How much race did matter after all became more apparent when it came time for the studio to recoup its costs. This production marked the first time that a made-for-television film was produced for VHS sales release, but as Zadan notes, this was where critical reception met the reality of popular culture and American perceptions of race:

> People just weren't getting behind the VHS release the way they needed to. There was also an unspoken racial issue about it being a "black show." Disney was counting on sales to make their money back, and it didn't look like it was going to happen. They needed chains like Walmart and Blockbuster, to put up giant cardboard cut-out displays—remember those?—of Brandy and Whitney, and the chains were reluctant. The Disney marketing people basically said to them, "If you want to continue getting an early look at our Disney animated movies, you have to promote 'Cinderella,' and if you don't promote it we're gonna make sure other chains get our products before you." It became like a threat, and finally they had to almost force them to put them up. But they did. . . . The irony of the ending to this entire story is that the first week we were in the stores we sold 1,000,000 units. At that point there was no such thing as a home video of a TV show selling 1,000,000 the first week. (Zadan, qtd. in James)

That Disney as a media corporation essentially strong-armed major commercial brands into carrying and fully marketing a production that was by all accounts a critical success at the time reveals the disconnect between something that has remained popular and the wider corporate culture that may well see it as a threat to its sense of normal or to its target audience. Although the legacy of the film remains strong twenty years on in Black communities and in other communities made up of people of global majority communities (James) and although, through their own accounts, white producers and stakeholders had their eyes opened to the need for more diverse representation, this *Cinderella* iteration remains a sole landmark in the wider Disney fairy-tale landscape. For whatever reasons, Disney veered away from a moment of more progressive imagining, solidified through deliberate multiracial casting even while moving the aesthetic from one filled with historical details embedded in fairy-tale fantasy to one of a more storybook village—a "world-that-never-was" (Thomas, 2). And yet this remains a moment excluded or separated from the wider Disney multicultural universe being built in the animated films. Perhaps worse, as the company has progressed through a process of making live-action remakes of its classics, the legacy of this *Cinderella* film has been to fade into a constructed obscurity through the lack of easy access to the film for decades compared with the rest of the corporation's productions. Again, the film was made widely available to stream only in the 2020s and, even then, only for those with access to the Disney+ platform. This production's differences become more and more markedly apparent as the newer films together worked to solidify what a live-action Disney fairy tale should be like, signaled through icons of ahistorical fantasy medievalist aesthetics and landscapes to confer both legacy and legitimacy.

Although there is a prince and Cinderella becomes a princess by marriage and even though there is plenty of magic, there is barely any fairy-tale forest landscape in this film other than that traveled through in the pumpkin carriage to the castle on the hill, as Brandy and Whitney Houston sing "Impossible" together before Cinderella attends the ball. The landscape does not build out into a wider world that is full of potential (and potential dangers); instead, it is confined to specific spaces: village square, home, castle, ball, carriage—the "urban" spaces of this world avoiding a challenge to the natural order of natural spaces that do not usually include Black people in the hegemonic imaginary. If we carry forward the notion of the chronotope, specifically, that time-space defines, announces, and constrains narrative possibility, even though this narrative exists in a fairy-tale time, the spaces it inhabits are confined and thus so too is the narrative. However, it is still groundbreaking that in 1997, in this particular enchanted carriage, with all the hope and wonder and possibility revealed through the Fairy Godmother's use of magic, *this* version of Cinderella is fully embraced by the fairy-tale potential for wonder, and that potential is a landmark depiction for all viewers, for both Black and white audiences. For the former, they are finally on the way to the kingdom Walt built themselves after generations of exclusion; for the latter, they are asked to widen their perceptions of with whom they might have to share access to wonder and therefore the potential access to power. These are gains in the construction and conception of Disney fairy-tale narratives that cannot be ignored, even if they are relegated to a niche corner of the larger transmedia conglomerate. However, it is a potential for magic that is not ultimately fulfilled in the same way as it is for other Disney princesses who wish upon stars and have their dreams simply fulfilled with a wave of a magic wand. As the method that marks this film as the most different from other fairy-tale films by

Disney becomes ultimately repeated in the only animated fairy-tale film to feature an African American princess, one cannot ignore the racialized implications of which princesses can have their dreams come true if they are willing to work for it.

This is ultimately the most distinct difference between this *Cinderella* film and the other fairy-tale films of the Disney canon that preceded it: the message that magic works through *work*, not dreams. Because this distinction is made specifically in an iteration built around multiculturalism and a Black Cinderella, it is not possible to just read this decision as an update for modern girls (i.e., not to just wait for their prince to come); there is also a racialized undercurrent. Cinderella is characterized first and foremost as a dreamer. From the opening dual soliloquy of "The Sweetest Sounds" sung with Paolo Montalban's prince, where Cinderella dreams of finding kindness and understanding, to "My Own Little Corner," where she embodies in her make-believe so many different possibilities of what she could be, Brandy as Cinderella passes on that dream of potential to viewers who see themselves in her. In this number she sees herself in roles that take strength and courage, confidence and skill, and imagination. She can be an heiress, a mermaid, a huntress—she dreams of roles across the world and of every background. In the reprise, she dreams herself at the ball meeting the prince, after her family has left her behind. But even though Cinderella's dreams are eventually fulfilled, the film undercuts the idealization of dreamers by emphasizing that one must do more than simply dream in order to make things happen.

Whitney Houston as the Fairy Godmother tells viewers right from the start that "dreamers never made a dream come true," and this is the message that is reiterated throughout the film. For the animated white fairy-tale princesses, true love and magic are enough to solve their problems and transcend their situations. For this Cinderella the magic comes with an asterisk. From the introduction to Bernadette Peters's number about how "falling in love with love" is for fools and that Cinderella should "know her place and be satisfied with what she's got" (paraphrased), to Cinderella's meeting with the Fairy Godmother, dreams and love are constantly indicated as not enough to make things happen to change one's circumstances. When Cinderella makes her wish at the window, the Fairy Godmother appears singing "Fol-de-rol and fiddledy-dee" and making comments that "all the wishes in the world are poppycock and twaddle" and "all the dreamers in the world are dizzy in the noodle." Although this is true to the original Rodgers and Hammerstein *Cinderella* lyrics, it is a far cry from the appearance of the Fairy Godmother in the animated feature. Where the white 1950 Cinderella sings about how dreams are wishes hearts make, Disney's Black Cinderella does not simply get to follow her heart's wishes and dream about a life filled with more, nor does she have it handed to her simply for daring to dream.

Whitney Houston's modernization of the role leads to a conversation between Cinderella and her Fairy Godmother in which Cinderella says, "I've always dreamed someone would come and take me away from here," and the Fairy Godmother answers, "Cinderella, if you wanna get out of here, you're going to have to do it yourself. The music's in you, deep down in your soul. When you find it, nothing will be able to keep you from walking out that door." After a conversation about why Cinderella has stayed with her stepmother, she says, "I've dreamt about leaving so many times," and the Fairy Godmother answers, "That's the problem with most people. They dream about what they want to do instead of really doing it." When Brandy then says, "Oh, I wish that—but I guess wishing's no good either," Whitney Houston replies, "Everything starts with a wish," and the two begin the musical's focal number, "Impossible." But instead of simply going to the ball, falling in love with the prince, and having him come find her (through a scene where the colorblind construction is truly tested as Paolo Montalban and Jason Alexander try the slipper on every woman in the kingdom), this Cinderella has to engage with her agency and make choices and take action to change her circumstances. At the end of the film, after being once again cruelly put in her place by her stepmother, Cinderella goes outside to speak with her father's spirit, saying, "Father, I know I said I'd never leave here, but after tonight I don't see how I can stay. . . . I deserve better. . . . I deserve to be loved," and she resolves to change her situation and gives up the idea of the joy she had with the prince with the reprise of "A Lovely Night." At this point, the Fairy Godmother shows up and the following exchange occurs:

Fairy Godmother: If you really love him, why don't you let
  him know?

Cinderella: How can I? Look at me?

> **FG**: Do you really think he fell in love with your fancy gown
>   and your pretty braids?
> **C**: I don't know anymore. . . . If you hadn't helped me—
> **FG**: You didn't need my help, you just thought you did.
>   Believe in yourself Cinderella, and trust him to love you
>   as you really are. (Transcription mine)

This messaging of believing in yourself was eventually incorporated into the Disney Princess brand and reappeared during the "Dream Big, Princess" campaign in 2016 (Epstein). But it does not really exist in Disney's fairy-tale films before this, as the animated films do not focus on agency and empowerment for their female protagonist. In this context, however, Cinderella's happy ending comes incidentally to her deciding to leave. We do not know if she was leaving her family or if she was going to follow the Fairy Godmother's advice, but the act of leaving changes her narrative resolution from waiting for rescue to one where she is taking control of her own destiny. This act of agency triggers a reprise of Cinderella's first meeting with the prince in the opening number, and the film ends with a major Whitney Houston number and a wedding up at the castle. At the end of it all, hard work is more important than a belief in dreams: To dream is not enough; one must do something to make that dream happen. And of course, one must believe in oneself—belief in Cinderella and encouraging her to believe in herself is the real magic performed by the Fairy Godmother, rather than waving her wand to fix Cinderella's problems. Yet, what could have been an empowering component woven into how Disney retells fairy tales, and its own fairy tales, is undercut by the fact that the only fairy-tale films that push this version of empowerment are the two fairy-tale films that feature Black princesses. The refrain of "It's Possible" becomes less about things magically happening and is more loaded with a legacy of "it's possible if *you* do something about it; no fairy godmother can fix it for you." This legacy of hard work, depending on oneself, and saving oneself from a bad situation, along with the different narrative approach and approach to setting taken in *The Princess and the Frog*, solidifies that Black princesses in the 1990s and 2000s have been treated differently—and are marked as different to the rest of the Disney fairy-tale canon—in a way that won't be further complicated until the live-action *Little Mermaid* is released in 2023.

"Almost There": Reaching for an "American Fairy Tale with an African American Princess"

The Princess and the Frog is adapted more directly from ATU-440, "The Frog Prince, or, Iron Heinrich," and was billed as a loose adaptation of both the Grimms' "The Frog Prince" and E. D. Baker's *The Frog Princess* (Clements, qtd. in Sciretta). On 11 December 2009 Disney returned to the format of the musical fairy-tale film, presenting viewers with its first animated adaptation of a European fairy-tale since 1991 and the first animated feature, fairy tale or otherwise, to feature an African American protagonist. The company had spent years trying to adapt the Grimms' story, with multiple versions in progress but without any luck, and purchased the rights to Baker's middle-grade novel in 2003 (Clements, qtd. in Sciretta). According to Clements, it was simply the concepts of the two narratives that seeded what became *The Princess and the Frog*—a transformation of a prince into a frog (the Grimms' narrative), and the twist that when the princess kisses him, instead of him becoming human, she becomes a frog (Baker's narrative twist) (Sciretta). All the versions in progress and input from various studio heads resulted in what director Ron Clements referred to as "an American fairy tale set in New Orleans in the 1920s" (Clements, qtd. in S. King) and "an American fairy tale with an African American Princess taking place in the 1920's during the Jazz Age as a musical" (Clements, qtd. in Sciretta). Although *The Princess and the Frog* was meant to be a return to many things—the musical, hand-drawn animation, fairy tales—the narrative choices made for it have ultimately marked it as fundamentally different from other animated fairy-tale retellings.

I include this narrative here for two reasons. First, it can be read as a rags-to-riches tale that sees the main character transcend class divides while she navigates family issues through pursuit of her dreams. Second, it is necessary to consider Tiana as a Cinderella character along with and against her foil, Lottie. Tiana's story is set in 1920s New Orleans, which imposes its own restrictions on the narrative; as an African American woman in this historical and geographic setting, Tiana can never have the almost royal lifestyle that Lottie leads as the daughter of a wealthy businessman. Sarah E. Turner notes that "this film represents a complex moment in a culture steeped in political correctness and an adherence to the politics of colorblindness" (Turner, 83). The central politic of the narrative encourages a colorblind pursuit of the American dream, but the film is also shaped by an awareness of the lack of Black representation in the Disney corpus. Class and race inflect the shape of and possibilities for Tiana's narrative in a way that is elided in the 1997 Whitney Houston–produced musical. Tiana does not aspire to become a princess; what she wants is to fulfill her late father's dream of owning her own restaurant. It is Lottie who dreams of becoming royalty, as the only thing that she does not have from the fairy-tale life she emulated from childhood is the title. Like the messaging given to Brandy's depiction of Cinderella in 1997, Tiana's journey emphasizes working over wishing, though this is counteracted in the song "Dig a Little Deeper," sung by the character Mama Odie (Jenifer Lewis), who is trying to tell Tiana that love and family are more important than her work aspirations to finding fulfillment in life. Lottie does not receive any such overt messaging, but she does try (unsuccessfully) to help Tiana and Naveen at the end of the film. Their marriage as frogs makes Tiana a princess, and when she kisses Naveen, they are both returned to human form. "Happily ever after" takes the form of Tiana's family and friends sharing meals together in the restaurant that she and Naveen own and work in together rather than in the castle on the hill. There is a significant leap in social status from waitress to restaurant owner and from single woman to princess by marriage. But the fulfillment of this *Cinderella* story becomes yet again marked by differences in possibilities presented for princess figures who are not white, which raises the question, Who does Disney as a corporation think that the transformative potential of its key central narrative is for?

Rather than deploying the medievalist fairy-tale aesthetic used by Disney,[5] if indirectly, to solidify the aesthetic connections between its films, this film is deliberately given a particular, non-European historical setting that jars roughly against the medievalist temporality of Disney fairy-tale narratives and continually references its own temporality, 1920s New Orleans. The film deliberately leans into associations with Black and Creole food and culture, Cajun culture, Mardi Gras, and jazz and

---

5 For more in-depth analysis on this aesthetic, see Anjirbag, "Enter the Castle."

ragtime music and ties its "American fairy tale" to the image of an African American princess. However, particular racialized dynamics associated with this time period and location limit the potentials for Tiana. Because the real history cannot be dissociated from this historicized temporality of the narrative, the narrative is consciously or unconsciously shaped by these limits. In other words, "even though Disney attempts to produce Princess Tiana as empowered, grounded, and down-to-earth, the colorful film still relies heavily on the reproduction of the ideology of whiteness that sanitizes the everyday lives of African-Americans and normalizes whiteness" (Gregory, 433). Whereas the medievalesque is a quasi-historical framing, a concept of a concept of a time and an evocation of a story of history, the 1920s in the United States is incredibly specific, with racial, class, and gendered dynamics that cannot be separated from depictions of it, even in fantasy worlds. New Orleans similarly has its own presence, both in terms of the historical and contemporary setting, especially after Hurricane Katrina (2005, with effects still felt more than fifteen years later). The film's producers had to balance history and fantasy, and, as noted by Jennifer L. Barker, "It is unlikely that Disney will ever try to produce animated films that focus on a serious engagement with reality or history; the sanitized aesthetic ('something for everyone!') necessary to appeal to broad markets is fundamentally incompatible with a realistic representation of history" (Barker, 483). Ultimately, though:

> Disney might not promote the twist as being due to the fact that Princess Tiana is black, since Disney princesses and the stories they embody are supposed to be timeless (which can be read as a coded description for raceless and without context). . . . *The Princess and the Frog* is a story in which the princess is in fact black, the setting is New Orleans, and the time period is the 1920s. These elements are important to consider at this historical juncture. (C. R. King et al., 156)

Although "in the place of the ugliness projected onto the crow in *Dumbo* through negative stereotypes, *The Princess and the Frog* renders blackness beautiful, appealing . . . to whites as well as blacks" (C. R. King et al., 158) and even though to viewers it might seem as if "we have entered a new era" (158), the combination of positive stereotypes and historical setting instead combine to embody three problems identified by King and colleagues:

> (1) Positive stereotypes are still stereotypes which present distorted and dehumanizing renderings; (2) the values at the heart of the dominant framing (such as beauty standards), rather than those of say African Americans, delimit what is good, worthy, and acceptable; and (3) positivity allows audiences to forget the difference that difference makes and enjoy the delusion of a society after racism and (hetero)sexism. (C. R. King et al., 158–59)

The difference in setting and overall aesthetic, as well as Tiana's race, complicates Tiana's incorporation into having the equivalent status as a Disney princess in the context of the rest of the Disney princesses (Dundes and Streiff). However, we cannot understate how the limited possibilities for Black people inherent in the time and place of the setting undercut the fairy-tale representation of the gains made in the 1997 *Cinderella*. In other words, it is necessary to think about what it means that Brandy's Cinderella had access to the wonder and magic of a fairy-tale realized in full, but the next time a Black fairy-tale princess is put front and center by the Disney corporation, she occupies a completely different world.

Before addressing the criticism of *The Princess and the Frog* and then reading it as a *Cinderella* story that helps to establish a pattern within the larger pattern of the Disney fairy-tale mode, I would like to acknowledge work done by Hannah Thuraisingam Robbins, who asserts that this film has valid, real gains, despite the parts that can be problematized from a critical lens. Thuraisingam Robbins argues persuasively that the ahistoricism that has resulted in criticism that rejects how the "film suggests a largely desegregated and romantic picture of New Orleans erasing the racist legislation in force when the film is set" ignores how the film actually centers the gaze of Black children by not subjecting them to depictions of overt racialized violence and antagonisms that are present in other films, such as, say, *Pocahontas*, where the central narrative is fully driven by racist conflicts. Thuraisingam Robbins reflects, "Black children are forced to encounter and understand racism from an early age, and I continue to struggle with the idea that they should only be allowed to consume American stories (of any era) through the lens of anti-Black violence." She goes on to say that "our critiques of ahistoricism must consider who those changes offer agency to. In this instance, white children do not *gain* agency from these changes and Black children are protected from the adultification of being forced to process the consequences of anti-Black racism in order to access a magical romance." In Thuraisingam Robbins's reading, *The Princess and the Frog* uses the nostalgia and escapism of the fairy tale to heighten the tensions between the real and the fantastic, and in doing so allows an ordinary Black woman to occupy the same space as Disney's fully royal European coded princess, a disruption in and of itself, and even prioritizes Tiana's dreams and cultural values while still following the patterns of other Disney princess films.

I do not disagree with Thuraisingam Robbins's reading of the film, and in fact, I agree that there needs to be an understanding of how wonder and violence are too often intertwined for certain audiences when pushing for accuracy and authenticity in historically situated media. But my concern here is how we understand this film in a wider context of patterns, how it fits or is made to fit Disney's fairy-tale mode, where it differs, and how its incorporation into the brand affects our understanding of the shape of fairy tales at large—what do we expect them to do, and who fits within them? Even though it is quite an ahistorical setting, the historical context still seeps through in certain scenes, and the constructions of race heighten these moments for an informed audience—and of course because of the nature of nostalgic reiteration, as the audience becomes informed and then returns to the film with that knowledge, history intrudes upon the fantasy in a way that is not present for other historically or historicism-inflected films. I look here to put Tiana's narrative in context with how only certain figures need to grapple with the tension between wishing and working or otherwise have limitations on their access to wonder and, as such, have their difference from the so-called canon be made even more markedly different.

The Princess and the Frog did not just have a long road through the various corporation studios. Critics from various corners outside the studio pushed back at the depiction of Tiana from the time the film was announced. In 2007 MSNBC reported on the production of "'an American fairy tale' starring a girl named Maddy who lives in the French

Quarter in New Orleans" ("Disney First"), and "reaction to the news of an African American princess ranged from joy to skepticism primarily because of Disney's history of mining racialized tropes. . . . The collective wisdom did not want to see Blackness associated with a frog, and other nagging stereotypes" (Haydel, 118). According to Richard M. Breaux:

> Originally, Maddy was to be a chambermaid, and cultural critics were quick to pounce on the phonetic similarities between—Maddy and—mammy. Maddy's occupation smacked of the ubiquitous mammy, the happy servant stereotype that dominated film and later television through most of the twentieth century. The result is a New Orleans waitress who becomes a princess, restaurant owner, and chef named Tiana. Two-dimensional, hand-drawn animated cels of the Princess cooking, cleaning, and serving food could be saved and remain in the film, and the storyline could be reworked to salvage Disney's image in the eyes of critics and many African American parents who had longed for the day that a Disney animated feature would include non-stereotypical African Americans and were ready to spend their money on *The Princess and the Frog* and Tiana merchandise. The revised *The Princess and the Frog* marked one of the ways Disney answered its critics and cashed in on its racist past. (Breaux, 398–99)

Breaux calls attention to how, when it comes to Disney and diversity, the "surface fix"—in this case, changing a chambermaid to a waitress and altering the name to not be so obviously reminiscent of a negative, racialized stereotype—is not enough to solve the problem. These changes might have allowed Disney to sidestep the criticism being levied at it and still reap a profit. However, surface fixes ultimately do not solve the deeper problems tied to equitable representation of difference. No matter what small amount of criticism the studio took on board, it does not change the fact that a fairy-tale narrative that centers Blackness and Black culture of a particular time, at its core also works to obscure that same Blackness: Much of Tiana's screen time is spent as a desexualized frog. Although Anika Noni Rose's voice acting carries Tiana's personality and character from human to frog, it does not change the fact that Disney's first animated film with an

African American princess lacks the Black princess's body on-screen. It does not stop with this film either; whereas the studio received some credit for casting Gugu Mbatha-Raw and Audra McDonald in the live-action *Beauty and the Beast*, these actors also spend the vast majority of their time as anthropomorphized furniture. It raises the question: How is Blackness being better represented in Disney films—especially the studio's quintessential fairy-tale films—if it is never fully seen or expressed on-screen? This problem seems to be compounded when actual people are involved, and not just voice actors, though without a large enough sample size—one animated feature film, one made-for-television film that was difficult to acquire (until its inclusion in the Disney+ streaming service in early 2021), and one feature live-action remediation not released until 2023—it is hard to say whether this is a deliberate pattern. Nevertheless, obscuring Tiana's human body, while the most consistently seen as Black human on the same screen is the villain Dr. Facilier, is another realization of the Blackness in absentia established in the Disney Renaissance; this is especially fraught because *The Princess and the Frog* as a production was meant to center Blackness in an animated fairy-tale feature film for the first time.

In some ways Tiana seems to be distanced from becoming yet another Black servant girl on-screen by virtue of her having a dream where she overcomes the prejudices and limits of her time by owning her own restaurant. However, she is still defined by the concept of *serving*. Where Brandy's Cinderella reaches the medievalesque castle on the hill and the implied happy life without need, want, or any more of the serving that defined her status in her stepmother's family, Tiana's fantasy is grounded in her historical reality. When she speaks about her dreams of owning a restaurant early in the film, she is ridiculed. When she tries to buy her restaurant after earning enough money for the deposit by making the beignets for Big Daddy La Bouff's masquerade ball, she is told that she has been outbid and out of luck unless she can top the offer by Wednesday. When she responds, "You know how long it took me to raise that money," the abrupt rebuttal is, "Which is why a little woman of your background would have had her hands full trying to run a big business like that. You're better off where you're at." Given the historical context of the film, the reference to "background" can mean only one thing: the color of Tiana's skin, which also compounds the class differences between herself and, say, her friend Lottie. The rebuttal to Tiana's attempt to work for her dreams is clear: Stay in your place.

Tiana's dreams are juxtaposed against those of Charlotte "Lottie" La Bouff, who is white, the only daughter of the wealthiest man in New Orleans. Lottie is always depicted in princess pink. *The Princess and the Frog* plays with the traditional opening. It erases the castle entirely, and the camera focuses on an image of the wishing star, or evening star, to the melody of Aniki Noni Rose singing, "The evening star is shining bright / so make a wish and hold on tight / there's magic in the air tonight / and anything can happen." As the second line of the melody is sung, the camera pans down to a large New Orleans–style mansion in place of the classic, canonical castle, meant to be in the city's Garden District, now famous for its historical mansions. The camera moves through the open window flooded in pink light in what is reminiscent of a tower, to where young Lottie and Tiana are listening to Tiana's mother, Eudora, read them "The Frog Prince" while Eudora finishes making one of many fairy-tale princess gowns for Lottie. This moment is significant because it brings to the fore the racial and class hierarchies "that sewing has exploited through the centuries . . . making visible the all too often unacknowledged seamstresses who labour on the array of princess dresses" (Do Rozario, 167). Young Lottie simply dreams of being a princess and marrying a prince, and she is willing to do *anything* for that dream, including kissing a frog. Young Tiana, however, is less than enthused by the idea, saying emphatically that there is nothing that could make her kiss a frog. Tiana and Eudora leave the mansion (with Lottie demanding the dress from the fairy tale she just heard and her father consenting before handing her a puppy). After a cable car journey that highlights their social distance from the La Bouffs and a touching scene showing Tiana's relationship with her father and the importance of cooking and sharing food as "a way to bring people together from all walks of life," Tiana is put to bed by her parents while she and her father talk about a dream of owning a restaurant and sharing their food with the world. Tiana spies the evening star out the window, saying, "Charlotte's fairy-tale book said, if you make a wish on the evening star, it is sure to come true." Her mother answers, "Well, you wish on that star, sweetheart," and her father continues, "Yeah, you wish and you dream with all your little heart, but you remember, Tiana, that that old star can only take you part of the way.

You've got to help it along with some hard work of your own, and then you can do anything you set your mind to." Her parents finish putting her to bed, and then young Tiana is seen at the window, staring at the star while clutching to her chest the picture of a restaurant on which her dad had written "Tiana's Place," whispering, "Please, please, please." The juxtaposition of the two young girls and their father's responses to wants and wishes is important. Lottie is able to have whatever she might want. Her dreams cross over from the fairy tale, and she wants to make a fantasy a reality, arguably in part because of a lack of want in her life. She is a princess in all but name. Tiana, however, has a dream rooted in a reality that might as well be fantasy for a Black family in 1920s New Orleans. Not impossible but fraught with man-made rather than magical obstacles. Tiana is also cautioned by her father to not just count on wishing and dreaming, which is incredibly different from the messaging Lottie, as a privileged white child, receives from her father, and it recalls Whitney Houston's Fairy Godmother's message regarding dreamers.

The juxtaposition between Tiana and Lottie continues when they are older. Tiana internalized her father's message about hard work, whereas Lottie has grown into a stereotypical Southern belle. Immediately before systemic racism and prejudice destroy Tiana's restaurant dream, the narrative follows Lottie's dream of marrying a prince. Lottie is distraught that at this point in the masquerade ball, Prince Naveen has not yet arrived, and she begins desperately wishing on the evening star—something she learned from the fairy-tale storybook in the film's opening scene. Tiana begins to say, "Lottie, you can't just wish on a star an' expect things—" and is cut off as the arrival of the prince is announced. Clearly, simply wishing *is* enough for some. Right before Naveen in frog form appears asking for a kiss, Tiana is on Lottie's balcony looking at the evening star and clutching the well-worn picture of the restaurant with her father's writing on it, again whispering, "Please, please, please." However, Tiana's wish does not go as straightforwardly as Lottie's seems to, for shortly after this moment Tiana does play along with the fairy tale, kisses the frog, and then is herself transformed.

Although she eventually gets her restaurant, Tiana's wish fulfillment does not transcend the racial and social hierarchies of 1920s New Orleans. She is a princess in name by way of her marriage to Naveen (which breaks the spell in the end), but she has none of the princess lifestyle that is constantly depicted as Lottie's social (and racialized) place in the narrative. Read alongside the messages about hard work and not being saved by anyone but yourself from the Brandy and Whitney Houston *Cinderella*, it seems as though the minds behind Disney cannot imagine a world where a white Cinderella and an African American Cinderella might want to wish the same wishes and dream the same dreams and even deserve to reach them in the same way. The African American princesses remain othered, shut out from the same kind of happy ending encoded and implied by the construct of the Disney fairy tale, whereas the white princesses retain their place in the larger Disney universe. Tiana and Brandy's Cinderellas are "different" Cinderella figures, but Disney remains the same old Disney in terms of ensuring that at no point do they risk alienating a target white audience while reaching for the market potentials of a diverse audience. This is a contradiction that cannot hold. The impact that Disney's *Cinderella* narratives featuring a Black fairy-tale princess have is the message that Black princesses cannot actually inherit the Magic Kingdom—they can only have one tiny piece of it. Thus the overall treatment of Black princesses in film narratives that adapt narratives associated with Disney's classic fairy-tale films is not without growth, but each step forward reveals deficiencies. The question of who belongs in the Disney transmedia multiverse becomes even more complicated as the geography of Disney's world expands.

Finding the Right Fit: Sneakerella *and Pushing the Boundaries of the* Cinderella *Narrative*

In 2022 the Disney Channel original movie *Sneakerella* debuted as a gender-bent and race-bent contemporary urbanization of the *Cinderella* tale set in Queens, directed by Elizabeth Allen Rosenbaum and starring Chosen Jacobs, Lexi Underwood, and Devyn Nekoda. Although my focus in this book is more largely the fairy-tale feature films, I am including a brief examination of this film because it does in some way prove that experimentation is possible and not as much a risk as the studio seems to view it to be. In *Sneakerella* the young El dreams about continuing his mom's work of getting people in "life changing" shoes, despite the efforts of his stepfather and stepbrothers to thwart him. El's mom used to have a shoe store that served the neighborhood, and she had a knack for getting people in the right pair of shoes for them—not ultimate fetish shoes like a glass slipper maybe, but definitely shoes that fit their lives and their needs. But after she dies, management of the store goes to El's stepfather, Trey. El is treated like a grunt, responsible for keeping the store tidy and functioning, and he is very much treated more harshly by his stepfather than his stepbrothers are. Meanwhile, El is quite the sneakerhead and dreams of designing and making his own shoes, something it is implied that his mother used to do as well, as she has all the proper cobbling equipment tucked away in the shop in a semi-hidden cupboard, which El has access to. El also has her talent of reading people according to their shoes.

El and his best friend, Sami, meet Kira, the daughter of sneaker mogul Darius King, at a sneaker drop. Hijinks ensue as Kira hunts for an original shoe design for her father to premiere at Sneakercon and El is grounded with no way to contact Kira—not that he realizes who she is in the first place. Meanwhile, El's stepfather ends up planning on selling his mother's store and moving the family to New Jersey. Once El and Sami realize who Kira is, they concoct a plan to sneak into a charity gala hosted by her father, in order to impress him with a shoe El has designed, inspired by his mother and the neighborhood he loves. El and Sami reach the gala with the help of Gustavo, who acts as a semimagical community garden caretaker playing the part of the fairy godmother to get them there. At the gala, El loses one of his shoes in the rush to leave by midnight, and Kira and her sister Liv start a social media campaign to find her "prince," that is, the shoe's mystery designer. Without recapping the rest of the film in full, eventually, all the little mysteries are cleared up, Kira and El are able to reconcile, Darius King names El his new sneaker designer, and El is even able to reconcile with his stepfather, who admits that he has been too hard on El and then promises to be a better father. The film closes with the revelation that one year after these events, El and Kira are still together and El's mom's store, originally called Laces, has not been sold. Instead, it is called El-evate and El sells his designs in the Queens neighborhood that the story starts in.

The reception to this film was a net positive, with the largest bit of criticism being that at times, the story "drags" (Amatangelo). It was nominated for eleven Children's and Family Emmys (Schneider) and called a "modernized, more tween-oriented telling" that "delivers a poignant take on the 1950s animated film it partially cannibalizes" (Howard). The diverse casting, the focus on tween lives, and the believability (with a bit of suspended disbelief of course) of what the main characters are setting as dreams, hopes, and goals make this a *Cinderella* narrative for a modern world, and the specific musical aspects draw frequent comparisons to Lin-Manuel Miranda productions (Menon). The film is of course a fantasy, but it is inflected with a degree of realism that allows the narrative to be shaped and driven by interpersonal relationships and renders the magical aspects of the story almost incidental. El is not seeking to transform as much as he is trying to fully realize his potential dreams. It is almost a pity that this film was relegated to the television screen and streaming rather than being a little more developed as a feature, where it could have had a wider footprint and impact.

And nevertheless, like Tiana, El's story is set in a hyperspecific geography and even temporality; this is not meant to be a story that just anyone can fall into and imagine themselves as part of. This is not even a wider New York fairy-tale narrative; the film is shaped by a single borough, a single neighborhood even, and becomes inflected with the history of that space. When put in context of the narratives of the ties between dreams and work, El does not even get told to dream big but work for it; instead, at one point Trey tells El that sometimes you just have to let dreams go. And once again because the entire narrative of this film is so hyperspecific, to the point where the diverse casting actually shines, it becomes hard to unsee that, once again, a nonwhite Cinderella figure is not being told that they can dream anything but rather that big dreams might not be for them. The reconciliation between El and Trey helps to undo some of this, especially given that Trey specifically apologizes for the ways he has been harder on or limiting El. But though I do think it is a film that does many things on lines of representation well, when held in concert with the wider interplay of specifically *Cinderella* narratives across Disney media, it is still the nonwhite and actually specifically Black Cinderella figures who have the narrative potential of a rags-to-riches narrative limited or otherwise reframed so that there are caveats to dreaming, rather than dreams being something they might be entitled to even if they have nothing else.

Is This Truly a Fairy Tale for Anyone and Everyone?

In holding these narratives together, what we see is a small study of how Disney uses the palimpsestic nature of fairy tales to build out the wider Disney fantasyscape. These depictions almost all draw on *Cinderella* iconography but specifically in ways that refer back to Disney's animated classic in such a way as to draw a comparison to that film as a seminal reference point, such as transformations and makeovers, magical and animal helpers, and less than ideal family or social circumstances. It is an interesting phenomenon to have so many narratives coexist as *Cinderella* narratives within one corporation without overwriting each other and without removing the primacy of the 1950 Disney animated film as *the Cinderella* story at the core of the narrative universe constructed by the corporation. It is also notable that there is an expansion in the image of how a Cinderella character is portrayed. As Shearon Roberts notes, "Good narratives make good cents" (Roberts, 4), and Disney is taking steps to "avoid appearing out of touch" and to provide "entertainment and memories that feel authentic to the customers it wishes to serve for decades to come" (14). However, when we examine the treatment of and messaging received by the "diverse" or disrupted iterations of the expression of the Cinderella character against the version that Disney has constructed as its classic or authentic version, there is an interesting, racialized difference to consider. Messages about and depictions of struggle, striving, and working hard characterize all the nonwhite Cinderella figures that I discuss here. This might be a coincidence, but we should consider the reiterative nature of fairy tales and their palimpsestic relationships to each other, especially here, where change is most visible because of the repeated similarities that help viewers recognize that they are indeed seeing a certain kind of story.

A Tale as Old as Time Retold

In 2022 a hybrid production of *Beauty and the Beast*, titled *Beauty and the Beast: A 30th Celebration*, was broadcast on ABC and later made available to stream on Disney+. This production blended the animated film with, as stated by narrator Rita Moreno, "musical sequences imagined as live-action spectacles." It starred H.E.R. as Belle, Josh Groban as the

Beast, Joshua Henry as Gaston, Martin Short as Lumière, Shania Twain as Mrs. Potts, David Alan Grier as Cogsworth, Rizwan Manji as LeFou, Jon Jon Briones as Maurice, and Leo Abelo Perry as Chip, all of whom are named in the storybook opening that starts the production. This version presented the first Black princess to be broadcast to a wide audience in a film format by the corporation since Tiana's debut in 2009, but she would not be the first Black Belle; in 1998, four years after the Broadway stage show debuted with Susan Egan in the lead role, R&B singer Toni Braxton spent six months as Belle on the Broadway stage (J. King). This production was Disney's second hybrid anniversary show after staging *The Little Mermaid Live!* in 2019, starring Auli'i Cravalho, of *Moana* fame, as Ariel. The hybrid productions are largely screenings of the animated films combined with theatrical productions of musical sequences, performed and broadcast live but then also retained for streaming purposes on Disney+. This type of programming builds on *The Wonderful World of Disney* programming legacy that first saw the Whitney Houston and Brandy *Cinderella* brought to life for primetime audiences, and it pushes the "politics of nostalgia" in a slightly different or, perhaps more accurately, wider direction through its casting choices. This time, the nostalgia is not just for a sense of so-called classic Disney framed by Walt himself, but rather, a nostalgia for one of the most critically acclaimed and beloved films of the Disney Renaissance era and all that this particular period stands for in the wider Disney corporate legacy.

In the creation of the musical production of *The Lion King*, director Julie Taymor leaned into a process of engaging "audiences emotionally and intellectually in a participatory experience" (Grossman, 125), in part by making expressly visible "the artifice behind theater" (Taymor, qtd. in Grossman, 125). In many ways the 2022 hybrid production of *Beauty and the Beast* strives to do the same. It uses the lot, the various stages, and even the audience to create a metanarrative that draws attention to the animation process behind the 1991 production, which is the hybrid production's point of reference as well as the point of reference for the following productions of the *Beauty and the Beast* Broadway stage show, the animated sequels, the appearance of Belle across other Disney and Disney Princess franchise media, and, of course, the live-action and CGI remediation from 2017. This artifice is made visible by using interludes narrated by Rita Moreno that showcase animation moments and behind-the-scenes footage of the original cast recordings for the 1991 film. The behind-the-scenes footage also highlights cameo appearances in the 2022 production: Belle's original character animator, sketching to open the show; original Belle voice actor Paige O'Hara in the role of the Bookseller; original Gaston voice actor Richard White as the Baker; and even award-winning composer Alan Menken, playing the piano during the moment in the song "Belle" when the character is singing to sheep at a fountain and showing them her favorite book. But beyond the Easter eggs and the narrated moments, the production makes a point of calling attention to the movement between animated film and staged moments, with the theatrical backdrop often featuring not color or finalized displays of the various settings but rather sketches from the animation process. This happens especially during the musical production of "Belle," which sets expectations for the entire show.

After an opening monologue by Rita Moreno that explains how the production will work, Moreno turns to the original animator who is onstage, apparently sketching Belle on a tablet. The camera that is recording all the action so far zooms into the flipbook style animation of Belle, which then becomes H.E.R. on the steps of the theater on the Disney lot in Burbank, California, beginning to sing the opening lyrics of "Belle." As she moves through the lot and through the reimagined choreography, it is clear that this is not just a transposition of the stage show to a televised audience. The props and scenery are all done in an animated sketch style that the cast interacts with, and the song moves from outside to inside the theater space, as H.E.R. moves through crowds of diverse audience members with various fan signs, including several young girls of different ethnic backgrounds dressed up in the iconic blue dress worn by Belle in the opening number. But the casting also stands out for its diversity, not just in the principal cast but also the ensemble. In many ways this staging feels informed by the care and intentionality that went into the 1997 *Cinderella*, and the impact is a subtle message about who is included as "part of this world." Yes, this casting definitely falls under the umbrella of colorblind casting. At times the casting of a Black Belle, white Beast, Black Gaston, South Asian LeFou, Filipino Maurice, white Mrs. Potts and Black Chip, white Lumiere and Black Cogsworth feels like a carefully balanced exercise in box ticking, and, unlike the 1997 *Cinderella*, racialized identity does not inflect the narrative at all. But, in a production that so heavily references itself as a celebration of an acclaimed and beloved "original," the casting choices do not take away the weight of having a Black woman playing Belle and dance numbers that include a young Black girl as young Belle or even the expansion of body types onstage in the ensemble cast. One wonders what might have been the impact of making an intentionally diverse live production of the stage show itself, instead of the hybrid, and how that could have created much needed space for diverse representations to breathe in the Disney mediascape through another "classic." But nevertheless, the diverse casting in this production, though long overdue, is a welcome addition to the Disney lineup. In the end, it shows that there is potential for the Disney fairy-tale mode to be broadened without affecting the company's ability to produce narratives in line with its core messages about magic, wonder, and imagination.

There is a potential case study in the making in examining more widely the effects of palimpsestic presentations of Disney's fairy-tale princesses as constant interventions in the corporation's own identity and self-created lore. But for now, the hybrid production of *Beauty and the Beast* is an example of how Disney's legacy does not in fact become overwritten through diversification and of how there are ways to innovate beyond the known, celebrating that which was groundbreaking in the past while widening access to the magic kingdom.

The Little Mermaid 2023: A Return to "Under the Sea"

In 2023, after many delays and both excited anticipation and controversy, the live-action and CGI remediation of *The Little Mermaid* was released, starring Halle Bailey as Ariel, Melissa McCarthy as Ursula, and Javier Bardem as King Triton. That the first Black princess to be centered in a live-action theatrical release premiered only in 2023, the year that also marked the celebration of "100 Years of Disney" for the corporation, is something that needs interrogation in and of itself (Smith). Like the 2017 *Beauty and the Beast*, the 2023 *Little Mermaid* tries to stay close to the scenes and numbers that are known and loved by generations of fans while still modernizing characters for a new generation of audiences. Not only is Ariel played by a Black woman, but her sisters, though seen little on screen, are also cast across racialized and ethnic backgrounds. Eric is played by a white actor, but his mother the queen is also cast as a Black woman, though there is no glimpse ever given of the king. Eric's story is expanded to cast him as an adoptee with aspirations to increase trade and contact with other kingdoms and islands. In the quasi-historical setting of a Caribbean that bears similar markers to the real one—and has all the trademarks of an international trade fueled by chattel slavery—more questions are raised than answered by an allegedly more well-rounded prince. And even though the photorealistic CGI is at times more uncanny than endearing, especially in the animation of Flounder and Sebastian, there is no question that Bailey is an Ariel for a new generation.

Bailey both vocally and physically embodies the role—her voice almost matches Benson's original recording even with her own reinterpretations of the songs taking the forefront in the new production. Like Brandy before her as Cinderella, she proves that the fairy-tale realm of Disney can be filled with princesses from beyond the canonical white proto-European world with which Disney historically populated its fairy-tale worlds. Seeing Bailey in the "Part of Your World" sequence—even just seeing clips from the promotional trailers that deliberately recall the animated film—she evokes everything about the strong-willed, bright, curious, beautiful princess that captivated audiences three decades earlier. This is not a Black princess who has been given caveats for how to wish for something unabashedly, unapologetically. Some decisions, such as writing additional songs to fill in Ariel's internal world once she has given up her voice, create space for more agency and perhaps even the tacit reflection for audiences that those who do not speak vocally still have wants, needs, and feelings and are full people capable of having a full life.

The production is overall beautifully balanced and rendered, but there remain missed narrative opportunities to have Ariel develop further. Ariel's internal monologue has expanded and there are more opportunities to show her curiosity and interest in the wider world, the human world in particular, but her motivations in the film become much more about her infatuation with Eric. Her iconic "I want" song, which longs for the experiences of the human world, is undercut by one of two scenes where her sisters are present. As they are cleaning up the harm to the reef caused by a shipwreck in a storm, the sisters insinuate that Ariel's absence has to do with her falling for a merman rather than her previously identified curious nature. Ariel's interest in Eric is apparent in her own actions, but to have her family frame her absence in this way also somewhat undercuts her general interest in the human world or, perhaps worse, can lead the audience to equate her interest in forbidden knowledge of the world above with her love of a human (also forbidden), which might cause her to be seen as more lovestruck than curious and intelligent. In effect, this limits the perception of her character, and it makes her a less fully realized female protagonist, especially when balanced against the attempts to widen Eric's character. As such, it does not quite hold up against how both Belle and the Beast were further rounded out as characters in the 2017 remediation or, even further, Linda Woolverton's treatment of the *Sleeping Beauty* narrative in the 2014 *Maleficent*, in terms of modernizing the narrative. But then again, does it have to? Can it be enough that a beautiful Black woman brought this character to the screen for a new generation? The question remains whether Disney will continue to put more, different bodies in the spaces of its classics or whether Bailey's portrayal of Ariel will stand alone for a generation, as Anika Noni Rose's Tiana and Brandy Norland's Cinderella (as well as Whitney Houston's Fairy Godmother and Whoopi Goldberg's Queen) did before her.

The weaknesses in this film have less to do with Bailey's performance, or even McCarthy's wonderful turn as Ursula, and are more related to structure. As I have written elsewhere, Disney's more recent world building uses historical details to invoke a feeling of authenticity, to ground its narrative settings in a sense of a historicism-inflected time and space.[6] To a knowing audience, the details of the Caribbean setting, trade routes, and larger global context will carry further connotations, similar to what happened with *The Princess and the Frog*. The film sidesteps the realities of Caribbean plantations and explorations, as it perhaps should as a media product for child and family audiences. To reiterate Thuraisingam Robbins's points, we need to be conscious of how demands for accuracy or authenticity have a tacit effect of intertwining the reflection of a Black child in fantasy media spaces with violence. And as such I would not assert that the 2023 *Little Mermaid* film should have

---

6 For further consideration of this time-space construction, see Anjirbag, "Enter the Castle."

been made to reflect anything more "historically accurate." But I am also conscious of the fact that Disney, like other media companies, has an impact on shaping audience perception of historical contexts. Whether thinking about Tiana, or Pocahontas before her, or even more general perceptions about what kind of people belong where and in what settings, who can be heroes, or who is inherently responsible for violence, the corporation is engaging in a pattern of shaping. Without paying more attention to how historicism-inflected otherworlds continue to populate the Disney mediascape, there is a risk that over time a pattern will be established of glossing "history" in fantasy spaces to whisk away, using Disney magic, the darker parts of real history that may be unpalatable to the corporation's audiences.[7]

Revisioning Tales Through the Fairy-Tale Mode: Whose Story Is It?

Across the Disney corporation the consistent reiteration of fairy tales becomes less about fairy tale as a genre and more about the fairy tale as a mode of storytelling: a flexible methodological pattern that might change and shift but ultimately makes Disney's kinds of storytelling, even across brands, recognizable and adhering to consumer expectations. What I term the Disney fairy-tale mode thus becomes a shorthand and a gloss: It is the method that makes other kinds of narratives fit the corporation's patterning while highlighting their differences, seen perhaps most clearly in the animated films of the Disney Renaissance (1989–1999). This is similar to the surface-level changes to its various *Cinderella* narratives that ultimately serve to reiterate a familiar pattern in the space between the recognizable similarities and differences, where the potential for fairy-tale transformations might be enjoyed from the outside by all but only directly accessed or imagined as possible for some. In this context the existence of *Sneakerella* as a race-bent and gender-bent version set in a hyperspecific location becomes interesting, but it is a drop in the ocean.

---

7   It should be noted that there is also a movement in Young Adult fantasy novels to use the genre to address historical evils. Works by such authors as Tracy Deonn, Natasha Bowen, and Justina Ireland (to name a few) use fantasy to face this history head-on.

El arguably faces some of the same problematic treatment as Tiana in that the hyperspecific setting of the narrative becomes as much a factor of how fantasies might play out and who the film is potentially trying to reach. In Disney's reiterations of *Cinderella*, we get not pluralism but reiteration of patterns that draw thematic boundaries around the narrative instead of complicating it. Without wider representation in terms of racial and ethnic representation but also in terms of ability, sexuality, and gender, people are implicitly excluded from what Dorothy L. Hurley notes is a necessary experience of seeing oneself in texts to develop positive self-image: "Through the ages, children have formed mental images of the princesses and other characters depicted in these tales from their representation. . . . Fairy tales, therefore, have an important role to play in the shaping of the self-image and belief system of children" (Hurley, 221). *Cinderella* is one of the corporation's most internally, intertextually played-with properties, but there remain strict boundaries around who has access to its fairy-tale magic or who viewers might be encouraged to imagine as being able to achieve the same wondrous potentials. Disney's consistent remixing and reinterpretation of the *Cinderella* narrative remains inherently political in what it considers normative representation, and, clearly, although all of us need to wear shoes, not all of us can expect or hope for a special pair to help us walk into a new life.

It is also not lost on me that, when considering remakes and remediations of the animated films, there is a wider pattern that needs to be commented on regarding who it is that actually shepherds and has controlling vision of these productions—wealthy white male industry insiders who leave their mark through expanded roles for princes, additional characters that do not really fit, and a seeming push to maintain a sense of fidelity—something not seen in the Woolverton-authored screenplay for *Maleficent*, for instance. Who makes stories, who brings them to life as whole mass-market productions, is just as important as who brings the characters to life on-screen. Although this too needs further consideration and analysis, it points to how the paratexts of creation regarding such productions are possibly equally important to how we consider the effects of these productions and their social and cultural placement.

Canon in the case of Disney becomes in part about aesthetic, in the sense of who or what is plausibly imagined in its brand of fantasy and how those spaces should be composed in the first place. By default, difference becomes more visible through comparison with more true-to-brand properties—things that have been around longer and reiterated across more generations. Artistic styles shift and different framing devices are used, and maybe there are a few unexpected twists in how the narrative eventually resolves. However, the sense of difference remains notable, even as these films become classics in their own right. When Disney remakes the animated versions as live-action feature films, the fairy-tale adaptations do not put Black, Indigenous, or other people of color in the leading roles of the white spaces of the so-called classic fairy tales (other than in the 2023 live-action and CGI *Little Mermaid* starring Halle Bailey), thus maintaining the hegemonic whiteness of the Disney fairy-tale mode. As such, people who might identify with the conservative middle-class white American construction of Disney's intended audience do not have to grapple with something that might challenge their own constructs of normalcy through an example of equitable and just hybridity. By making the "multicultural" films different, even just in terms of surface-level glossing of difference, the corporation does not risk alienating a significant portion of its audience[8] and is also able to expand its appeal to a broader, more global audience. And still, these surface-level differences are recognized as different from the constructs of a more normal, "classic" Disney, and that visibility of difference thereby makes these properties somehow still not equivalent properties, despite the status they gain with time.

8 This question of alienation comes up particularly regarding the casting and marketing of the 1997 adaptation of *Rodgers and Hammerstein's Cinderella* and is discussed explicitly on the record by executive producer Craig Zadan (see James).

4

GRAND OL' DISNEY MYTHIFICATION

*Re-Orienting the World Within
the Magic Kingdom*

**Disney Orientalism and the Fairy-Tale Mode:
When "West" Rewrites "East" (and Everyone Else)**

In 1992 Disney's animated *Aladdin* became the corporation's first foray into telling a story not inflected with European medievalisms since its animation division was reinvigorated. During the song's love ballad, "A Whole New World," Aladdin takes Jasmine sightseeing around the world, with familiar landmarks in play such as the Nile, the Sphinx, and the Great Pyramids of Egypt and the Parthenon in Greece. Finally, as the song closes, Aladdin and Jasmine are sitting above what looks like the Taimaio (Imperial Ancestral Temple) in China, watching fireworks and a dragon dance. As the song goes, Aladdin opens up Jasmine's eyes to a new world—and as the decade progresses, Disney does the same through both the expansion of animated film narratives and the expansion of the theme parks globally. For the corporation's target audience, a "whole new world" was about to be discovered. Disney was going to take them there, one way or another.

Disney's own "habits of whiteness" (Young) and inherent and historical anti-Blackness did not stop the corporation from trying to incorporate, or rather subsume, other forms of otherness into the corporation's storytelling remit. In Chapter 1 I discussed how the imposition of the Disney fairy-tale mode became a method of incorporating what Disney framed as "new" kinds of narratives into its animated feature film presentations without having to push forward into authentic, collaborative cross-cultural storytelling. It was not just about using Wasko's "Disney formula" or Disney's evolution of its own fairy-tale texture or chronotope but about actually culturally relocating narratives (and implicitly, cultures and peoples) to make them fit within Disney's world. The net effect, of course, was totalitarian, not democratic, and reflected ideological colonization impulses as seen through Bradford's description of language as a colonizing structure (as discussed in Chapter 1).

Disney's version of the Middle East, of ancient China, of precolonization and even colonization era North America, as conveyed in the language of Disney imagery, aesthetics, and narrative, is what reaches audiences, not stories told authentically from these spheres, which is at odds with the inherently multivocal, pluralistic concept of a fairy-tale web. On some level the corporation tacitly acknowledges that it must prove that it has done the homework required to tell authentic, believable, sanctioned versions of these stories. A lot of marketing efforts since the 1990s have focused on research trips, culturally specific actors and actresses, attention to specific details, and the like—all the way up through the production of *Moana* in 2016. There is another implication in what kinds of narratives Disney tells through a culturally specific or, rather, othered lens. The corporation thus acts as an arbiter of what is culturally significant or what kind of source narratives are translatable to a believable equivalent of the corporate practice of relying on European fairy tale and British classic literature. Disney decides what is important enough to share with a global audience filtered through US-audience preferences and also what that core US audience will find believable as culturally authentic. Importantly, it does this while also having a pattern of sidestepping critiques of racialized characterizations and simultaneously still making overtures to more diverse representation.

Sara Ahmed analyzes orientalism by tackling the idea of "orientation" implicitly embedded within the distinction between "orient" and "occident," and how "the Orient is not only imagined as 'being' distant, as another side of the globe, but also is 'brought home' or domesticated as 'something' that extends the reach of the West" (Ahmed, *Queer Phenomenology*, 120–21). To put this in the context of race and space, Ahmed further explains that "racial others become associated with the 'other side of the world,'" and through such "embodiment of distance . . . whiteness becomes what is 'here,' a line from which the world unfolds" (121). As such Disney's "habits of whiteness" (to again lean on Helen Young's phrasing) are shaped "through orientations toward others" (121). As Ahmed notes, "Whiteness may even be orientated 'around' itself, whereby the 'itself' only emerges as an effect of the 'around'" (121). Essentially, Disney's core whiteness has always been to some extent "invisible and unmarked, as the absent center against which others appear only as deviants or as lines of deviation" (121). It was *made* visible as the corporation engaged in the process of *making race* as a media construction (Saha, 168–71) since 1989. In other words, the oriented steps into hyperspecific locations and time periods for "different" stories become the very things that make visible both Disney's "habits of whiteness" and its central orientation as a white space.

I am using orientalism as a framework in this chapter, taking after the work of Ahmed to think about the orientation of Disney, or the oriented position of the corporation in relation to the world it interpolates and presents, or, more accurately, re-presents to its audience. This audience, by the time the Disney Renaissance arrives, already has an expectation of what the texture of a Disney film is (Tiffin, 6) or of what a Disney film should *feel* like, as well as where and when it is located. Disney engages in exoticism on both a temporal and a geographic level. If "real" Disney, or "original" or "classic" Disney, is the Disney of castles and forests and fairy godmothers and other European-rooted fairy-tale traditions and hallmarks specifically marked by medievalisms and other historicisms that recall various European pasts, then that is the position around which all other productions are oriented. That is the center that they are different to, or different from, and part of this exoticization process—to make the Disney-other, or the Disney-exotic compared with the Disney-real—is that the Disney-exotic has to exist both some*where* and some*when* else that viewers are then brought to. This framing becomes an almost implicit invocation of teleological narratives of progress. The othered cultures exist in the then; Disney-real exists in its own now—the fairy-tale world and natural world simulacra that can be entered (for a price).

The push of an "other" to an "ancient" time allows for the supplantation of Disney-other by Disney-real, and it becomes a form of natural progression for those already primed to be receptive to teleological narratives of progress about both the progression of history and colonization (as most WENA culture already is). Even if, as I have written elsewhere, Disney leans into medievalism and other historicisms to solidify its central aesthetics,[1] a past to our audience orientation in the contemporary present, that medievalism and historicism are still situated as progressed further through time than the "ancient past" of the settings of such Disney Renaissance animated films as *Mulan* and *Aladdin* (though, as I discuss in Chapter 5, temporal setting is a little harder to pin down in the *Aladdin* films) or even *Moana* several decades later. Disney-real thus supplants Disney-other through the perception of temporal progress, and the temporal shift helps to further distance these films that have a different representation from the corporation's core aesthetic. To return to Ahmed, "making the strange familiar, or the 'distant' proximate, is what allows 'the West' to extend its reach" (Ahmed, *Queer Phenomenology*, 126). As such, in the Disney Renaissance and beyond, Disney engages in a process of simultaneously othering certain kinds of stories and "bringing them home" or "domesticating" them within the Magic Kingdom construct to extend its corporate reach. In this chapter I attempt to disentangle how Disney orients certain films as different from its core aesthetic.

Breaching the Great Wall: *Mulan*

In 1998 Disney Feature Animation released *Mulan*, a film meant to mark a departure from the studio's previous princesses and modes of storytelling on multiple levels. Not only was *Mulan* meant to present a different kind of heroine to Disney audiences, but it was also supposed to take Disney viewers to ancient China, instead of Disney's more familiar proto-European settings, through an "authentic" look into a different culture using a vastly different animation style. *Mulan* is a retelling of a narrative that exists outside the Anglophone sphere and that has its own cultural presence and history, and as part of a plethora of already existent historically rooted films, it is an example of the wobbly line between adaptation and appropriation. The film exemplifies the nuance between cultural appropriation and appropriation as a

---

1   See Anjirbag, "Enter the Castle."

method of adaptation, where, rather than signaling "a relationship with an informing source text," as a direct adaptation would, an appropriation instead "frequently effects a more decisive journey away from the informing text into a wholly new cultural product and domain" (Sanders, 35). *Mulan* cannot be theoretically divorced from the problems and implications of cultural appropriation. It reflects Disney's process of incorporating narratives from outside its recognizable aesthetic into the wider Disney universe while marking the film as different enough, through animation style, framing, music, and overall presentation, to remain distinctive in the context of the wider canon. In *Mulan* the dual impetuses of claiming authoritative ownership over difference and of marking difference as *different*—the net effect of the deployment of the Disney fairy-tale mode—come to the fore.

With a profit of $120.6 million domestically and $176.5 million overseas, *Mulan* is considered a financial success for Disney. As Jing Yin notes, the film also has embodied a popularity in popular culture that "confers [on the corporation] authority to tell the story of *Mulan* globally" (Yin, 286), embodying a process of appropriation of non-Western cultural materials by the US culture industry that ends with the reformulation of the perception of the non-Western (in this case Chinese) culture in the minds of a world audience. Yin's study of Disney's *Mulan* and its source material, *The Ballad of Mulan*, demonstrates how a cultural artifact can be abstracted and Westernized and then can supplant the original culturally authoritative narrative. The changes from the ballad to the film reveal a process through which "Chinese cultural values were selectively disposed of and replaced with Western ideologies that simultaneously pacify feminist criticism and reinforce the racial/cultural hierarchy" (286), a process that works to "transform ethnic materials into a timeless or universal classic" (289). The assumption embedded in this process is that only the dominant (Western) culture can be universally understood and that the values of that culture are the default standard to be imposed on the rest of the world. Such domination under the guise of universalization also "imposes the perspectives or values of the dominant on the dominated, and does not allow the dominated to use their own perspectives or values," reinforcing the construct of the dominated group as Other and the dominant group as the natural, standard self (289). These changes alter the social and cultural values of the ballad in such a way that the cultural currency of the narrative reinforces negative stereotypes of and orientalizes Chinese people.

Mulan's framing as a film depicting something Other—other than the "normal" Eurocentric pattern of adaptation of fairy tales and cultural stories—begins from the moment the iconic castle and signature production logo appear on-screen with distinct auditory cues courtesy of Jerry Goldsmith's score. The castle fades to black and then a background reminiscent of rice paper or parchment takes its place; the opening credits unfold against a scrolling, animated stylized calligraphic depiction of mountains, trees, and clouds, culminating in a depiction of the Great Wall of China, an easily recognized monument from and a symbol of "the East" and "China" in Western culture (Dong, 170). As the clouds scroll across the screen, in red typeface the words "Walt Disney Pictures Presents" appear and disappear before the title of the film itself, "Mulan," is projected above the same clouds in a larger black typeface with a heavily stylized dragon underscoring the name. It is only as this contextualizing text fades out that we see the beginning of the calligraphic-style Great Wall, onto which the title descends before it fades. The calligraphic depiction then fades itself, to be replaced by the Great Wall depicted in Disney's more traditional, realism-based animation style—what Paul Wells refers to as "visual orthodoxies of its own making" (Wells, 120)—that its viewers have been conditioned to expect from previous Disney animated features. This opening framing is important because it frames exactly what the viewer is about to see. This is Disney's presentation of a (traditional) Chinese cultural story and its presentation of (traditional, historical, ancient) China. The film's exoticism is framed by the music and the distinct animation style, but it is made acceptable, Western, and relatable through the use of the Disney name and Western typesetting to communicate this information. Even with the nod to difference, the narrative does not begin properly until we move away from the "old," "ethnic" drawing style, exchanging it for the contemporary, Western drawing style. Elements that seem traditional to WENA audiences are used to convey a sense of simultaneous separation from and connection to a specific culture—the idea that this story is being told with permission and research in a way that does not "violate the integrity of a culture" (Cai, 38). The pull between authenticity and otherness is continually reiterated throughout the film through the visual and musical effects.

The Disney adaptation emphasizes a sense of individuality in the character of Mulan; it adds a romantic interest and a magical talking animal sidekick and uses the revelation of Mulan's sex as a plot device, leading to her disgrace and dismissal from the army (Yin; Dundes and Streiff). Disney has its heroine defy her family by confronting her parents when her father says he will serve in the army despite being injured (indicated by a limp and use of a cane throughout the opening of the film). Further, before running away in the dead of night with the family horse to join the army in her father's stead, Mulan steals her father's sword and armor and chops off her hair in a vivid and dramatic scene underscored with heavy 1980s rock synthesizer, bass, and drums; she leaves the hair comb from the visit to the matchmaker in place of the scroll bearing the orders for her father. Her absence is discovered thanks to her grandmother's implied connection with the family gods, leading to her parents running out into the rain. Her father collapses into the puddles, Mulan's hair comb falling from his hands to the ground. Her mother goes to help her father stand up, saying, "You must go after her. She could be killed," and her father replies, "If I reveal her, she will be." This sets up the kind of situation that Disney revels in: When no human help can be provided, enter the magical or animal sidekick—in this case a small dragon voiced by Eddie Murphy named Mushu. The incorporation of Murphy's Mushu into the film also allows Disney to rest on a secondary note of diverse inclusion, though, as already discussed, relegating African American or Black representation to anthropomorphized comic relief does not truly serve to include more diverse representation.

The moment Mulan leaves her family deploys an orientalist lens by juxtaposing Mulan's individualistic, heroic nature against her traditional Chinese community, which the film constructs as archaic and brutal. The film narrative is constructed to encourage viewers to understand that Mulan, an Americanized, independent, feminist female character, knows better than the traditional society grounded in filial piety into which she was born. Such orientalization and exoticization reappears when Mulan causes an avalanche with the army's last rocket to bury the approaching horde instead of aiming it at the leader of the Huns, Shan Yu, as ordered. Mulan (as Ping) is injured for her efforts. When the doctor reveals that Ping is female to Shang and Chi-Fu, it seems that Mulan's father's worry is justified. Chi-Fu calls Mulan a treacherous snake, condemns her for committing high treason, and tells Shang and Mulan's companions, "You know the law." Although in this scene the words *kill* or *execute* are never uttered, the implication is clear, as Shang does initially draw Mulan's father's sword from the scabbard on her horse's saddle. A clear narrative comparison is made between what viewers are meant to recognize as the feminism of the contemporary United States and the implied cruel patriarchy of ancient China. The relative orientations of liberation and global positioning are emphasized, as Chi-Fu, who is used to symbolize in many ways the worst stereotypes of effeminate and backward Chinese males, is the instigator of the sentencing and upholder of what viewers are meant to judge to be a bad law (though the law is never actually mentioned) from a backward culture. Instead of being killed, Mulan is simply left behind, able to play the American-style hero once again in the film's conclusion, where her independence becomes sanctioned by the emperor himself. Through this narrative pattern of defiance accompanied by success and thus justification of said defiance, against the backdrop of a pastiche of Hollywood orientalisms that signal "ancient China" to viewers, American cultural values promoting independence and individualism (read: freedom) are held up as not only justifiable but also superior to the values of obedience or filial piety—or the "Oriental tyranny" (Yin, 290) of Chinese culture that is depicted in this film's attempt at multicultural hybridity.

The film's depictions of China are stripped of context and contain historical inaccuracies, such as the episode with the matchmaker, the presence of the Huns, the presence of the shrine to the ancestors, the clothing, and the presentation of villains as darker skinned. All these choices mean that "rather than completely removing all the original cultural elements, Disney's appropriation accentuates the Otherness of non-Western materials so as to cater to the Western audience's desire for exoticism" (Yin, 290). The matchmaker scene in particular plays on orientalized stereotypes of meek Chinese women controlled by their families, forced to marry and to embrace a second-class status in society; it is against these representations that Mulan's more American, independent characterization is directly constructed. Perhaps most important, Disney's iteration perpetuates orientalized stereotypes by conflating racial and gender perceptions, where the oriental Other is both effeminate and irrational in the characterization of Chi-Fu, and this depiction serves to motivate the conflict (Yin; Dundes and Streiff, 5; Dong, 172–73) and advance the plot. Chi-Fu

> epitomizes the vilification of asexual, effeminate, and homosexual men, a portrayal exacerbated by the stereotype of Asian men as hyposexual. He personifies the antithesis of hegemonic masculinity in which men dominate other men or conquer women. Asian males are particularly vulnerable to unflattering, effeminate portrayals that reduce them to caricatures within a fixed binary hierarchy prescribed by heterosexuality ideals and race. (Dundes and Streiff, 5)

Chi-Fu's mannerisms, build, and features construct him as the antithesis of other depictions of orientalized masculinity: Shang, the Emperor, and Shan Yu. Shang is this film's epitome of physical masculinity, with a clean-cut, muscular physique—a Disneyfied Bruce Lee. In comparison, Chi-Fu is slim and narrowly built, is rarely seen without writing implements, and wears voluminous clothing reminiscent of the apparel worn by the women in the matchmaker sequence. He shrieks in panic when he sees a panda and is pictured wearing a towel like a dress accompanied by a second towel wrapped around his head, reminiscent of how women with long hair might dry it after washing it. His facial hair is limp and wiry, sprouting from his chin only, in direct contrast to the Emperor's long and flowing beard, which, as Dundes and Streiff note, "confers masculinity" (Dundes and Streiff, 5). This is, of course, a different masculinity again from that embodied by Shan Yu, the film's villain, who is shown with "fang-like canines" that "match his similarly shaped fingernails, emphasizing the threat he poses" (5). In addition to fangs and talons, Shan Yu's villainy is marked by his darker skin, along with the rest of the Huns, compared to the relative paleness of the heroic characters. To complete the orientalizing effect, no white characters exist to offer a visual backdrop for either Mulan's heroism or Shan Yu's evil. The audience never has to balance any frame of visual-cultural hybridity, because the symbols of difference, heroism, villainy, and masculinity are all read in the closed system that is this Disney version of ancient China. Disney controls all narrative potential and therefore how the perception of this culture might yet be shaped in the eyes of its audience. "Stripped of context" refers not only to the inaccuracy of specific details but also to the lack of global context in the instance of a quintessentially American company appropriating a Chinese cultural artifact in order to incorporate the culture more firmly into Disney's world. Orientalizing stereotypes act as shorthand for the process of overwriting both the source material and the culture and reframing them to fit the schema already known and recognized by the target audience.

Mulan was scored by Jerry Goldsmith and included original songs written by Matthew Wilder and David Zippel—themes of which were then incorporated into the score by Goldsmith. It should be noted that Goldsmith's own website proclaims him a master of "ethnic scoring" and identifies "ethnic instruments" as part of how he constructs the signature sound of the film score (Goldsmith), feeding into the orientalizing and coloniality embedded directly into the soundscape of the film itself. A close listening to the themes of the soundtrack that are meant to signal "oriental" or "ethnic," specifically the rising and falling seven-note structure often heard when transitioning to scenes featuring the title character, reveals that these musical riffs are voiced primarily on various woodwinds (saxophones, oboes, and flutes), mid-voiced brass instruments (trumpets and French horns), and harps. The "oriental" sound is created by using not culturally specific instruments, that is, instruments that would reflect the musical culture and tradition of China, but the instrumentation of WENA symphonic and other popular musical productions. As such, heavy percussion, sweeping use of string sections, mid-voiced brass, and woodwinds give voice to the score. This problematizes the depiction of the music as ethnic on several fronts. First, we must question what "ethnic" means in this context: Is it that it is simply signaling a non-Anglo-American/European sound, and, in context, viewers are meant to infer that, here, "ethnic" means not just "not white" but "from a specific not white part of the world"? Or is this scoring considered "ethnic" because it uses melodic voicing that an American public has already been trained to recognize as "Asian" or "Other" through a longer orientalizing tradition? Furthermore, does "ethnic" then become synonymous with "Asian" or a homogeneous and all-encompassing construction of otherness that is not actually culturally specific but defined simply by not containing the signifiers of the hegemonic culture? Although the DVD special features include a reel of clips of artists sketching in what is presumably China and interviews with the directors describing research trips to discover how to represent this culture with integrity, the same signification of that level of authentication is not applied to the creation of the soundscape.

The deliberate inclusion of such details as traditional calligraphic forms and watercolor painting in the *Mulan* introduction are used to set the scene before being superseded by a more traditionally Disney-style sense of animation, but they do not disappear completely from the visual texture of the film. Echoes of the same visual signifiers from the movie's introduction can be seen when we meet Mulan's father for the first time as he stands in front of the family shrine and she rides off to town. The outline of his body, the strokes denoting his features, and the outline of the building behind him are strongly foregrounded, standing out like ink on a silk screen or rice paper, whereas, in comparison, the trees in the background take on a soft, blended texture, such as that of dispersed watercolor ink on fibrous paper. This effect is repeated when Mulan's mother stands in front of the building where the potential brides are meant to be prepared to meet the matchmaker. The strokes outlining her figure and features are so sharp in contrast to the softer textures of the background that she appears almost to be standing in front of a scenery backdrop. The stylization is seen again, notably, in the swirling snow of the avalanche that buries the Huns, in effect, softening and blurring the violence of the scene. This stylization and use of visual texture—referred to as "poetic simplicity" by producer Pam Coats (Dong, 168)—appears throughout the film to subtly remind the audience where the narrative is situated and to keep the visual construction of the animated world intact. Although this seems to be a testament to the research efforts of the production team, it is also a technique used to visually highlight where a distinction is being made between the cultural background of the audience and the one being represented on screen, particularly when it comes to drawing attention to a clash between cultural values, where the values more familiar to the target audience are meant to be seen more favorably.

These effects come together in the musical sequence of "A Girl Worth Fighting For" to signal cultural difference, to contextualize culture and otherness, and to indicate how the viewer should relate to the cultural material presented in the film. Framed by a song that embodies a male voice of identity and desire in a female-driven and female-named film, this scene also uses a change in animation style to signal difference as related to cultural knowledge, identity, or information through the deployment of Chinese calligraphic brushstrokes. This othering effect communicates a sense of authenticity embedded in the information imparted through the particular scene, such as cultural definitions of gender roles, but also heavily slants the reception of the information so that it is identified visually as different and separate from the rest of the Westernized adaptation of the cultural narrative.

"A Girl Worth Fighting For" is situated in the film directly after Mushu engineers the moving of Mulan's unit to the front to further his own goals. As the army laments needing to march long distances, Ling suggests in song that, instead of thinking about their discomfort, they "think of instead / A girl worth fighting for." When Mulan, as Ping, looks askance at the suggestion, he repeats the assertion: "That's what I said / a girl worth fighting for," pulling out a scroll from his armor and opening it. The scroll unrolls to reveal an orientalized depiction of a woman reminiscent of the idealized women off to see the matchmaker at the beginning of the film; she hides her face behind a fan, with writing in presumably Chinese characters vertically to the left of her. The camera then zooms in on this parchment, and, as it takes over the screen, this background is presented as having the same color and texture as the only other time we have seen this kind of stylized drawing in the film—the introduction, which set the scene of ancient China—in contrast to "normal" Disney fairy-tale visual retelling. The written characters unravel themselves into stylized depictions of Ling, Chien-Po, and Yao as they all describe their ideal woman: pale, quiet, meek, willing to admire them, good at cooking—essentially subservient to them and existing to improve their quality of life.

As the song continues, the visual narrative leaves the scroll and stylized animation to return to the "normal" animation style of the film, achieving a particular effect through this momentary shift. In the film opening the calligraphic style is used to solidify a localized connection between the orientalized and constructed culture and the adapted narrative, thus bringing the viewer into Disney's version of ancient China. What is seen here is a continuation of that connection, but with an added element. The song contains a message that reiterates an alleged cultural message encoded previously in the film in the song "Honor to

Us All"—a woman's worth is dependent on her ability to win a husband through her physical appearance, knowing her duties, and keeping to her place in society. This message is meant to be jarring to those positioned within a Western, feminist audience. Co-directors Tony Bancroft and Barry Cook deliberately targeted this audience and are on record as saying they were motivated in part by wanting to disrupt Disney's pattern of heroines relying on a man to save them, in order to create a role model for their daughters (Bruckner). The audience is meant to relate to Mulan's sense of isolation and not quite fitting in where she is meant to "belong" based on her outward appearance in this culture when she sings, "How 'bout a girl who's got a brain / Who always speaks her mind?" and is promptly rebuffed.

This is not the only time that Mulan becomes the outsider; however, it is one where the culture represented in the film is most clearly othered compared with "Western" values. The audience separates the "Chinese-ness" of the film from the appealing, hybridized heroine. The Chinese-ness becomes identifiable when the lyrics of the song are compounded by and associated with the stylized, albeit orientalized imagery. In comparison, Mulan, who is confused and made an outsider by the messages in the lyrics, simultaneously embodies the independent teenage heroine searching for her place and the ideal of an authentic yet palatable hybridization of Western ideals dressed up in a projection of what the dominant power holder in this iteration of globalized storytelling thinks the othered culture should look like. This is an example of orientalizing and embedded coloniality: The patriarchal values of the song are partnered visually with images that encourage the viewer to connect antiquated gender roles with a particular culture, which is then in turn identified as not contemporary, especially compared with the values embodied in the character of Mulan. By deliberately using a different style of animation to represent this mode of thinking about a woman's place in society, as described by men who are conferred a higher status and more autonomy in this depiction, the animators separate the message from the rest of the film and assign it to the originating culture. In essence, through animation style, this shift communicates to the audience that this is not something that belongs to *us* (Disney/WENA hegemonic cultural norms); this belongs to *them* (the culture that is being borrowed from and othered). Here, I argue that Disney uses its assumed "self-created authority" (Parasher, 44) to indicate that patriarchal thinking is inherent in Chinese culture, which is antiquated and not compatible with the sensibilities of a progressive and contemporary young woman (or audience). In this way, a seemingly innocuous or comical song actually undermines any possibility of incorporating ancient China and Chinese culture into Disney's contemporary sensibility through its rather blatant othering and orientalizing. A culture that it alleged to try to represent with integrity instead is actively depicted as less progressive than "Western" culture, and "Western" culture is elevated as more progressive as a result.

In several interviews *Mulan* directors Tony Bancroft and Barry Cook have referred to the culturally specific research that went into the production of *Mulan* (Bruckner; Dong, 173). However, the relative lack of success of the film in its proclaimed origin culture points to an area for improvement in terms of how Disney approaches cross-cultural storytelling where the end-product would be accepted by the culture from which the original narrative came (Dundes and Streiff, 2). Despite the signaling of "research" to authenticate Disney's presentation of "China" in interviews, DVD extras, and shifts in visual style, the film still presents a rather superficial multicultural retelling. Tellingly, Yin evaluates the "transformation of a Chinese story to a 'timeless' canon" as "a mimicry of Chinese culture" to inscribe "a sense of authenticity in the film," one where the source material is "decontextualized, deracinated, and displaced" and cultural elements are reduced "to the extent that only the most superficial ones were strategically retained to ensure a façade of otherness" (Yin, 291). That "sense of authenticity" is key to Disney's multicultural or cross-culturally adaptations beyond the 1990s, especially in terms of selling diversity to a global audience, but it was still problematic in this early iteration of that mode of storytelling. Yin further asserts that such a process of adaptation or appropriation, what I would call bending the traditional ballad to fit the Disney fairytale mode, essentially robs *Mulan* of "original meanings" and through "resignification or appropriation does not just distort certain authentic meanings" but "contributes to establish, maintain and reinforce certain ideology . . . while it challenges, contests, and emasculates others" (291). Disney wields global power through narrative transmission rather than exchange. Disney also attempts to shore up its image as the authority on global storytelling and as the arbiter and definer of how global stories are told by incorporating—literally and figuratively—stories from outside its direct cultural sphere into its larger oeuvre, subsuming cultural narratives and overwriting them into what it considers to be more universal or global. The process of subsuming a cultural narrative—untethering it, redefining it, and then broadcasting it to a particular culture and/or the world as the authoritative version of the narrative—can be seen clearly through an examination of the production and reception of a film such as the animated *Mulan*.

Whatever the intent behind Disney's culturally specific research might be—and I am not going to try to read individual producers' and creative directors' minds here—how that research is perhaps implemented in practice opposes its stated intent. Such research becomes about the performance of research as a way of adding intrinsic value to a product rather than creating a culturally authentic product. That performative value of having done research, of trying to get it right, results in only superficial change, not a deeper shift in the way narratives are retold, and does little to fix the representation issues embedded in Disney culture. The research is not really concerned with the depth of knowledge or the context it might provide, but it is useful in that creators can point to it as evidence of having tried. This is evident in the degree to which the images produced fail to translate back to the source culture as authentic; when considering transcultural adaptation, Disney primarily understands the surface level of the image and not the underlying sociocultural and historical politics. Nor does it need to; the point, after all, is not to authentically reflect something new or different but rather to provide a point of contrast that returns the knowing viewer back to the core aesthetic, to remind the viewer of the comfortable positioning and orientation of Disney-real. This continued in the 2010s, most notably with the production of *Moana* in 2016 almost twenty years later,[2] and even again in different ways with the production of the live-action and CGI remake of *Mulan* released in 2020. But even though the efforts made in the production of the 1998 animated *Mulan* reflect specific orientalizing tendencies and the incorporation of a specific temporality and geography, that is not the only

---

2   A dialogic reading of these two films can be found in Anjirbag, "Mulan."

method the corporation has used to create the effect of a sanctioned inclusion of other cultures and peoples.

From Neverland to Atlantis and Everywhere In-Between: Constructs of Folklorized and Ambiguous Indigeneity

Disney has a long history of misrepresenting Native Americans and contributing to Indigenous erasure,[3] which in turn contributed to decisions made in the Disney Renaissance and post-Renaissance eras. From outdated stereotypes immortalized in Neverland to an ancient civilization still living beneath the earth's crust and myriad actual cultures located in "real" historical times, which include so-called pre-historic "Inuit" and "Polynesian" cultures, Virginia Algonquins at the time of North American colonization, and contemporary Hawaiians, Disney's constructs of Indigeneity span the globe—above it, beneath it, and on it across time. In 1953 Disney released its own adaptation of J. M. Barrie's classic *Peter Pan*. Although not a fairy-tale film, *Peter Pan* solidified the stereotype of Native Americans visually for generations of children and families; this stereotype then continued to be reiterated across the company's live-action productions in pastiches of the so-called Wild West. WENA cultures have broadly not been able to let go of a particular frontier fantasy; the perpetuation of this fantasy has contributed to the erasure of Native American and other Indigenous peoples as living cultures rather than as symbolic relics of a mythic past that has been "naturally" progressed beyond. And importantly, as a US-centric company that literally built its own versions of the world on stolen Indigenous lands, Disney needs to relegate all those who might have inhabited the spaces that became Disneyland and Disney World to the distant past, people who have been replaced through a natural form of progress making. To touch on the history in a real way would mean creating a collision space in a colonized present; therefore Indigenous representation has to be positioned largely outside the bounds of the progression of history, lest the true progression of history intrude into the white space of Disney and reorient it.

---

3 See Byrne and McQuillan; Jhappan and Stasiulis; C. R. King et al.; Parasher; Parekh; Putnam; Tulk; Ward; Wasko; and Whitley.

In Disney's *Peter Pan*, "Indians" are based on stereotype, caricature, and even the colonizing factors of Barrie's own time, but nevertheless the film set a low bar for growth in the 1990s for Disney's multicultural project, as Prajna Parasher explains:

> The diverse, decimated communities that provided the material for this erasure [of Native Americans] became homogenized into Pidgin English, plains Indian teepees, and more than anything else, the substitution of the terror and horror of a warring exploitive past with a jokey, incompetent present: Jim Crow Indians. The animated version *Peter Pan* incorporates a standing theatrical tradition; its own particular inflection is the lack of any shading or irony. . . . The figures—braves, squaw, chief, princess—are immediately recognizable as Disney which in itself displays a caricature history that was at inception specifically racist. (Parasher, 43)

Disney's construction is part of a long tradition of novels, serials, comics, films, traveling shows, and other media that depict Native Americans and their encounters with European and then American colonizers, leaving their imprint on the imaginary of Anglophone and European popular cultures (Parasher). The construction of the Frontier or Wild West had already produced a working language of images and symbols by which to communicate pattern narratives and tropes. It is from this history that Disney's depiction of Native Americans in *Peter Pan* can be explained, but the contribution to Indigenous erasure must be noted. Following the original erasure of Indigenous peoples through genocide and the further erasure perpetrated by the necessary pivot to being "show Indians" for things such as Buffalo Bill's company (Parasher), the attempt to just move from caricature to history-flavored realism resulted in its own form of continued erasure of real Native Americans at the time of *Pocahontas*'s release, and the film's legacy remains one of obfuscation of history in favor of a neat, cute "fairy-tale" narrative.

Rewriting Matoaka's Story

Even though I am not going to deconstruct the many problems with *Pocahontas* here, I do want to briefly highlight the conversation that existed at the time of the film's release and continues to the present. This conversation can better explain the divide between intent and impact, and why it is so difficult to not only change the internal Disney ethos of constructing multiculturalism but also to make the problems in Disney's shaping of otherness more visible. Although *Pocahontas* is a quasi-historical narrative appropriated into Disney's cultural construction of multiculturalism and is not itself rooted in folklore or fairy tale, the film is important to this overarching discussion on two points. First, in recasting the narrative to be palatable to its audiences, Disney engaged in the folklorization of history, overwriting the historical narrative in popular cultural memory.[4] Second, the critical reaction from specifically the Powhatan Renape Nation and other Indigenous peoples and their relative lack of power to speak back to the corporation and exert cultural autonomy over their own history are, along with the response to criticism of *Aladdin*,[5] useful in establishing the baseline corporate response to criticism of cultural content in this era.

Disney's narrative about a "heroine who bridges the gap between two cultures" (Parekh, 168) presents an ahistoricized, simplified fantasy of multiculturalism that results in a "reinscription of an old colonial practice; utilizing the 'Other' in the business of spiritual awakening of the European, who still dominates the American continent," and defines the narration of American history as one of "cultural contact and conflict, of transplantation and displacement, forged constantly by violence and violation" (168–69). Parekh continues, "Powerful myths that emerge out of these narratives engage, at affective levels, in reinscribing or revising notions of identity and difference within the circumscribed realms of hegemonic control and authority" (169). In other words, communicating the history of the North American continent after European contact is fraught with racialized and hierarchized dichotomies. To make *Pocahontas* an uplifting or heroic story in any regard is to rewrite history, as Disney has done. This is compounded by the propensity of Disney fairy tales to replace their precursors in the public imaginary, leading to the reality that Jack Zipes refers to as the corporation's "cultural stranglehold on the

---

4   See Leece Lee-Oliver's chapter on *Pocahontas* for a more stringent exploration of Mattaponi Oral tradition and the recounting of the history of the settlement of Jamestown.

5   See chapter 5 and Anjirbag, "New Agrabah."

fairy tale" (Zipes, "Breaking," 21): Disney's "signature has obfuscated the names of Charles Perrault, the Brothers Grimm, Hans Christian Andersen, and Carlo Collodi. If children or adults think of the great classical fairy tales today . . . they will think Walt Disney," and "[Disney's] spell over the fairy tale seems to live on even after his death" (21). Although Zipes's observations specify the relationship with Disney films and versions of fairy tales, the same thing holds true for legends from other traditions, as seen with *Mulan*, and from history, which is made abundantly clear by *Pocahontas* and its sequel, *Pocahontas II: Journey to a New World*. Together, the *Pocahontas* films recast a colonizing history that turns a narrative about a Native American's imprisonment, marriage, and subsequent death away from her people into a fuzzy story about love and multicultural friendships; the films also fail to "[dislodge] whites from the position of power," despite *Pocahontas* ostensibly "undercutting the authority with which [whites] speak and act in and on the world" (Jhappan and Stasiulis, 152). Disney took a historical figure and developed its own folklore around her, which has subsequently overwritten the real historical context. Such recontextualization at the price of real history has concrete effects for the people misrepresented, as seen by the Powhatan Renape Nation's response to *Pocahontas*.

Following the release of the film, Chief Roy Crazy Horse of the Powhatan Renape Nation posted a response to *Pocahontas* on behalf of the tribe, the members of which would have been the descendants of the people loosely depicted by Disney. On the now archived website, he writes:

> This year, Roy Disney decided to release an animated movie about a Powhatan woman known as "Pocahontas." In answer to a complaint by the Powhatan Nation, he claims the film is "responsible, accurate, and respectful."
>
> We of the Powhatan Nation disagree. The film distorts history beyond recognition. Our offers to assist Disney with cultural and historical accuracy were rejected. Our efforts urging him to reconsider his misguided mission were spur[n]ed.
>
> Of all of Powhatan's children, only "Pocahontas" is known, primarily because she became the hero of Euro-Americans as the "good Indian," one who saved the life of a white man. Not only is the "good Indian/bad Indian theme" inevitably given new life by

Disney, but the history, as recorded by the English themselves, is badly falsified in the name of "entertainment." (Chief Roy Crazy Horse, "Pocahontas Myth")

The page goes on to present the history of Matoaka—Pocahontas's real name—including the circumstances of her capture, imprisonment, renaming, and eventual death. The page closes: "It is unfortunate that [with] this sad story, which Euro-Americans should find embarras[s]ing, Disney makes 'entertainment' and perpetuates a dishonest and self-serving myth at the expense of the Powhatan Nation" (Chief Roy Crazy Horse, "Pocahontas Myth"). The website also held details about a play staged by the Powhatan Renape Nation called *The One Called Pocahontas*, which told the true story of this historical figure (Chief Roy Crazy Horse, "One Called Pocahontas"). It was the tribe's only answer to the overwriting of this section of the continent's history, and the website documented Chief Roy Crazy Horse's side of how the film came to be and how Disney's failure led to the formation of the play performed on 2–4 August 1996. The Powhatan Renape position is clear: The production by Disney was a misrepresentation of a painful history, despite offers to collaborate in a responsible way with the corporation.

Shirley "Little Dove" Custalow McGowen, an early consultant on the project, is listed as "Native American Consultant: of the Mattiponi Indians" in the credits among the crew. She was later quoted as saying, "I wish they would take the name of Pocahontas off that movie" (Custalow McGowen, qtd. in Rogers; see also Ward, 33–56). And yet, looking at the media produced by the corporation itself, including a documentary titled *The Making of Pocahontas* originally included in the Special Edition DVD, in which the lengths of research and consultancy are described by the filmmakers, one might think that the company had gone above and beyond to honor the truth and that if deviations were present because director Mike Gabriel conceptualized the film "as a love story, not a historical character" (Gabriel, qtd. in Rogers), these changes were made with the consent of said consultancy. Paired with the involvement of actor and activist Russell Means (Oglala Lakota) (Dutka; Rivas; "Disney Magazine") and the casting of Irene Bedard (Cree, Inuit), the film had more than a patina of authenticity. This documentary is notably not included with the film extras on the streaming service Disney+, whereas deleted scenes and a multilanguage reel of "Colors of the Wind" are, which indicates that there is a much broader conversation to be had in future scholarship regarding Disney peritext and what happens to narratives surrounding certain films when such supplementary materials are removed from easy public access by the corporation and become digital ephemera as the corporation tightens control of a film's full paratext.

Criticism of the films was not limited to the time of release. Organizations such as Lakota Children's Enrichment (see Dunne) and historians and activists continued to problematize the film through the 2010s (see Mansky; Kenzie Allen [Oneida], qtd. in Bodenner). Part of the reason that *Pocahontas* remains in the public consciousness is the further research and documentaries produced on the Jamestown settlement and Matoaka, but Disney's recursive nostalgia also played a part, because Disney is "a powerful agent in the imaginative construction of history as our collective memory" (Stripes, 88). This "collective memory" and how it exists for people outside Native American contexts become particularly visible when considering a twenty-year retrospective piece published in *The Atlantic* in 2015. Author Sophie Gilbert considers the Pocahontas character "a radical reimagining of the Disney heroine, [and] the movie she starred in was itself attempting to both re-explore history and to encourage empathy as a guiding quality for young viewers" (Gilbert). Gilbert draws not only from her own experience of the film but also from Means's controversial statements that *Pocahontas* "is the finest feature film ever done about American Indians in the history of Hollywood" (Means, qtd. in *Disney Magazine*) and animator Tom Sito's assertions that the film was made with due diligence and historical consultation at the forefront. The dissonance between the perceptions of Sito and Gilbert and the perceptions of people closer to the material reveals the distance in impact on various groups by Disney productions versus the intention or the appearance of "research" on behalf of the corporation, and it also leads to insights into the orientation of the film: Who was this narrative truly for?

The gap between nostalgia and intent, or the ability to buy into the corporation's intentions and the felt impact by misrepresented groups, is a considerable distance. Where one side sees self-erasure or effacement, the other side can, in a detached and decontextualized manner, point to the presented evidence of "we tried." And yet Matoaka is forgotten several times over—not only renamed Rebecca in her lifetime after her marriage to John Rolfe but also known in perpetuity as Disney's Pocahontas. Giving a historical figure the fairy-tale treatment is one thing; doing it when the figure in question is someone who represents an already clouded and mistold and misrepresented history is quite another, because "in dealing with topics that have both a historical basis as well as a mythical force, Disney films reflect and ultimately promote a certain frame of imperialist ideology that pervades modern or even postmodern thinking, an ideology that rationalizes the appropriation and often blatant misrepresentation of the history of the Other" (Parekh, 170). However, the fact that twenty years since the film's release there is still considerable debate over its true impact, despite the breadth of own-voices critique and further scholarship, begins to illustrate just why Disney's multicultural experiment is far more complicated than just diversifying the images represented by the corporation. Although Disney stepped firmly away from real figures or histories after *Pocahontas*, the 2000s did not show much further grasp of the depths of complications of representing various Indigenous cultures to the wider world, as seen in the *Brother Bear* films.

One Big Happy Animal Family

The *Brother Bear* films (2003, 2006) feature a young man named Kenai who is turned into a bear. On the UK version of Disney+ (as of 15 May 2020), *Brother Bear*'s main character, Kenai, is described as "Inuit" in the description and plot summary on the film's page, but for *Brother Bear 2* the description and summary specify a setting in "the Pacific Northwest at the end of the Ice Age." This framing does several things in terms of prefacing the films' internal logic and spiritualism and providing viewers with a particular lens through which to view the film and thereby interpret what they see and create meaning. But most importantly for this discussion, the different framing sets the scene for the films to also reproduce a dehumanizing effect and erasure by producing yet another depiction of Native Americans or First Nations people as of a long ago past that no longer exists, while "[sidestepping] the problematic terrain of colonial history altogether" (Whitley, 94).

The opening of *Brother Bear* uses a framing effect of an older male storyteller relating the tale of "his brother who became a bear to become a man." The animation then shifts to a past scene where the narrator, whom we learn to identify as Denahi, is a younger man, with his brothers Sitka and Kenai. The "human"-related portions of the film are rife with symbols of "prehistoric peoples": furs, bones, implied ritualized dancing, cave paintings (more reminiscent of those found in Europe than the area the film is set in [Parasher, 46]), mammoths, and a shaman. A deliberate connection is implied with the animal or natural world, a variation on the already problematic "ecological Indian" stereotype (Gilio-Whitaker, "Problem"), which drives the central conflict of the film, triggered when Kenai receives his totem, the "bear of love." He is upset with it because he wanted something more masculine, and his dissatisfaction seems to come to a head when his eldest brother, Sitka, is killed by a bear. Kenai kills the animal he blames for his brother's death and is subsequently transformed into a bear by Sitka's spirit in his eagle totem form.

As a bear, Kenai meets Koda, a cub separated from his mother through Kenai's actions. By learning to love Koda and understand how his actions caused the little cub to be alone, Kenai is able to become human again. As the moderator Najela of the Tumblr blog "Writing with Color" notes, token representation that involves animal transformations are

> dehumanizing because these are the very few POC [people of color] characters in the Disney franchise and they spend most of their time as animals. It wouldn't be quite so bad if there were more Black Disney Princesses [referring to *Princess and the Frog*] or Inuit Characters, but the fact of the matter is that there aren't. They are the only representatives of their race in the Disney franchise and the likelihood of having more characters to represent these ethnicities is slim. ("Animal Transformations and Dehumanization")

Najela further points out that the secondary part of the animal transformation trope is that these underrepresented figures are turned into animals because they somehow "need to be taught how to love," which, other than tenuously in the case of the Beast and Merida's mother in *Brave*, is not the case for other Disney characters who undergo some form of transformation ("Animal Transformations and Dehumanization"). There is something utterly dehumanizing about folding a nonwhite character into an animal body and teaching them to love as part of the progression of a narrative that is about the connections between humans and the natural world. Furthermore, learning the thing that Disney sells as intrinsically human—love, especially the fairy-tale variety—is part of the characterization of these characters as they are taught through love to become "human." In the case of Kenai, this is part of solidifying his innate connection to the natural world through his animal transformation.

The connections between this particular Indigenous people, who are never specifically identified in the film itself, and the natural world or animals are reinforced several times. Not only does Sitka's spirit appear as both human and eagle, but there is also a particularly important scene where Koda tells the story about his mother defeating a hunter to the other bears at the salmon run. During Koda's narration, Kenai relives his own memory of his brother's death from the perspective of Koda's mother and understands the wrong he committed to be transformed into a bear in the first place. The connection is reinforced yet again when, after Kenai tells Koda the truth about his mother, Kenai notices the similarities between a bear paw print and a hand print, and uses the brush of his paw to turn the paw print into the hand print he once wished to place on a cave wall as a symbol to his people that he had learned to live a life guided by his totem. This scene reinforces the idea that Kenai must become his totem, a bear, to understand the importance of love as a human, a theme that comes up again in the second film: By changing and embracing the natural world, we become more our human selves.

Brother Bear steps away from a full embrace of an uncomfortable moralizing New Age spiritualism by turning to comedy, such as in the vignettes peppered throughout the end credits. But these outtake-formatted clips make the exoticized human-animal connection more weird through the image of Koda performing martial arts or the image of the moose brothers leading a yoga class, which performs an incredibly crass moment of appropriation. As the animals are led through an approximation of a plow position, or Halasana, supine on their backs with their legs reaching over the tops of their heads, the leader of the class tells them to "shift into salutation to the sun." While probably a throwaway line meant to poke fun at the very human fad of yoga in WENA contexts, the decontextualization of a spiritual tradition in such a way as to have it performed by animals is questionable and uncomfortable, adding another layer to implications of what kind of people are more intrinsically connected to the natural world. Just because we can retrospectively justify the reasoning for why or how these decisions might have been made, especially considering the gags, it does not mean that the gags are uncritically okay to have been presented in the first place, nor should they be simply glossed over as part of the hybridity that underlies the presentation of diversity in the film. There is a positionality inherent in joke making: Who is punching? Is it upward or downward? Who is going to feel the impact versus who gets to apply an exoticizing gaze to the situation?

The depiction of Inuit culture is less prominent in the *Brother Bear* films than the implication of Inuit, or broadly "Native," beliefs. This is not dissimilar to a vein of New Age spirituality that turns to an appropriative amalgamation of "Native American" or "First Nation" beliefs. Prajna Parasher most accurately describes this kind of depiction as "set 'respectfully' amongst the Inuit, the characters are generic enough to be Eskimos and with a nod toward the preoccupations of our era (multiculturalism, shamanism, totems, matriarchy, transformative power of love) move through a story line that struggles between Cartoon Network and religious docudrama" (Parasher, 44). This is most apparent during Kenai's transformation scenes and in the way that music is used alongside depictions of "the spirits" descending from the aurora borealis. The "Transformation" theme, sung by the Bulgarian Women's Choir, was translated into Inuit, and the score itself incorporated "world music," signaled by the incorporation of particular percussion to communicate a general sense of "Native American" culture, much in the way the storyline itself was developed as an original tale based on "a lot of research on Native American myths and legends" and the discovery that "they had a lot of stories about being transformed into animals" (Dudley). As noted by Janice Esther Tulk, "The choice to translate one song into an Inuit language . . . combined with background research trips to Alaska (especially Denali National Park) to paint landscapes for the animation, suggests that the film-makers were consciously representing an Eskimo or Inuit culture group" (Tulk, 126). However, the most "authentic" presentation of culture, the translation of "Transformation" into Inuit from its original English by Phil Collins, is ultimately given its supernatural feel by the Bulgarian Women's Choir, simply because Mark Mancina, co-writer of the film score, "was a fan of the choir" (128–29). The then-president of Walt Disney Music, Chris Montan, acknowledged that "people viewing the movie likely will not know the language," but this was not an obstacle because "it'll feel real to them at least, and they won't even probably know why" (Montan, qtd. in Tulk, 129), another example of the tension between believability and realism embedded in the company's approach to authenticity. Notably, "Transformation," which was so integral to the otherworldliness of the first film is not used again for Nita's transformation at the end of *Brother Bear 2*. Music more generally in both films lyrically tends to invoke the "great spirits," both in Tina Turner's "Great Spirits" number in the first film and in Melissa Etheridge's opening number for the second, which is reprised to close that film. The imagery that accompanies both of these songs includes depictions of "tribal" life and its implicit closeness with the natural world, solidifying again a more general sense of ambiguous Indigeneity that simultaneously erases specificity of culture and continues to assign Native Americans and First Nations to a prehistoric, legendary past, erasing them too from modernity.

The Mask of Mythical Ambiguity

Ambiguous Indigeneity appears again in the *Atlantis* films (2001, 2003), cross-coded with Blackness. Atlanteans are constructed in both image and culture to be interpreted as nonwhite. As noted by Tumblr "Writing with Color" moderator Brei ("She Is of a Mythical Race"), Princess Kida is further coded as Black through the casting of a voice actress who is "a black actress most famous for voicing black animated characters" and because "Kida has African features such as: brown skin, full lips, broad nose . . . bone structure and hips wider than any previous European princess. Disney also tries to incorporate features of the voice actor into the design, meaning that to divorce Kida of her blackness would be to divorce Cree from her ethnicity as well." In outlining how Disney deploys ambiguous race coding or racialization so that viewers read Kida as a woman of color, Brei continues, "I do condemn Disney for not explicitly stating so and relying on magic and white hair to distance her from people of color. (Not that I don't like magic in my Disney films, but none of the other films use magic as a crutch for racial ambiguity)" ("She Is of a Mythical Race"). This ambiguity is crossed with the historical setting, which also creates space for this deployment of magic in a "plausible" setting. The setting of the film is the United States in 1914—with all the implications of industrial and archeological profiteering fully present and a good dose of white savior and white discovery narratives included. In an interesting twist, Milo Thatch's companions are the most diverse cohort of secondary characters based semirealistically on the real diversity of the United States at the time: a very round and somewhat grotesque Frenchman; a Black and Native American doctor; a teenage female Puerto Rican mechanic; an Italian florist-turned-explosives expert; and an elderly white female radio operator. And yet, despite handling the concept of American period history arguably better than in 1995, *Atlantis: The Lost Empire* stumbles when it comes to how these people interact with Atlanteans and how the Atlanteans themselves are portrayed. This is again based on the fact that, although Disney has in this film created an incredible aesthetic of diversity, how that aesthetic was conceptualized and deployed, particularly regarding the Atlanteans, stems from a lack of a deeper sensibility regarding multicultural depiction.

To animate a science fiction derivative of a myth with its roots in classicism that has then reappeared in myriad ways in art and literature and, importantly, representing people lost to the surface world (allegedly) since before Plato's time, the animators seem to have landed on "prehistoric" as the best visual coding for an advanced society. Signaling "native ancient culture" and also making sure it came across as "mythical" became a matter of composition: skin and hair color, apparel that seemed to be a hybrid of loincloths and the more robelike draped garments of the Classical Mediterranean, pet dinosaurs, a magical life source, an intrinsic conflict with the values of Atlanteans and those of the visitors from the surface world, and—key to any discovery of an ancient civilization—a loss of culture that can only be remedied by outsiders.

Somehow this exploration of a lost culture becomes even worse in the sequel, *Atlantis: Milo's Return*, which was released straight to DVD and reads as though it were three episodes of what would have been a television series, with some bridging animation thrown in. The premise of the sequel is that Milo is helping Kida rebuild the lost city with the knowledge he returned to Atlantis, but the explorers from the first film return to see if the Kraken that recently started to sink ships off the coast of Norway could be an Atlantean war machine. The film's three distinct parts become a pastiche of tying Atlantean technology and knowledge to Gothic and Lovecraftian horror and folklore, science fiction, Norse myth, and North and Central American Indigenous cultures.

The second "episode" sees the group travel to the Southwestern United States, where they encounter a "Native American" wind spirit who is flanked by a red-eyed sand coyote named Chakashi, who is protecting an ancient sanctuary of the Nashoni people from looters. The Nashoni are a fictional tribe, and the hidden city, which is vaguely reminiscent of Mesa Verde's pueblos, also has statues reminiscent of the Atlantean guardians who protected the city from the lava in the first film. The statues, the pottery, and other artifacts are all vaguely Mesoamerican (reminiscent of imagery also seen in the architecture and motifs of *The Emperor's New Groove*), and upon seeing it, Milo comments, "It's a blending of every culture from Idaho to Peru: Nashoni, Aztec, Maya, Olmec," and Kida replies, "The Crystal Guardian's teachings influenced all these cultures." Chakashi explains that the Crystal Guardian, whom a large central statue depicts, was a "great teacher and protector" who "revealed many secrets to the Nashoni: the path of the stars, the time to plant, how to heal themselves." There are two problems in this construction, the first being the blending of a fictional tribe with very real tribes with very specific cultural and technological developments and historical trajectories, by making the Nashoni equivalent with the Aztec, Maya, and Olmec, all ancient civilizations in their own right. The second problem is the implication that all the mentioned North and Central American Indigenous cultures come from somewhere else, as derivative of Atlantean culture, rather than being their own entities with distinct, real histories. Separately, each problem would need redressing in its own right, but combined, these problems contribute to the thinking that these were not sophisticated cultures with their own histories and in their own right and therefore the Disney narrative replaces and erases real historical and cultural development. Such a construction reinforces the idea that these other cultures, focalized through the appearance of Chakashi, somehow were in need of mystical help to survive and thrive, and so are and were teleologically "behind" both the modernity of Milo's world or the development of fictional ancients in the case of the Atlanteans. This construction is predicated on the idea that Indigenous cultures could not have developed things themselves and contributes to an erasure of Indigenous culture, which scholars and activists such as Crystal Echo Hawk (Pawnee) point to as also contributing to systemic disenfranchisement and "the invisibility and erasure of Native Americans in all aspects of modern U.S. society" (Nagle). This has a continuation effect of reducing potential futures for young Indigenous and Native American youth who do not get to see themselves as real people in the present (Elliott-Groves and Fryburg). By using real elements to connote authenticity in the construction of this racialized fantasy of the nonwhite precursor to a European presence on the North American continent, such elements become deconstructed and distanced from their real contexts, and the people who have cultural ownership of those elements become irrevocably connected to the fantasy and further erased.

The pattern of representing Native Americans and other Indigenous peoples as located in the long ago and far away, as stereotypes, or as somehow inherently magical or connected to fantasy spaces is not resolved in the films made in the 1990s and 2000s. Criticisms such as those directed at *Pocahontas*, *Brother Bear*, and *Atlantis*, as with *Peter Pan* before them, shapes the "research" approach in *Moana* in 2016, but from the analysis of these films, it is possible to see the problem with uncritically misrepresenting history and mythologizing people who still exist today. It raises the question over and over again, Whose stories are these, and whose stories should they be? However, just like the cultural imperialism and orientalism featured in *Mulan*, this is again only one aspect of the complexities of multicultural representation by Disney, and this is all further complicated still when taking into account the other strain of orientalism common in the Anglo-American world, the construction of a fantasy Middle East, as well as colorism and anti-Blackness.

I Am Moana: Glocality and the Disney Fairy-Tale Mode

Moana (2016)[6] takes a mild step away from both the ambiguity of racialized depictions of the 1990s and 2000s and a bigger step away from the return to whiteness as a core aesthetic as seen in the live-action fairy-tale remediations. This film goes to great lengths in both the internal film aesthetics and the marketing paratexts to signal how Disney is depicting

---

6 I do an extended reading of *Moana* in Anjirbag, "Mulan."

a real culture authentically—and this time with sanction, input, and permission. But it avoids "real" history because *Moana* proffers an intervention in history to explain a gap in oral histories and Polynesian and Oceanic wayfaring traditions. And yet in this film's attempt to elide or avoid real history by sidestepping the real effects of settler colonialism on the geographic area that the narrative explores through narratively predating, it only serves to draw more attention to what is being vanished, as did rewriting the settler-colonial history of Jamestown several decades earlier, something explored in more depth by Jenny Banh, who catalogs the different levels of colonial erasure that *Moana* engages in.

How *Moana* engages with, to return to Sara Ahmed's phrasing, "making 'the strange' familiar" (Ahmed, *Queer Phenomenology*, 126) allows us to think about the function of the Disney fairy-tale mode in relation to the idea of glocality in fairy tales as considered by Anna Katrina Gutierrez. Gutierrez locates how localized adaptations of fairy tales in various contexts push against narratives of universalization, and she highlights how such adaptations engage in a "nuanced dialectic between global and local concepts" (Gutierrez, 9). But what happens in *Moana* is not a nuanced conversation; it is almost the inverse. Elements of specific cultural legends and myths are made to fit a Disney narrative through the enforcement of the Disney fairy-tale mode over the specific details, location, and even historically situated distant-past setting. Despite any visual, superficial gains, Disney still orients this film as aesthetically different, belonging to a hyperspecific time and place, a place that must by necessity fade to the storied past for the Magic Kingdom proper to arise.

Moana's opening is meant to signal the entrance to another culture, time, and place. As the Disney castle appears, the opening notes of the first song of the soundtrack, "Tulou Tagaloa," are heard and the narrative moves forward from that musical framing. Instead of "Once upon a time," we are offered "In the beginning there was only ocean," as the creation story of the world of the narrative unfolds on brightly colored tapestries. These tapestries are composed of repeating motifs and textures that recall woven fabrics and fibers that signify a particular kind of idyllic island life (Herman). Eventually, the digitally generated tapestries give way to Disney's trademark computer-generated animation aesthetic as Moana's grandmother terrifies a group of children—all but Moana—with the impending fall of darkness and destruction of their home. So again, just as in *Mulan*'s opening, there is an auditory cue of otherness, a zoomed-out view of the culture we are being introduced to, and then, once the scene is set, we settle in on the zoomed-in view of our title character. As young Moana claps at her grandmother's story, the viewer is firmly rooted in a sense of place as the textures of the tapestries depicting the story are echoed in the textures of the wood and fibers surrounding Moana. Viewers are encouraged to accept the location and its validity through the visual signaling of culture and so too accept the validity of the narrative.

The integration of visual texture in the opening parallels the use of calligraphic brushstrokes in the opening of *Mulan* as a frame, with the woven, fibrous tapestry setting the scene before being superseded by a more traditional Disney animation aesthetic. But despite the graphic shift, these elements do not disappear completely from the visual texture of the film. The visual effect of using different animated textures to simultaneously enhance world building and signal difference is used slightly differently in *Moana*, presumably because the medium is CGI rather than hand-drawn animation, but to no less an othering effect. Just as the creation myth emphasizes a connection with the natural world and affirms a mythical idyll, the visual textures of the film itself, especially those that depict interaction with natural elements, are highly stylized. The sand and the ocean have a heightened realism, especially when characters interact with them directly. The coconut fronds and the grain of the timber are also emphasized, as is the movement of Moana's hair. The idyllic nature of Montunui is made so real that the spiritual elements are secondary to how much the visual signifiers convince the viewer of the believability of the world they are witnessing. Because those visual elements track with the ideal of island life—sand, ocean, coconuts—that a WENA audience has been conditioned to expect from an "island narrative," it adds to the expectation and the idea that the story being communicated is culturally authentic; through that hyperrealism by means of visual texture, Montunui and thus Disney's presentation of "Polynesia" become plausible.

Ultimately *Moana* allowed Walt Disney Animation Studios another chance to nudge at the geographic boundaries of the brand while folding yet another culture into the confines of the Disney universe and the Disney Princess franchise. *Moana* stands out in other ways than just the culturally specific stylization lent to the animation itself, the integration of Polynesian voices from the Oceanic Story Trust, and the involvement of Opetaia Foa'i in the production of the film's songs. The typical princess narrative is disrupted; although Moana has a demigod traveling companion, she retains her agency in the film, which also passes the Bechdel test, showing how easy it is to make a film that does. Moana is the first new non-white princess since Tiana, and Disney's first attempt at an Indigenous "princess" since Pocahontas. However, Moana's story is still structured in the Disney fairy-tale mode, just as Mulan's story was. The question at hand is, Was the execution any better, or more "authentic" or "authorized," as the corporation would like to claim and has tried to assert? Or is this instead, as Ida Yoshinaga describes it, yet another example of "symbolic expropriation," where the "Native stories and other cultural information are extracted into the narrative factory of capitalism . . . [and] then attempts [are made] to replace those community stories and information with its canned product within hegemony's highly commodified symbolic marketplace" (Yoshinaga, 188–89)? Criticism of *Pocahontas* and *Mulan* at the time of their release may not have permeated the US mediasphere to the same extent as the praise, but the criticisms leveled at the production and presentation of *Moana* were wide-ranging in the public sphere and easily accessible online. Despite its best efforts, Disney can no longer completely control the narratives about altruistic cross-cultural storytelling and cultural authenticity that are part of the marketing strategy around multicultural texts. In fact, an understanding of the relative positionalities inherent in the concept of glocality allows for more nuance in terms of understanding what happened when the studio was forced to contend with criticism of films such as *Moana* for misrepresenting cultural heroes and deities, rewriting traditional legends in ways that omitted key figures.[7]

Disney's production of *Moana* reflects many of the same techniques deployed to connote authenticity in the production and marketing of *Mulan* about twenty years earlier. The main focus of the marketing campaign leading up to *Moana*'s release centered the formation of the Oceanic Story Trust by Disney and its validation of the film (J. Robinson).

---

7 See Diaz; Flores; Gilio-Whitaker, "Disney Refines Its Cultural Competence"; Herman; Ka'ili; Ngata; Ngata and Kelly; and Schilling.

Where the films differ, however, is that, whereas *Mulan* relates a version of an already well-known and often retold Chinese story, *Moana* is an act of literal myth making, inserting a Disneyfied invention into a perceived gap in Polynesian history. Disney's creation and use of the Trust to craft and verify its "authentic" elements in the film generated an abundance of culturally specific criticism regarding how authentic Indigenous voices are used in such productions. This kind of criticism is strongest and most valid from within that wider community. Especially worth noting is a growing body of responses in op-eds, public and academic presentations, and engagement through the Mana Moana Facebook page, which addresses not only representation in *Moana* but also depictions of Indigenous peoples from across the Pacific in Hollywood and Western media culture and the reality and impact of such misrepresentations. Such criticism included interrogating the colonial positioning of relationships between various Indigenous peoples across the Pacific arena and the Western mediasphere. Often "admiration" is almost synonymous with entitlement to said culture by a corporation such as Disney (Ngata and Kelly). Pohonpeian and Filipino scholar Vicente M. Diaz writes:

> Who gets to authenticate so diverse a set of cultures and so vast a region as Polynesia and the even more diverse and larger Pacific Island region that is also represented in this film? And what, exactly does it mean that henceforth it is Disney that now administrates how the rest of the world will get to see and understand Pacific realness, including substantive cultural material that approaches the spiritual and the sacred. (Diaz)

Māori educator Tina Ngata (Ngāti Porou) asserts that *Moana* is not an Indigenous story: "Having brown advisers doesn't make it a brown story. It is still very much a white person's story" (qtd. in Herman). The lack of transparency in the creation of the Oceanic Story Trust means no one knows how much individuals were or were not able to push back against the corporation. The Trust's existence serves to authorize what becomes Disney's "authored" construction of a proto-prehistoric "Polynesia." This is a very different dynamic from, say, a major corporation putting funding behind an already existing storytelling culture so that they have the resources to put their stories before a wider audience in the way they choose. Disney's construction comes to stand for this culture in the wider world, validated by that construct of the "Trust." In an open letter to Taika Waititi, who did early work on the first version of the screenplay, Ngata further outlined how the corporation has continued to profit from problematic depictions of otherness since the 1990s and mentioned her own fears for her own culture in that light, noting in particular that "while we continue to promote and demand culturally appropriate platforms and relevant contexts for telling our own stories—the mass-consumptive power of machines such as Disney has the absolute ability to eclipse our voice and position" (Ngata). Both the creation of the Oceanic Story Trust and Waititi's early involvement were meant to ratify Disney's cultural authority to tell this particular story in the public eye, but the concerns of Ngata and others prove that this is far more complicated than having a relative handful of people sign off on the film. Especially given the prolific use of coconuts to emphasize either idyllic island pastorals or ridiculous coconut-armor-wearing pirate opponents, the coloniality embedded in the narrative, despite the alleged attempt at being culturally accurate, becomes that much more noticeable and in need of being widely problematized.

Two of the major critiques of *Moana* are the romanticization of the primitive set against the larger, often violent colonial history of the region and the current neocolonial relationships of many Pacific Islands, and the depictions of the character Maui. Putting aside momentarily the Maui skin-suit merchandise, which was quickly pulled from shelves and was problematic for many reasons (Diaz; Sonoda-Pale), Maui, as drawn by Disney and brought to life by Dwayne "The Rock" Johnson, has also been criticized as unintelligent, a buffoon placed for comic relief, and as perpetuating negative and offensive stereotypes of Polynesians as overweight (Schilling). The demigod is a heroic figure across Polynesia and is depicted in story, comics, and other culturally specific media as a teenager nearing manhood, a sort of trickster figure, well-dressed, charming, and intelligent. Despite these and other criticisms, however, this reshaping becomes sanctioned because of the specter of the cultural authority board that was supposedly meant to have authenticated this film.

Despite the oversell on how this film would be different, it was still marked by myriad controversies both before and after its release. The pushback and subsequent removal of a racist costume (Herreria) and Disney's public if performative attempts to be true to the cultural roots of the narrative borrowed for adaptation mark a shift in Disney's historically closed approach to filmmaking. The film credits the twelve individuals who made up the Oceanic Story Trust as story and cultural consultants, and much of the prerelease marketing stressed the Trust's involvement and the extensive cultural research undertaken by the directors and animators. However, as both Jenny Banh and Ida Yoshinaga explore, this research is quite surface level and leads to a level of "erasure and invisibility," where audiences can be "lured by the histories [they] find entertaining, but not the histories [they] find inconvenient" (Banh, 133). Nor do audiences need to look further at how the corporation might be continuing settler colonial practices and thereby undercutting any level of projecting cultural sensitivity or positive engagement.

By drawing Disney into a dialogue about how it writes otherness and where the corporation's authority might end, communities that are historically misrepresented and appropriated—as Oceanic, Polynesian, and other Indigenous peoples have been—can begin to "write back" (Bradford, 31) against the hegemonic projection of culture in contemporary spaces. Despite the tensions of "collaboration" that I have highlighted in this section, it remains that Disney inserted itself into Polynesian myth (Herman), and ultimately *Moana* has become the WENA-sanctioned "culturally authorized" face of Polynesian and Oceanic culture in the Disney universe, though a face certainly rightfully characterized as "a beautifully visualized but historically hollow monolithic hodgepodge of diverse Pacific Islander spiritual traditions and misattributed scientific breakthroughs" (Yoshinaga, 192).

Missing Equity While Aiming for Diversity and Forgetting Inclusion

At heart, none of the films discussed in this chapter address their depicted audience. They instead make a point of commodifying difference to play to a particular audience instead, forcing other cultures to fit into preconceived ideas that will reflect the biases and expectations of both Disney and the greater specter of WENA cultural positioning. There is no sense of what any culture from outside Disney's own point of view actually designates as an important narrative to tell on a global stage. It is interesting to me that even though the Disney Renaissance is a period of greater diversity in representation, as we look back at it, we can see how badly the concept of equity is misunderstood at a corporate level and the persistent, ongoing legacy of that misunderstanding. Although the terms *equity*, *diversity*, and *inclusion* are often rattled off together, especially in institutional spaces, the goal is ultimately to expand diversity and inclusion until equity is achieved, until it is not a matter of inviting people to have a seat at the table but rather having multiple tables and rebuilding them so that everyone can just take a seat. Otherwise the efforts to diversify or include risk becoming just tokenizations and exoticizations rather than redressing the issues that underwrite current or legacy hegemonic models. This is not to say that the Disney Renaissance should not have happened or that institutions should not try to change. But it does again make visible the fact that surface-level fixes are not the same thing as disruptive change that can remake norms and rebuild what are considered standard practices. But despite the widened skin-tone color palate needed to animate these films, the space of the Disney fairy tale—the unfettered magic and wonder, the realization of dreams without caveats—remains closed to people who are other than phenotypically European and tends to play on misrepresentation and stereotype. Without thinking more deeply about how Disney is positioned within narrative space, even as it constructs narrative space, the Disney fairy-tale mode becomes less a universalizing narrative tool to be imposed over other kinds of stories and more a device that makes visible Disney's previously invisible or less visible true positioning.

5

IS IT A DISNEY WORLD AFTER ALL?

Repeating and Extending Past Places

Glocality and Stepping into Hyperspecific Otherness

Disney returned to fairy-tale narratives in 2009 with *The Princess and the Frog*, a move that signaled both the idea of a return to a core narrative pattern (with the twist of a princess becoming a frog instead of her kiss releasing the prince) and the creation of what would be Disney's first Black fairy-tale princess in a feature animated film. Of course, we do not see Tiana as a Black fairy-tale princess for most of the film; she spends more time depicted as a waitress or a frog than as someone for whom all the potentials of fairy-tale magic and wonder were opened.[1] But what happened afterward? In the 2010s the reformulation of the Disney brand begun in the Disney Renaissance continued, particularly through the reiteration of the older Disney canon supplemented with both sequels and new properties. The next three animated fairy-tale films to be released by Disney were *Tangled* (2010), *Brave* (2012), and *Frozen* (2013). The trend of live-action remakes kicked off in 2014 with the release of *Maleficent* and was followed by *Cinderella* (2015) and *Beauty and the Beast* (2017). In effect, the three princess films of the 2010s helped to reinvigorate the Disney Princess brand and the ideal of the Disney

---

1 A similar if slightly inverted version of this happens in Pixar's *Soul* (2020), where the Black main character is displaced from his body, and his visualized Blackness is puppeteered by another character voiced by a white actress, creating a bit of a body-snatcher situation with an implicitly racialized dynamic.

fairy-tale narrative, specifically by expanding and reiterating Disney princesses and Disney fairy-tale realms in particular. Not only did this approach create an instant cross-period dialogue between the contemporary and more classic Disney, but it also marked an aesthetic "return to normal," an affirmation that Disney would be returning to what it was renowned for, even if the known stories were updated one way or another. Future scholarly work should focus on the live-action remediations of the animated Disney fairy-tale films, especially looking at how these productions are changed, framed, and updated and even at who holds the power to remake them and who is weighing in on casting and aesthetic decisions. But for now, I am going to turn my focus to where new worlds were built, or known worlds were expanded.

After *The Princess and the Frog*, there isn't another Disney fairy-tale or folkloresque film that includes, let alone centers on, nonwhite people until *Moana* in 2016, followed by *Coco* in 2017, and the live-action and CGI remediation of *Aladdin* in 2019. These last three are importantly not classic European fairy tales being populated by people who are not phenotypically European—that does not happen in feature film until 2023 with the remediation of *The Little Mermaid*. Rather, these films are narratives that, like the animated features of the Renaissance period and the 2000s, relegate nonwhite people and narratives to geographically and temporally specific locations. As the geographic and narrative spaces of the brand are extended along with the reiteration of canonical narratives, the canon both expands and contracts. Concepts of diversity and multiculturalism become more complicated, and people criticize Disney in more visible ways with more tangible effects. Although some might see such movement as consistent shifts in what the ultimate goal is, I would argue that the constant need to reconsider voice, power, and sanctioned representation speaks to a shift toward a greater complication of how identity is constructed in the contemporary globalized world.

As noted in Chapter 4, Vicente M. Diaz asks a pertinent question regarding Disney's claims to authorized cultural authenticity: "Who gets to authenticate so diverse a set of cultures?" (Diaz). Although Diaz's question is posed specifically with regard to Polynesian cultures and *Moana*, it is a question that bears asking in every instance of a diverse or multicultural tale. To return to animator Marlon West's assertion that Disney does not do "realism" but "believability" ("Big Changes"), this is the period, both in terms of what is happening within Disney studios and the wider global context of calls for rights and equity in the face of oppression, where the implied question of "believable to whom" must be pressed harder and where in the context of "authentic to whom" Disney has expanded the both real and imaginary geographies of the Magic Kingdom. WENA countries have imposed a racialized spectrum from the age of exploration through the eras of colonization, settler colonialism, and imperialism to dominate and describe other people in relation to whiteness. These categories of poorly constructed racialized identity are becoming more loudly and more frequently challenged in myriad ways from pluralistic multivocal points of view around the globe, especially in the collision space of globalized media storytelling. Disney becomes a microcosm in which to examine this effect and the power dynamics informed by coloniality that still exist through a multinational corporation rooted in a specific context trying to tell global stories. Despite good intentions and perhaps improved execution, Disney nevertheless continues with its pattern of attempting to define other cultures in allegedly authorized and sanctioned ways to create an authorized Disney presentation of incorporation into the larger Disney universe.

These complexities are more easily seen by looking at films such as the animated *Aladdin* in relation to its live-action *Aladdin* remediation, the live-action *Mulan*, *Frozen II*, and *Maleficent: Mistress of Evil*, all of which involve confronting both individual and cultural difference in some way while trying to maintain a narrative that conforms to the Disney fairy-tale mode. The problematization of both *Aladdin* and *Mulan* is relatively straightforward, as they are narratives adapted from outside Disney's core cultural scope. *Frozen II*'s narrative is directly in dialogue with narratives of colonial expansion perpetuated by European countries. Just as these three films are not separated from the racial politics of the real world, neither is *Maleficent: Mistress of Evil*, though it involves not an appropriation of a cultural narrative but rather the incorporation of nonwhite bodies into a fairy-tale fantasy setting where Disney is most at home. These films allow an exploration of how the set of fairy-tale heuristics that have become synonymous with Disney's particular method of narrative construction have or have not shifted. Put another way, as the world that Disney represents has grown wider, what do any changes signal in terms of the connections already established in the

Disney Renaissance between the fairy tale and hegemonic constructions of power on racial lines? By taking this line of inquiry, we might be able to more firmly determine who the bigger, better, more global, incorporated Disney brand is for. The evolving methods of both narrative development and how the corporation engaged with difference from a seat of hegemonic power have shown that Disney tacitly acknowledged a need to change from the methods of the 1990s and 2000s but also that there remains room for growth.

By reiterating the classic canon and expanding it with new narratives, Disney was also expanding to incorporate potential competitors, essentially dominating the market for all forms of entertainment by apparently using the adage "If you can't beat 'em, join 'em" as a corporate strategy. Instead of competing with burgeoning franchises aimed at a more adventure-driven market, such as *Star Wars* and Marvel, Disney bought the companies behind the franchises in 2012 and 2009, respectively (Whitten; Mendelson), with even more franchises becoming part of the House of Mouse following the 2019 Disney-Fox merger (VanDerWerff). Like this literal incorporation of other companies, where each company sits somewhat separately under the larger Disney corporate umbrella—its own region of the Magic Kingdom—more recent film narratives try to extend that practice to geographies and cultures. However, unlike entertainment companies, cultures are not primarily economic entities, and such a method of incorporation does not prove either seamless or always welcome.

As Disney continues to use the idea of research to communicate its intentions to produce more authentic images, it becomes more apparent how signaling authenticity on an image-based level is not guaranteed to result in automatically recognizable, embodied storytelling that resonates with the people it claims to represent. Disney is actively engaging in a process of "making race," to return to Anamik Saha's term, but while also sidestepping historical and contemporary realities and contexts in favor of a "believable" realism. Although not fully using Saha's cultural industries approach to address the corporation's body of work, my approach in this book has made visible how Disney partakes in the cultural industry, shaping "the media products we consume, and, in turn, ideas about racial and ethnic difference" (Saha, 6), and in turn contributes to how both "media discourses of race" and "race itself" are made

(7). At best, for Disney a patina of authenticity and collaboration is presented; at worst, viewers witness the imposition of a colonial ideological structure in a world marked and shaped by continued cultural imperialisms. It seems as though Disney's more contemporary approaches to telling more diverse stories use the following strategies: including what "we" (Disney) think of as and construct as "them" (*Aladdin*); hyperspecific cultural appeasement that falls flat (*Mulan*); performing collaboration to authenticate its productions (*Moana*, discussed in Chapter 4); and geographically extending the borders of established magic kingdoms to explore contact-based conflicts (*Maleficent: Mistress of Evil* and *Frozen II*). These different strategies are not uniform in their application; however, together they highlight how the power dynamics intrinsic in Disney's fairy-tale narratives have not been redressed even as specific narratives or specific production patterns might have changed.

The Disney Renaissance's constructions of diversity replicate exoticized images of cultures and ethnicities outside Disney's cultural purview, and as I have written about extensively elsewhere,[2] both *Moana* and the 2019 *Aladdin* remediation continue that trend.[3] Returning to the idea of the corporate structure paralleling what Clare Bradford describes in *Unsettling Narratives* as the confining structures of language and then weaving in the idea of omnipresent coloniality, what we see is a transaction that declares itself to be intercultural but is in fact, intentionally or not, one-directional between the hegemonic positionality of the corporation and the cultures it engages with, producing an exoticist dialogue inflected by the Disney's values and economic goals. Although some might find the characterization of Disney's cultural transmission as one-directional to be an overstatement, I would point to the pattern of reiterating Disney properties through cyclical rereleases or remaking them in such a way that palimpsests are created; rather than replacing the other, older images, the images represented in the older films remain in the public consciousness and are decontextualized from earlier criticism. Those who find themselves on the wrong side of such representation must still contend with asserting their identities around other peoples' misunderstandings of such misrepresentation. After all, *Disney* said that

---

2 See also Anjirbag, "Mulan"; "Reforming Borders"; and "New Agrabah."

3 As does the live-action *Mulan*. See Anjirbag et al. for more.

it tried to be *authentic* and did the *research*. Disney simultaneously confers authority upon itself to tell such stories by using different aesthetic techniques, signaling to traditional forms of art, travel, and music, and by crediting Disney-constructed consulting boards to justify why and how it now "owns" the authoritative version of a particular story and has the cultural right to represent other people (Anjirbag, "Mulan"; Parasher, 44).

Disney's appropriation of other cultures, especially when it is done in such a way as to speak for a marginalized group, becomes a part of its method of storytelling. Historically, misrepresented groups were limited in the ways they could push back against the hegemonic dominance of the corporation such that racist materials would never see the light of day. The brushing aside of the concerns of American Islamic communities over the depictions embedded in the creation of Agrabah in *Aladdin* was, perhaps, prototypical. Although an offending lyric from the opening of the film was removed, greater concerns regarding the hodgepodge of "the Middle East" were brushed aside under the explanation that Agrabah was fictional.[4] To look at this issue from only this perspective misses how Anna Katrina Gutierrez analyzes orientalization or othering as both script and spaces:

> The Eastern character of orientalised fairy tales may create the impression that the global space corresponds to the Orient and the local space corresponds to the West, but this is not strictly the case. A Western narrative set in the Orient indicates that the East has the potential to be the global power, yet the imbrication of Oriental images and words with motifs of otherness reinstates the West's ruling position. (Gutierrez, 73)

Replacing "Orient" with a broader construction of otherness that can be extended to mean cultures that the West—here meaning Anglo-American hegemonic institutional structures of power—sees as Other to itself, we can read this as an assertion that, even if the narrative of dominance and subjugation cannot be completely undermined, there is still space to reimagine and reformulate the power dynamics by changing elements of scripts and spaces to challenge the status quo. Gutierrez's

---

4 See C. R. King et al., 143; Tiffin, 216–17; and Wells, 122.

construction draws on theories of glocality, the dialogic construction between the global and the local. It allows for more nuance in terms of understanding what happened in such films as *Moana* when the studio was forced to contend with criticism for misrepresenting cultural heroes and deities, rewriting traditional legends in ways that omitted key figures.[5] But it also becomes a way for us to understand better what is happening in films like the *Aladdin* and *Mulan* remediations, especially when considered along with the ideas of orientation that Sara Ahmed emphasizes are key components of how orientalism becomes constructed and expressed: that processes of incorporation emphasize relationships to the familiar, and what the familiar is oriented around especially as it collides with the unfamiliar (Ahmed, *Queer Phenomenology*, 131–32). For Disney, this means considering the position of the company and who is making production decisions during the attempts to increase perceptions of authenticity. Rather than overwriting the old with the new as a corrective, locating the remediated versions of the animated films in more historically and geographically specific settings adds a dimension to the making of identity in relation to both Disney's world and the world at large from a multivocal plurality of positions and orientations.

Another "Arabian" Night, Another Missed Chance for Growth

Disney's multicultural projects of the Renaissance period participate in something that C. R. King and colleagues identify as "commodity racism," a primary mediator in a global, postindustrial order, where the legacies and realities of racism make the system functional, meaningful, and profitable but their presence must always be held under erasure, where difference is desired and demonized, and where too often alternatives, rather than being oppositional problems, become absorbed as fads or fashions, readily accessible for co-optation and commodification (C. R. King et al., 139–40). Commodity racism explains Disney's focus on image over the absence of deeper deconstruction of "racial structures and their unspoken center—whiteness"; it offers "positive images that

---

5   See Diaz; Flores; Gilio-Whitaker, "Disney Refines Its Cultural Competence"; Herman; Ka'ili; Ngata; Ngata and Kelly; and Schilling.

stress humanness and inclusion as they celebrate diversity and singularity" (140) and, as such, have contributed to and "converged with the fragmentation of the consuming public into niche markets" (140–41), reflecting a desire to cultivate "'ethnic' markets" (141). Disney's animated *Aladdin* and the live-action remediation exemplify this strategy, making "a dual move in an era marked by multiculturalism," "simultaneously [hailing] a broad, purportedly raceless audience and [targeting] ethnic consumers, thus reinforcing racialized differences and their entanglements with power" (141).

In playing with the idea of a bigger, more vast "whole new world," the corporation has in fact managed to flatten that world, if not erase large swaths of it through misrepresentation in both the animated and the subsequent live-action *Aladdin*. One of the most disappointing aspects of this project has been realizing how much the orientalizing legacy remains present in Disney's (mis)representations of multiple cultures even as the corporation goes to great lengths to signal better representations and incorporation of cultures in other areas. The 1992 *Aladdin* faced significant criticism from the American-Arab Anti-Discrimination Committee (ADC) regarding the use of "stereotype and misrepresentation" (C. R. King et al., 141) in the film. Preferring "fantasies of an exotic and alien generic Arabia as a backdrop for a formulaic romance to a culturally accurate and historically anchored story in an actual time and place" (141), *Aladdin* also notably reiterates orientalisms directly after the First Gulf War.[6] The heroes are light skinned; the rest are dark skinned, swarthy, accented, and with exaggerated features. Even though the visual stereotypes were not addressed, the ADC's criticism did result in the removal of the most egregious stereotypes from the opening song, "Arabian Nights." In retrospect, this was at best, as King and colleagues describe, a "half-measure," as it maintained the reference to barbarism and therefore the incorporation of Arabs into the Disney universe as its barbaric Others, but "without the overt and violent overtones" (142) and while also making oblique public commitments to diversity.

Phrasing such as "the Persia of Arabian legend" describes a notion of geographic and historical specificity abandoned by Disney, which is not in itself necessarily a bad thing. However, it also points to a depth and

---

6 See C. R. King et al.; Macleod; and Wise.

nuance in construction of identity that Disney has made more difficult to contend with for those who embody such an identity because of how exactly Disney has abandoned that geographic and historical specificity. Just as other Disney films depict reimaginings of imaginings of other periods fleshed out with historicizing detail, so too does this film, albeit not as a US-centric imagining of a fantasist's Persia in the Arab imaginary but rather as an imagining in the US imperial visual language of orientalized barbarism that serves as a stand-in for nuanced representation of the various peoples who call that region of the world their home. The temporal constructions of Westernized history demand a Eurocentric point of view that positions everything in relative geospatial temporalities to Europe and, later, the Anglophone world. Such a construction has thus flattened and merged the specific regional histories of Iran, Persia, Iraq, Kuwait, Syria, India, and so on. Discussions about the animated *Aladdin* move between vague descriptors of "Middle Eastern" cultural representation and more firm standpoints of "the Arab world," revealing a lack of recognition that these are both generalizations that are then broadly applied to the diverse peoples and cultures of that region. It seems almost accidental that this derivation of a story from the *Arabian Nights*, which locates its story in a derivation of Baghdad, does pick up on one of the threads inherent in the original source—"the culture of medieval Baghdad" (M. Warner, *Stranger Magic*, 8)—although it does not deploy anything further in terms of tapping into the rich material of the underlying source narrative. This remains a problem in the live-action remediation. Disney's *Aladdin*, in all its iterations, fails to use the same historicism that marks its European-rooted medievalist fairy-tale and folkloresque narratives. Historicity left its mark on the quasi-medievalist, historicized spaces of *Beauty and the Beast*, *Maleficent*, and *Cinderella*, and those same medievalist impulses need to be considered in terms of both iterations of *Aladdin*. What I explore here is how specific historicizing details—whether building shapes and architecture, names, or landscape—were deployed to evoke not a *realistic* depiction of a medieval-era Middle Eastern kingdom but what Disney's target audience would find *believable* in such a geographically and temporally located imaginary space.

Effacement is a different occurrence than the flat-out erasure of Black bodies discussed earlier. Instead of simply not representing a group of people, effacement limits and defines how individuals of various backgrounds might be interpreted and classified by those who would largely only encounter them through media. Effacement refers to a thinning out or a disappearing of something, here not by *not* representing it but by forcing pluralities of identities and experiences to fit a singular representation or belonging in a singular space. This term describes what Disney has done to the Middle East, North Africa, and the Indian subcontinent, in the particular kind of orientalizing and exoticizing present in both *Aladdin* film productions. Effacement and erasure are problematic in different ways; despite burgeoning and growing film industries in India, Iran, and across the Middle East and North African (MENA) countries, all of which have had their own successes with building fantasyscapes full of influences from across the old paths of the Silk Road, the 2019 live-action remediation of *Aladdin* instead chose to build a medievalized, orientalized fantasyscape. Disney's moves toward alleged better representation instead promulgated the same old problematic stereotypes and resulted yet again in a faux "Middle East" once again poorly constructed by "the West."

As with the remediations of *Beauty and the Beast* and *The Lion King*, the live-action *Aladdin* is more re-creation than reimagining, but in such a way that could be best thought of as a "cleaned-up palimpsest" (Kunze, "Why Belle Loves Books"). From its opening frame to its attempted course correction in the characterization of Jasmine and its attempts to apparently walk back the whitewashing of the animated film in the casting of the narrative's heroes, Disney has attempted surface-level fixes to the problems flagged when the animated film was first released and through criticism in the intervening years, while still sticking as close as possible to a scene-by-scene replication of iconic moments with some additions to the narrative. However, by looking at the world building, the musical numbers, and some of the casting controversies, it becomes more apparent that the attempt to deconstruct the orientalism of the previous iteration, despite some progress, does not quite hit the mark.

Despite the addition of the harbor to recast Agrabah as a multicultural stop on a Silk Road–esque trading route, which could also be used to explain the magpie approach to cultural appropriation deployed in the film, the net effect is an amalgamation of Middle East and South Asia that ultimately feels more like the orientalized pantomime of the eighteenth century. The Middle East and South Asia have been folded together beyond the animation transplanting a Taj Mahal–inspired castle out of Agra, India, and into an Iraq-esque desert. This is made apparent through the various paratextual materials released by Disney, including interviews conducted by those working on the film. The Walt Disney Studios promotional video *World of Aladdin* includes sound bites from director Guy Ritchie describing a "team of cultural advisors," anecdotes about shooting in Wadi Rum, Jordan, and production designer Gemma Jackson talking about the multiple influences she incorporated into the set building of Agrabah. Producer Dan Lin describes the decision to shoot "on location" as a step taken to make sure the studio was "as authentic as possible," but the clip ends there, never clarifying what exactly the film is being authentic to. Lin goes on to say that "our world of Agrabah is truly a global trading port, heavily influenced by Arabia, but also influenced by other neighboring cultures as well" ("Disney's Aladdin"). The historicism of the medievalist remediations of the proto-European fairy tales was signaled by details corresponding to specific historical periods. Historicizing details are tied to implications of geographies rather than time, because in the invented kingdom of Agrabah, *time*, or temporal location within a specific flow of history, matters less than the indication of *where*. This is the orientalism of *Aladdin* narratives fully realized in the contemporary. The invented exotic location is not one that can be fully reconciled with WENA constructions of temporality, because that would break the magic of the exoticized construction, which *must* exist out of time for it to remain believable to a part of the world that cannot and does not grapple well with the real region's more complex history, for doing so would unseat its own concept of its own supremacy. Agrabah is constructed based on stereotype, with "authentic" details chosen to address the gaze of WENA cultures, even as it effaces genuine representation through the construction of an imaginary region, separate from its other temporally located fantasies that, if being truly historical, would exist in a parallel temporality.

The geographically situated historicism comes to bear in the construction of the sets, which were predominantly built on soundstages in the United Kingdom, especially on the backlot of Longcross Studios (Moon). These sets draw influences from souks in Marrakesh and Burmese monasteries and from historically orientalized depictions that signal "Persia" or "India," layered together. Production designer Gemma Jackson, across several interviews, has spoken about the vastness and the depth of the sets made to aid in the construction of the storyworld and about the decision by the producers ultimately to not film on location in Morocco or to use a "real" location for the fictional city. Her statements on the matter include:

> In the end, I think it's great that we didn't because I think I was freer just to pull things from where I wanted them, I didn't just have to be Moroccan, I could go anywhere I liked in my imagination.
>
> I loved Iznik ceramics, I love Turkish and Persian miniatures. . . . There's the Orientalist paintings that I used, a lot of the Victorians used to go on those wonderful journeys and do these fabulous paintings stuffed full of detail.

and

> The reference that I had was a real mishmash—obviously you can't lift anything directly or you'll get done by everyone right, left, and center so you have to steal a bit of this, a bit of that and a bit of the other, and mix it up and make it your own. (Jackson, qtd. in Sinha-Roy, "Agrabah")

There is a lot to unpick in those statements from someone at the production level of the film who is responsible for film and narrative as concept and realizing it for the viewer.

On the surface this is another iteration of the Disney marketing pattern: signaling research done without defining what exactly is "authentic" about the film or the narrative. There is also the question of what it means to be "influenced by Arabia." The term *Arabia* properly refers to a geopolitical designation of the Arabian Peninsula, made up of the countries of Saudi Arabia, Oman, Qatar, Kuwait, Yemen, and the United Arab Emirates and also including Bahrain, the Socotra Archipelago, and several other islands. To use such a nonspecific geopolitical designation as the root of the film's inspiration displays the deployment of orientalism rather than research-driven improvement in world building. Most concerning, in some ways, is Jackson's lack of reflexivity over her statements regarding her influences and how these statements alone demonstrate a certain centering of the construction of otherness from the perspective of someone who exercises control over the shaping of culture on a global stage. Jackson's sources seem to be primarily her imagination and elements of a mixture of cultures, regardless of whether or not these influences are geographically or culturally aligned with producer Dan Lin's statement about being inspired by "Arabia." The elision of Turkish ceramics (Iznik ceramics) with "Turkish and Persian" miniatures, along with "Orientalist paintings" and "Victorian paintings" speaks more to how this part of the world is constructed in this production designer's perception than research that would have yielded, perhaps, a different texture to the world building of the film. Pulling details from already orientalized depictions and folding together South Asian, Persian, and Arab cultures do not provide more broad and accessible representation; rather, they do not allow any of these cultures to see a recognizable reflection of themselves.

The goal, then, for Disney is neither historical accuracy nor cultural accuracy but rather Martha Bayless's notion of a "history-flavored Otherworld" (Bayless, 40), with a slightly different "flavor" than its usual fare, or "believability" over "realism," with no further thought given to who in fact "authenticates" that "flavor" for the masses. The historicism of specific details that ratify the expression of the Disney fairy-tale mode becomes more complex and complicated when also dealing in postcolonial temporalities, and the WENA positionality of the corporation cannot be overlooked or understated. Such elision might not matter when presenting this othered world building to Disney's core audience base; however, as the corporation has gone even more global, such acts are far more noticeable. There also seems to be a lack of reflexivity in Jackson's statement that she could not "just lift anything directly," without realizing that the "mishmash" she describes is still appropriative and still decontextualizes cultural elements by placing them outside their proper contexts. This is perhaps most disappointing because, although this is Disney's first attempt at a live-action depiction of the *Aladdin* narrative and although WENA film and theater are peppered with orientalized versions of this story, other versions of this kind of fantasy space do exist from Bollywood and other film industries from the part of the world that

Disney is struggling to depict, and plenty of experts know how to do this "authentically;" they just seem to have not been employed here.

The live-action *Aladdin* film also courted casting controversies, namely, Naomi Scott's casting as Jasmine and the alleged use of brownface in the extras. Jasmine is meant to be a Middle Eastern or Arab princess, but Scott herself is half South Asian, half Caucasian. Such casting raises concerns about that idea of effacement, that all brown people are somehow the same, and it also calls into question the idea of a US corporation–produced "hybrid Middle Eastern–South Asian world" (Sinha-Roy, "How Disney Handled the Casting"). Disney Vice President of Multicultural Engagement Julie Ann Crommett spoke to the decision to cast Scott, saying:

> There was a real intention for Agrabah to become the center of the Silk Road and reflect the diversity and movement of what we can loosely construe that time period to have been, which was a golden age as well for the region. . . . There are South Asian individuals who associate with Aladdin and with Jasmine as well, and I think there was a sense of we should reflect some part of the community in the principal cast so that we're actually being inclusive of who sees themselves and identifies with this text. (Crommett, qtd. in Sinha-Roy, "How Disney Handled the Casting")

Crommett displays the problem with "single stories," in this case using ambiguous brown bodies to stand in for all brown bodies of an ill-defined region. People find themselves in productions because a twisted mirror is better than no mirror at all, but this has less to do with some universal appeal of the character of Jasmine and more to do with the lack of other options for people of other backgrounds to find themselves reflected in Disney's fantasy spaces and fairy-tale narratives. Crommett continues:

> What we've done intentionally with Naomi's character as part of the plot is that her mother is actually from a different land, and it's very clear in the movie that her mother is from a different land that's not Agrabah and that's drawing on a lot of her motivations in terms of how she sees the future of Agrabah as a welcoming place that embraces people from other places because her mother

> was from somewhere else. And we felt that was really important
> for so many reasons to speak to the idea of trade, intersectionality,
> intersectional identity, as part of the broader Arab experience and
> South Asian experience by extension. . . . That opens up a really
> beautiful conversation and I think nods to all the different audi-
> ences who possibly saw themselves in the original animated film.
> (Crommett, qtd. in Sinha-Roy, "How Disney Handled the Casting")

Crommett continues to reflect both a misunderstanding of why so many different audiences "possibly saw themselves" in the animated *Aladdin* and a shallow understanding of the term intersectionality—perhaps reflecting the danger of concepts from critical race theory being embraced without proper education of their contexts in capitalist spaces. Intersectionality is not something that can be imposed; intersectional identities are inhabited and negotiated on a day-to-day basis and are not something automatically projected through a mixed-race character who is still supposed to somehow serve as the only representative princess for an entire region with a plurality of cultures within it.

This is not the first time that the broader corporation had cast an actress of South Asian heritage as Jasmine; Karen David played her for the incorporation of Agrabah into the television series *Once Upon a Time*. However, the Walt Disney Studios paratextual material that was released accessibly to the public on YouTube did not itself specify exactly to what the world building was being authentic. Instead, explicit references to such things as "the Silk Road" and "hybrid Middle Eastern–South Asian" came in interviews for more tabloidesque publications, resulting in a nonspecific glossing of a diverse part of the world that was also specifi-cally targeted with marketing for *Aladdin*.

As seen through the missteps and the focus on the image presented—a surface-level simulacrum of the world only slightly deeper than the construction of EPCOT rather than the various cultural and his-torical contexts surrounding both the Disney production and the history of the narrative itself—Disney's live-action *Aladdin* continues to trade in stereotypes and negative fantasies. Instead of drawing from a "real" cul-ture or series of cultures and trying to lend a narrative authenticity, the film draws from a faux construction of many interwoven cultures. This creates a problem in which—unlike in *Moana*, where people could say,

"We're really here and this is wrong"—Disney can rely on the construct of fantasy and turn to the point that Agrabah is not a real place to combat criticism instead of acknowledging the poor reflection. After all, people are not meant to "be" from Agrabah or the fictional lands that might touch its borders, because it is fictional. In terms of being a "cleaned-up palimpsest" (Kunze, "Why Belle Loves Books"), the question remains, "Cleaned up" for whom? In whose eyes could this be considered better, and how could the film that had the most opportunities and resources to hire experts in creating *this* kind of fantasy world in an authentically informed way have missed those opportunities so completely? The orientalism of the old and the orientalism of the new still exist in a way that does not disrupt the problem of historicity constructed in the other fairy-tale remediations.

Whose Reflection? *Mulan* (2020)

Where "the Silk Road" is invoked in the paratexts for the *Aladdin* remake, it becomes an explicit setting marker (albeit one without a specific time-line attached) in the *Mulan* live-action remediation released in 2020. Like many of the more contemporary Disney films, the different setting is announced from the title card: The iconic river and castle are set amid a different landscape, and the façade of the castle has been overlaid with an image similar to what is later seen in the film as the palace in the Imperial City. But the film is deliberate about specifying geography in a way that is uncharacteristic of Disney films; the on-screen text that identifies both "the Silk Road" and "the Imperial City" goes past the flavor of historical context invoked in the live-action *Aladdin*. It drops the story directly into a historical-geographic context, even if the temporality is still left up to context clues and never explicitly stated. I am tempted to call this film somewhere between an overcorrection and a cross-cultural industrial-political appeasement. Although the cinematography is stunning, there is a distinct impression that, if the 1998 animated film is an instance of Disney writing "ancient China" into its own filmographic language, then the live-action film might be thought as, in the most generous sense, Disney attempting to speak "wuxia" from a complete outsider's perspective. Not every interpolation or remediation must aim at being a frame-for-frame reproduction, but the changes in this film seem to completely invert the social, gendered, and interpersonal politics of the animation while also retaining some of the colorism and structural orientalism of the animated film.

One of the most significant changes is that the live-action film is entirely framed by the narration of Mulan's father, telling the legend of his daughter but also highlighting the ways in which she breaks and defies her society. This is a quite different lens on her actions than that constructed in the animated film. After the title card, the film opens with the father's voice framing the narrative—something that on the surface parallels the storybook openings of other fairy-tale films or even the woven tapestries that open *Moana*. But this framing sets a different tone. As the sun rises over a pastoral landscape, the father says, "There have been many tales of the great warrior, Mulan. But, ancestors, this one is mine." The scene shifts to the young Mulan practicing with a staff in a field as he continues, "Here she is. A young shoot, all green, unaware of the blade. If you had such a daughter, her chi, the boundless energy of life itself speaking through her every motion, could you tell her that only a son could wield chi?" The scene shifts from the field to lush green steppes, showcasing even more of the landscape, visually reiterating the difference of the setting, and the father adds, "That a daughter would risk shame, dishonor, exile?" This is in contrast to the context of the Chinese ballad where Mulan joins the army with her family's blessing. Finally, the scene moves toward Mulan's village as the father's monologue closes, "Ancestors, 1 could not," and viewers see a moment where a young Mulan wields her chi before the village to the disapproval of all. Later, Mulan hears her parents discuss how she needs to be taught to fit the role of a daughter or risk dishonoring the family, and this is followed by a conversation with her father telling her that she must hide her gift, to "silence the voice" of her chi—something that parallels another father-daughter moment in *Frozen* and something that deserves further study, though 1 cannot fully interrogate it here. At this point the "Mulan" title card is finally shown, and the film begins.

Let's put aside the fact that the explanations for the "magic" system are heavy-handed and that the insertion of Xianniang as a foil to Mulan as a woman who is a more competent user of chi leads to a gendered dynamic where women with power are inherently seen as evil and in need of destruction. From just this introductory segment, there is still much to consider about how this film declares itself as a diversion from what has been established as Disney norms in a way that is different still from its animated counterpart. One thing that the Disney fairy-tale mode facilitates is making other cultures or modes of storytelling "speak Disney"—narratives are bent and twisted to fit the mode. But here, we see Disney almost trying to speak another visual language. The 2020 *Mulan* plays with the signs and schema of wuxia films, populating the screen with accomplished and recognizable martial arts film stars, focalizing on the athletic feats of its artists in the choreographed battle scenes, and using landscape as a character in and of itself to heighten both dramatic and mystical affect.

But the tension between the schema of wuxia and the Disney fairy-tale mode cannot be resolved. The animated film knowingly leans into the Americanization of the main character; her independence and her strong will become a part of her heroic character without being undermined throughout the film, despite the fact that one of the most significant changes between the ballad and the Disney film is that in the ballad Mulan leaves with her family's blessing and does not hide her identity (Yin 295). By maintaining the disguised nature of the animated film but also using the depiction of a highly patriarchal culture as a baton with which to beat the audience, Mulan becomes doubly undercut. Disney's construction of ancient China is not liberated in this remake; the stereotypes are just solidified in a different way, and the physical landscape of the real China lends a heightened authenticity to the film. Although the animated film is focalized around Mulan—hers is the first voice that we hear—the conceit of this being her father's story continues throughout the film. He narrates key moments as she enters the army, emphasizes her femininity, and when she comes to terms with herself. Between both his voice and the words of the general who becomes an extension of her father on screen, Mulan is barely heard in comparison. In fact, the only places that the sounds of the animated film seep through are in the moments when the score highlights the catchy, familiar songs that are no longer sung, absorbed instead into an epic landscape.

We hear Mulan most when she speaks with Xianniang: first, when the other woman challenges Mulan to show her true self to claim her full strength, and later, when Mulan is expelled from the army and Xianniang asks Mulan to join her, because she will have no place otherwise, echoing the sentiments expressed by her parents that Mulan must "learn her place." Finally, Xianniang saves Mulan as the film moves toward its final climax, and with her dying breath tells her, "Take your place, Mulan," telling her to claim the space she deserves to occupy despite what she has been told her whole life about hiding herself. But this moment of solidarity between the two women again becomes undercut in the film's resolution, where, after Mulan has found her voice with the Emperor and has had her honor recognized by the Emperor in her village, the film ends not with Mulan's voice but with her father's framing narrative: "The girl became a soldier, the soldier became a leader, and the leader became a legend." How Mulan feels about this, how she chooses anything for her own life going forward, remains unseen. Disney's feminist, international, fairy-godmother-free heroine of the 1990s is absorbed into a film that is in the end neither wuxia nor Disney, and the film never quite resolves where it stands or what kind of story it is trying to tell, or to whom.

Building Out Fairy-Tale Worlds Further Through Sequels

Whereas the *Aladdin* and *Mulan* remediations reflect a turn to historicism, this is not the only method Disney used to either reaffirm or extend its depictions of a wider world. It also played on the loose genre distinction between fairy tale and fantasy to expand on its fairy-tale world building, constructing what are more properly fantasy narratives with loose ties to fairy tale or the folkloresque. In considering *Maleficent: Mistress of Evil* and *Frozen II*, both released in late 2019, it is more possible to examine how, several decades beyond the commencement of the Disney Renaissance, Disney's narratives continue to reproduce coloniality even when ostensibly producing narratives that seem to be about dismantling empire. Released within a month of each other, both *Maleficent: Mistress of Evil* and *Frozen II* have narratives that are inherently rooted in the idea of expanding the worlds that viewers were introduced to in the first films. Kimberley Lau demonstrates that "race is critical to the development of the European fairy tale" in that it "undergirds" the form as it "slowly coheres and settles into the familiar genre so easily recognizable today in its popular iterations" (Lau, 7). Here, I show how the same is true of Disney fairy tale, made most easily visible when the fairy-tale worlds expand to become wider, more complex fantasyscape settings with more opportunity for collision and conflict.

Maleficent: Mistress of Evil takes viewers to Philip's kingdom on the other side of the Moors from where the conflict of the first film takes place. *Frozen II* sees the kingdom of Arendelle expanded from the boundaries set in the first film, exploring new geographic space and attempting to reveal obscured histories and to right the wrongs of the past—both within the film narrative and in terms of Disney's course correction following its exploitative use of Sámi culture in the first *Frozen* film. Taken together, *Maleficent: Mistress of Evil* and *Frozen II* seem to point in a direction to where the corporation might head. Yet, in their effort to fix problems of representation and engage in deeper dialogues, the two films also reveal new areas for improvement in narrative development.

Fantastic Creature, Racially Coded:
The Fight for the Moors in Maleficent: Mistress of Evil

Maleficent: Mistress of Evil provides an interesting case study in terms of what the development of better constructions of otherness in Disney fantasyscapes might look like while still indicating how the studio's medievalist fairy-tale aesthetic contributes to a simultaneous undercutting of its attempts at greater inclusivity.[7] This film exemplifies the necessity of being not only aware of but also conversant in the politics of representation, how the Disney fairy-tale mode cannot gloss over those politics, and, most of all, how diverse representation is about more than simply inserting more Black, Indigenous, and/or nonwhite or global majority bodies into Disney fantasyscapes or otherwise using fairies or nonhuman creatures as stand-ins for nonwhite representation, which Nalo Hopkinson has noted has been a trend for a long time in speculative fiction (Hopkinson, 101). *Maleficent: Mistress of Evil* is of interest in this discussion precisely because it is a return to the proto-European medievalist fantasy space in which Disney is historically most at home, especially when it comes to adapting fairy tales. It is simultaneously a sequel to the remediation and another version of the *Sleeping Beauty* story, where this time it is not a child who is cursed but a king. Although the film has more nonwhite bodies on screen, it still retains the invocation

7 See Anjirbag, "Enter the Castle."

of Europeanness through its landscapes, costuming, architecture, and other details, such as weaponry, to invoke a particular historicism. This film is a return to what Disney has based its aesthetic identity on; thus opportunities to think more deeply about racialized identities that were missed—both in terms of the fantastic creatures and the physical bodies on screen—become more visible.

In the first *Maleficent* film, Maleficent is no longer an uncomplicated antagonist, and her victim is also now her adopted daughter. This story has been pulled out of the narrative realm of fairy tale and placed firmly into the space of fantasy. It has been expanded beyond the structure and duration of the classic European fairy tale and opened up to new narrative possibilities and, importantly, a world where further stories can take place. Despite the changes, the setting remains constant: the quasi-European romanticized forest dotted with enchanted creatures and stunning castles where wonder just waits to unfold for the special chosen few who are allowed to enter. These spaces have been white with a small handful of token nonwhite characters visible in small parts in more recent Disney films, but they overwhelmingly lean into a particular myth of the medieval to construct their aesthetic. *Maleficent: Mistress of Evil* expands the idyllic magical world established in the first film, adding a darker component through the kingdom of Ulstead and its queen. It complicates viewers' ideas of what evil might look like, while also being one of three films from the wider corporation since 2017 to openly deal with the problems of imperialism and colonialism in its narratives,[8] including depicting genocide and experiments on the magical creatures by the humans looking to encroach into the Moors for the resources the land holds. However, diversity and the representation of different ethnicities and races within a layered, othered context are still handled without understanding the politics inherent in diverse representation.

There are more nonwhite faces among the human ranks of soldiers and peasants, namely, Percival, the Captain of the Guard of the Royal Family of Ulstead. Percival is played by David Gyasi, mimicking the casting decision used in the live-action *Cinderella*, where Nonso Anozie embodied the role. However, the bulk of ethnically diverse representation in *Maleficent: Mistress of Evil* remains problematically in the

8   See Anjirbag, "Reforming Borders"; and Anjirbag, "*Maleficent*."

nonhumans, a continuation of the trend of representation through "coded images" or "phasing in" (Hopkinson, 101) of nonwhite bodies where the normative expectation would be the continuation of an aesthetic guided by whiteness. Although the choice can be read as one made to visually signal how human encroachment into the natural world has affected Dark Fey globally and how they have been reduced to inhabiting one single island together to preserve themselves and their culture, it results in multiple layers of exoticization. The humans have expanded with no regard for the natural world or other beings, and the Dark Fey have become the exoticized, de facto "indigenous" guardians of nature and the other magical creatures in opposition to human expansion. This construction also repeats a trope in Hollywood film of equating Indigeneity with naturalism and, by extension, magic,[9] thereby reducing the recognition of Indigenous peoples as people outside the scope of the film. Juxtaposed against the contemporary struggles of the Water Protectors at Standing Rock (Zambelich and Alexandra), the struggles of the Waiapi guarding the Amazon rainforest (Hawk), and many other real conflicts between Indigenous peoples and protection of ancestral lands, this characterization of the Dark Fey is an inept, dangerous parallel to embed in a fantasy film screened internationally. Although Indigeneity is not a singular descriptor of a racialized identity, because it is a broad descriptive category that encompasses multitudes of identities that have become racialized and effaced through the effects of colonialism, the flattening of the Dark Fey alongside the singular wants of all the fairies, despite their differences, overall reflects a homogenizing colonial construction. This elides the idea of cultural, historical, and contextual specificity as paramount to understanding resistance to settler colonialism, as explored by Patrick Wolfe. Wolfe notes:

> Where survival is a matter of not being assimilated, positionality is not just central to the issue—it *is* the issue. In a settler-colonial context, the question of who speaks goes far beyond liberal concerns with equity, dialogue or access to the academy. Claims to authority over indigenous discourse made from within the settler-colonial

---

9 See Keene, "Dear JK Rowling"; and Keene, "Magic."

academy necessarily participate in the continuing usurpation of indigenous space (invasion is a structure not an event). (Wolfe, 3)

The postcolonial exoticization deployed in *Maleficent: Mistress of Evil* implies that Indigenous peoples who might fight in various ways for their various homelands are a monolithic entity over vast geographies, an ideological construct that overwrites a reality of multiple peoples in various spaces, even shared spaces, who resist settler incursions and settler colonial reconstructions of history and historicized narratives. That is what Disney has visually built in this nest that is meant to be the originating home of the Dark Fey. It also plays into the trope of the "vanishing Indian," as explored by Raymond Orr, Katelyn Sharratt, and Muhammad Iqbal, who outline how settler societies "discount and eliminate" Indigenous peoples in order to "diminish [their] existence" in an effort to "access land and resources" (Orr et al., 2078). The nest is a literal removal of the Dark Fey from the wider world, held in parallel to Queen Ingrith's open land and resource grab.

It is interesting to consider this narrative and worldbuilding construction in terms of the idea of race as a species within the construct of the film itself running simultaneously to the idea of racialization as a way of implicitly and explicitly denoting a hierarchy among groups of humans, especially when *Maleficent: Mistress of Evil* is almost explicitly about race in terms of Queen Ingrith's mission to exterminate all the nonhuman occupants of the Moors. Hopkinson writes:

Science fiction, fantasy, and horror literature can be as naive about race and as conformist about gender norms as much pop culture can. Yet it is surprising, because so much spec fic is about race. So much of it is about the longing for the "authenticity" of being indigenous, of being part of a magical tribe. It's a literature full of impossible creatures, sentient beings who have powers that exceed our own, and so on. Yet there are still few human people of color in spec fic. There are SF/F/H writers who say quite bluntly that science fiction allows them to deal with touchy issues without the hassle of the messy real world power politics. In fantasy and science fiction, "race" will often literally mean a humanoid of another species, from another planet or reality. One clue that they are really coded racialized humans is that so many of them can interbreed with humans. (Hopkinson, 105)

The Dark Fey are certainly humanoid, as are other fairies that the audiences are meant to develop an emotional connection with. And although the love story that has a chance of begetting the next generation is located strictly within the fully human characters (the potential of a generative union between human and fairy being violently disrupted through Stefan's abuse and maiming of Maleficent in the first film), much is made of the idea of a cross-species mother-daughter relationship between Maleficent and Aurora, including this being frequently challenged as legitimate by Ingrith. *Maleficent: Mistress of Evil* thus perpetuates and continues to normalize the kind of positive stereotyping that strips people of their real lives and selves, reducing them to mythic occupants of symbolic spaces while also relying on a double-layered coding of race and racialization in its depictions of a more diverse world.

Furthermore, to facilitate Maleficent finding her place among her people, the narrative of *Maleficent: Mistress of Evil* also leans on the magical Negro trope, in which a supporting Black character aids white protagonists with special insight or powers (Glenn and Cunningham; Kelly). Chiwetel Ejiofor plays the peace-seeking Conall, a foil to Ed Skrein's warhawk Borra. Conall's death is the catalyst for Maleficent achieving her full potential, whereas Borra lives beyond the film's concluding marriage scene. Deployment of race-based positive stereotyping is compounded by the fact that Japanese musician and actor Miyavi plays Udo, who primarily fulfills the role of teacher and spiritual leader for the young; he is only briefly heard speaking in the capacity of teaching young Dark Fey to fly, something that could be considered through the lens of model minority discourses where people with certain minoritized identities are considered more acceptable because of how they both serve the status quo and do not prove "disruptive" to the hegemonic structures in place. Positive stereotyping of nonwhite peoples in fantasyscapes in which complex leading roles are dominated by whiteness undermines any purported disruption of hegemonic hierarchies of racialized identities. In short, it is not enough just to have nonwhite bodies on-screen. How producers and film writers use and work with those bodies within the narrative to shape and construct full fantasy landscapes and aesthetics is more important. Although some might argue that a fantasy landscape would be better off attempting to use a colorblind lens, the fact that these tropes are recognizable even on a first watch indicates that they have become encoded for future viewers. Positive stereotypes are still stereotypes and still harm minoritized communities. Disney might have done better in its past in terms of on-screen diversity in a fairy-tale fantasy world, but that is a low bar.

That domination of whiteness also appears in what reads as a genocide scene in the final battle of the film. After weaponizing the tomb bloom, Queen Ingrith traps the Moor folk in the church under the pretense of them attending the wedding and releases a powder through the organ that strips magic away from the Moor folk. As the organ plays, trapped fairies are murdered en masse inside the church, in ways that in modernity can only recall the atrocities of other historical and current and ongoing genocides: the systematic and brutal elimination of the Other through bad-faith manipulation of one people by a brutal and oppressive regime. Hope Wabuke's commentary on the fantasy of violence in *Westworld* becomes relevant here; this scene cannot be disentangled from this historical context and reading, and this fantasizing about such brutality—especially because it remains ongoing around the world in various contexts as an offset of the legacies of both colonialism and imperialism, and the current capitalist global state—should be questioned. Even though the scene does exemplify the depths of Ingrith's deplorable hatred and warmongering, one wonders why the film does not come with a warning for openly depicting genocide or why this was not questioned more deeply.

In addition, in *Maleficent: Mistress of Evil* it becomes clear that Disney does not know what to do with a strong, literally empowered and powerful woman capable of leadership. Despite, or perhaps because of, how Maleficent embraces her full potential, there is no space for her in that new world being built from the end of the imperialist, violent conquest led by Queen Ingrith. Maleficent's fully realized, othered self must step away from leadership over a twice-united kingdom, leaving her adopted human family to take over leadership—not unlike how *Frozen II* also resolves the problem of Elsa. It will be interesting to see whether this decision is made again in a future film, thus establishing a narrative pattern. Nevertheless, a young queen who married an appropriately human male takes the throne; they look out across the lands of the three kingdoms of which they are now rulers (Aurora united two of the kingdoms in the first film), and children and the continuity of cis-hetero patriarchal rule are implied. Maleficent is left to roam the skies with her "real" children—those who are the Dark Fey and thus othered like her. The ending leans into medievalist tropes of fantasy that undo some of the more potentially subversive moments of the first film and reestablish hard lines around ideas of who gets to rule and belong in the magical kingdom. For better or worse, *Maleficent: Mistress of Evil* is a step forward for Disney in its storytelling and construction of its fantasy aesthetic, though it remains to be seen where that step leads and whether or not Disney can recast its traditional fantasy aesthetic to push past the hegemonic constructions it thus far invariably upholds with regard to race and ethnicity and even gender.

Re-Inserting "Indigeneity": Frozen II *and the Northuldra*

Frozen II attempts in some ways to walk back the problematic appropriation of Sámi culture in *Frozen*. Controversy regarding the first film arose on the internet when viewers noticed the similarity of Kristoff's clothing to that of traditional Sámi reindeer herders; later, photographs of the script circulated on Tumblr in which Kristoff is explicitly identified as "a young Sámi boy" (carrieasagiri). Other aesthetic references made to the Sámi included Kristoff's reindeer companion Sven and the use of the song "Vuelie," written specifically for the film by South Sámi musician Frode Fjellheim. "Vuelie" draws on a formerly outlawed vocal tradition, joik, and is adapted from another song by Fjellheim, "Eatnemen Vuelie" (Simonpillai). The selective deployment of culture in *Frozen* to cement an aesthetic that could be identified in such a specific way was almost the opposite of what happened in *Brother Bear*, where Disney deployed an ambiguous sense of "Inuit" or "Pacific Northwest Native American" and then avoided any direct reference that might steer the studio into facing claims of appropriation. However, following the controversy regarding *Frozen* and the cultural appropriation claims that circulated on the blogosphere, Disney, directors Jennifer Lee and Chris Buck, and producer Peter Del Vecho took steps to avoid a second round of allegations of appropriation in the sequel.

The themes of *Frozen II* are, broadly, reparations, cultural erasure, the harms of colonial betrayal, and how kingdoms (read: nations) can obscure the truths of their histories. These topics are embedded in the narrative in part by making the sisters half-Northuldran, a fictional tribe hidden by a magical mist in the north that Arendelle has forgotten about. As in the past, Disney looked for a team of experts from the group that it was about to weave into one of its magical fantasyscapes, but this time the usual course of action in which Disney had complete control over the process and terms was disrupted. The process was made open and non-confidential, and involved a treaty between the corporation and the Sámi people. Unlike the Oceanic Story Trust process that saw the corporation put together a team of experts to "vet" *Moana* to the consternation of many, for *Frozen II* there was a collaborative effort between the Sámi parliaments of Norway, Sweden, and Finland and the Saami Council to put together a group of experts, called Verddet. The process also involved a formal contract between Disney and the Sámi people that codified Disney's "desire to collaborate with the Sámi in an effort to ensure that the content of *Frozen II* is culturally sensitive, appropriate, and respectful of the Sámi and their culture" (qtd. in Simonpillai). This contract covered use of garments, the reprise of "Vuelie" sung by the Northuldra in *Frozen II*, and magical elements, such as the Northuldra connection to nature spirits. It also guaranteed the release of a version of the film in the Northern Sámi language, not dissimilar to the creation of versions of *Moana* dubbed in Tahitian, Hawaiian, and Māori (Milligan).

The idea of a formal agreement or treaty is a massive step forward, considering the previous accusations of appropriation regarding Disney's prior properties involving the depiction of various Indigenous peoples. Managing Director of the International Sámi Film Institute Anne Lájla Utsi called the move "a good example of how a big, international company like Disney acknowledges the fact that we own our own culture and stories. It hasn't happened before" (qtd. in Simonpillai). Noting the wider impact that such a move has for other Indigenous communities, Jesse Wente, the director of Canada's Indigenous Screen Office, noted that "it's in keeping with how Indigenous nations have tended to negotiate with other entities in the past. I think it's a great precedent for how Indigenous nations might deal with a corporation the size of Walt Disney, as well as governments and other agencies, around the use of their cultural and intellectual property in popular entertainment" (qtd. in Simonpillai). The contract marks a particular step forward in terms of providing a blueprint for better interactions with Indigenous communities regarding cultural and intellectual property appropriation by other entities with more cultural capital on a global scale. Of course, whether this remains a practice or becomes a "habit" of representation for the corporation remains to be seen.

Furthermore, the narrative of *Frozen II* examines the options for what one might do if, as Anna did, one became aware of the ways in which their people had propagated harm against others. Anna becomes radicalized by learning the truth of who she and Elsa were and how and why they lost their parents and then by thinking that she had lost her sister—all because of her grandfather's betrayal of the Northuldra. Her instinct upon realizing that she has lost everything and everyone she loved is to tear down the dam—the thing that started the whole cycle—even if it destroys Arendelle in the process. In contrast, Elsa is the one driven by nostalgia to save the place where she was never truly accepted. Having fallen through her own river of memories in the glacier Ahtohallan, and—through her sister's actions of causing the dam to break, thus releasing the magic it was holding—surviving what was meant to be her last action, Elsa and the Nokk, the water spirit, race the wave that is about to hit the fjord that Arendelle is built on. Elsa uses her magic to stop the wave from wiping out the kingdom before riding back to where Anna is, still thinking that her older sister and her home have been lost forever. The historical truth provokes "the next right thing" from Anna, to borrow the language of her grief ballad after the death of her sister. Conversely, Elsa's time in her own memories, confronting not only her family's past as rulers but her past selves, allows for a moment where the audience watches Elsa forgive herself and also own her full self and become a quasi-divine power that intercedes in the moment that her kingdom might face the consequences of its past actions. The film concludes with Elsa stepping aside as queen to live with the Northuldra, leaving Anna to rule Arendelle, with the idea that "a bridge has two sides." There is something too simplistic in such an ending. In Elsa's saving of the kingdom of Arendelle, which was built on a lie,[10] Disney seems to say that the answer to righting the wrongs of the

---

10   Something that has recurred across the Disney transmedia universe, such as in *Thor: Ragnarok*; see Anjirbag, "Reforming Borders."

past is not *actually* destroying the source of harm but rather simply being willing to do so, as Anna was. Elsa's "divine" powers, then, can serve as a deus ex machina and sweep in to stop the waves. However, the solving of imperial wrongs and reconciliations cannot *believably* simply fade away through the bond between two sisters, just as the animosity between human and Dark Fey cannot fully dissipate through one marriage, as implied by the end of *Maleficent: Mistress of Evil*.

Essentially, both *Maleficent: Mistress of Evil* and *Frozen II* try to provide examples of dismantling warlike hegemonic powers—but they come from a place of literal cultural imperialism by way of Disney, so, as "fixes" for embedded coloniality, they read a bit reductively. It is not enough to address lack of representation simply on visual levels, and *Maleficent: Mistress of Evil* and *Frozen II* start to try to disrupt the "normal order" of Disney storytelling. Instead of relying on the Disney fairy-tale mode to plaster over narrative gaps that do not necessarily fit, these films try to unpack the implicit colonizing tendencies in fairy-tale narratives that confront otherness. And yet, to reach this place, the resolutions of both films still point to a clumsiness regarding how to handle and resolve the problems of empowered and powerful women, explaining Elsa's powers as her being the "fifth element" that acts as a bridge between the humans and Nature and explaining Maleficent's powers as her being the last descendent of the Phoenix, and having both basically die to be reborn before stepping down from their places as de facto rulers. This narrative strategy points to where Disney struggles to balance the old Disney fairy-tale mode with the new, to truly reimagine new, open fantasy spaces, with new possibilities for all, despite paying lip service to "not being defined by where we are from but by who we are," as in the wedding ceremony at the end of *Maleficent: Mistress of Evil*.

An Expanded Disney World: Cultural Specificity and the Fairy-Tale Mode

All the films discussed in this chapter display different methods of how "research" or "collaboration" might exist in the structures of Disney narrative construction, and, importantly, even though the films came out sequentially, their productions in many ways overlap. What this means is that in this grouping of films, we are not watching a progression of change in the contemporary but rather nonlinear trajectories of various changes that are more accurately compared with earlier periods and reflect linear changes in the company itself. These changes about how Disney engaged with its critics can thus be categorized: not understanding genuine engagement (*Moana*); "engage" but "cheat," as is the case with *Aladdin*, because the location is not real and so there is no need to "play fair" in terms of accurate representation; leaning so far into another style of filmmaking that the Disney texture becomes lost (*Mulan*, 2020); a formal treaty outlining cultural property (*Frozen II*); and a return to the medievalist fantasy/fairy-tale model, where Disney can claim full authority with no need to think more deeply (*Maleficent: Mistress of Evil*). All these different strategies and methods are distinctly Disney strategies that at their heart are about maintaining the corporation's authoritative control of the narratives it presents. That control amounts to a distribution of power where Disney is still "naming" these various depicted peoples, defining them for the world at large, and reacting to or pushing past various criticisms. Returning to Vicente M. Diaz's question of "who gets to authenticate," the end decision maker remains the corporation in all these scenarios. However, in the last few years, it has become clearer that Disney's authority is perhaps less publicly infallible than it might have been in the past.

As the Disney fairy tale itself pushes past the traditional European sense of what it used to tell to now include its own classics redone regardless of their source material, the tension between difference and the Disney fairy-tale mode remains and becomes more complicated. These films make clear how changes in Disney's production methodology are, perhaps, slowly emerging, as seen in the varied methods of creative design enacted across just these films from 2016 to 2020. The most promising thing emerging from the past five years of filmmaking by Disney is truly the formal legal agreement between Disney and the Sámi, as that has the broadest sense of something impactful for the industry at large. But I would be remiss not to note that all these films address hidden histories in some ways, not just the idea that there is more than one way to tell a story but that people hide the past or hide parts of themselves and that things are forever out of balance until that obfuscation is rectified, something that is continued, in a way, with the 2021 *Raya and the Last Dragon*. It will be interesting to see what comes out of the next five to ten years of Disney productions in this light, especially because there does not seem to be an end in sight for either reimagining classics and doing so "more authentically" or generating more new narratives rooted in non-European geographies.

One possibility is that, in the search for expanding the different worlds represented by the corporation, Disney will start to let go of its adherence to the fairy-tale narrative or the folkloresque. A step in this direction would be something like *Raya and the Last Dragon*, a fantasy film that drew on Southeast Asian cultures for its aesthetics (Clark). Although the film has dragons, magical objects, and high adventure, the narrative actually strives to tell a new story[11] rather than retelling something that must be forced into a particular frame to be appealing to Disney's audiences. But all the same, Raya is still cast as a warrior princess with her coterie of sidekicks, and the resolution of the film still comes from the idea of personal relationships solving and/or remaking the fantasy world into a better place. In addition, the corporation once again emphasized culturally specific research, including research trips and the formation of a "Southeast Asia Story Trust" (Clark). The Disney fairy-tale mode is still present here, and it can make it more difficult for cohesive, robust, diverse storytelling to really thrive. The expanded world and different kind of story were steps forward, but I have to return to the point about falling back on the same gambit of a Black-coded dragon as a character, though this time the voice was supplied by Awkwafina, a woman of Asian descent using a blaccent, rather than casting anyone Black in the role. If movement toward diversity or inclusion requires deployment of negative stereotypes or otherwise perpetuates continued erasure, then equity in representation and by extension the opening of the Disney fairy-tale mode to all can never be fully realized.

---

11 With the caveat that, though *Raya and the Last Dragon* was new for Disney, the parallels between this film's world building and the *Avatar: The Last Airbender* media and world building have been widely noted.

CONCLUSION

Space for a New Tale? Future Disney and a New Fairy-Tale Narrative

Once upon a time, or so the story goes, there was a little girl who lived in the woods. The deer visited every morning, and in the summer she played under the old apple tree and explored the paths through the trees where the bobcats once roamed. She danced in the thunderstorms that carried summer into autumn, and when the deep snows covered the forests and the ice made those paths impassible, she wrapped herself in blankets and read fairy tales, searching for an elusive, magical mirror that might make the paths she wandered clearer, in this forest where her family had only recently put down roots. And that is where this story begins.

Or maybe the story goes this way:

Once upon a time a young woman left the forest she called home and went on a long journey to pursue a dream. It was not the first time she had done this, but every time she had returned home prior, she realized she still hadn't found what she was looking for. Where she looked for a reflection of herself she only found refraction, twisted mirrors that only showed what she was not. She learned to think that was enough—that it would be enough to peer into these images of other people's stories, even if she knew they would never reflect her. But one day a few years from her thirtieth birthday, she sat on a train and the world gave her what she had stopped looking for: a reflection of her family, or herself, in a story. And having seen a true reflection once, having felt seen accurately, in some small way for the first time in her life, the imperfect and twisted images would never be enough again. Maybe that is where this story begins.

Or, perhaps, the real tale is this:

Once upon a time a little girl knew her family was different but was not quite sure how or why. She just knew that whereas other people had family very close by or did not have to explain who they were, or why their hair or eyes were a certain way, or where they were or weren't from, her family instead was different. She retreated into books, looking for the possibilities of happy endings, a world where wonder existed around different corners. Alongside the books, she retreated into a world where her differences seemed more acceptable: Disney's world, where even if the stories weren't about her, she could at least be in the background, in some way a part of something bigger, a world where mermaids were real, carpets could fly, and dreams of Americana were gifted like new fables to any child waiting to believe that these possibilities might belong to them too, even if they didn't fit in elsewhere yet. A place where she might have the space and opportunity to live out that elusive dream, built of its own magic and wonder. Maybe that, too, is where this story begins.

Where it continues is in the classroom. I have been lucky enough to be able to lecture on fairy tales, adaptations, children's media, and Disney in classrooms in the United States, the United Kingdom, and Europe, thinking with undergraduates, graduate students, and public education groups about the different power dynamics embedded in the works produced by an international corporate media conglomerate and why it is so important to look at these details. In the classroom our analysis reaches beyond good and bad versions, beyond the idea of whether Disney did better or worse. Instead, we continue to ask the question, Who is missing? And in endeavoring to see the answer to that question, we better understand the power of representation in media, to both reflect the world we think we know and to proffer routes to remaking it in more expansive, more equitable ways. This might be one way to consider the 2023 *Little Mermaid*.

We can think about the creation and construction of this film somewhere in between the contexts and approaches used for the 1997 *Cinderella* featuring Brandy and Whitney Houston and the live-action remediation of *Aladdin*. Although, yes, as already discussed, the 2023 *Little Mermaid* does fall into some of the same traps of historicism that *Aladdin* did, it also unapologetically puts nonwhite bodies into the magical underwater kingdom space that is Ariel's home and populates the land above with nonwhite human beings. One of Disney's worlds becomes opened up to new audiences, to new dreamers, and to new possibilities. We will, I'm sure, keep pulling at the threads of this film and its realization from different critical contexts. However, it does not diminish the fact that Halle Bailey's Ariel, and the world she is surrounded by, marks a sea change for the Magic Kingdom, the idea of who populates a fairy tale. Importantly, the fairy tale, the wonder, the magic, all stay intact. The world does not break; the fairy-tale mode holds—which tells us many things, but, perhaps especially, that this was always possible.

When I thought about what this book might be, there was a part of me that really saw its scope as being from *Mermaid* to *Mermaid*—a look at what had or had not changed in a little over thirty years of movie making. I approached this as someone who has grown up as someone for whom Disney was a defining factor of an American identity formation and, really, my introduction to fairy tales and a larger love of fantasy as a space that can both reflect the world as it is and show the potentials of what it might yet become. The 1989, 2019, and 2023 *Mermaid* productions, each in their own way and when grouped together, exemplify different new potentials for storytelling, whether in terms of format, the kinds of stories told, or who can feature in them and what their outcomes might be. The potentials are arguably the most important factor when it comes to fairy tales or tales of wonder. At their heart, these are stories that ask, What could be, or what could have been? And in so doing, they motivate us as audiences to ask more questions about the world we live in and what we think is possible in it. Cristina Bacchilega and Pauline Greenhill write that "the fantastic was not simply relegated to (presumed) mere entertainment and escape, but was part of cultural formations of proper actions and behaviors and of potentially transformative resources for the oppressed or marginalized" (Bacchilega and Greenhill, 4), and that fairy tale and folktale operated on intergenerational levels of communication and was not just "primarily for children" (4). Just because Disney has not been fully grasping that potential since 1999 or so, it does not mean that the last few decades of fairy-tale or folkloresque film have not still been operating on an intergenerational level. After all, when reiterations or remakes do not exactly match nostalgic memory of a beloved film, it is not children who are protesting online or causing backlash that creeps into news cycles. But despite the various backlashes, change has still been slow, nonlinear, and imperfect, and that alone shows that there is—with the right leadership, the right creators, the right mind-sets behind the wheel—potential for the company to grow into itself for a new audience.

And this is true not only of Disney but also for every studio that decides to tell stories in the contemporary through the narrative lens of fairy tales, the folkloresque, or even fantasy more widely.

Considering the variant potentials of fairy-tale films made by studios other than Disney, Pauline Greenhill and Sidney Eve Matrix write:

> Each traditional fairy tale retelling forms a copy for which there is no original. Every version offers a snapshot—a view of that story in time and space that refers to its sources and predecessors. . . . With their own specific meanings and uses, fairy tales speak with as well as about their tellers, audiences, contexts of performance, and sociocultural backgrounds. (Greenhill and Matrix, 1)

They go on to note that "the mirror of fairy tale film reflects not so much what its audience members actually are but how they see themselves and their potential to develop (or, likewise, to regress)" (Greenhill and Matrix, 17). In traveling from *Mermaid* (to *Mermaid*) to *Mermaid*, that mirror becomes slightly more visible than it perhaps once was. By examining as a distinct corpus the past three decades of Disney's fairy-tale and folkloresque films, we see that even this studio's frame around the mirror of its particular tales is changing. More than thirty years after the premiere of the film that relaunched Disney animation, *The Little Mermaid* was remade as a hybrid stage show/showing of the animated feature. This iteration was broadcast live on ABC and starred Auli'i Cravalho, Shaggy, and Queen Latifah in the live portion, three actors stepping into a previously whitewashed space. Although the hybrid anniversary format with radically updated casting would be repeated in 2022 with the anniversary presentation of *Beauty and the Beast*, in retrospect the 2019 *Little Mermaid Live!* looks almost like a litmus test: Can the company substitute darker faces for the ones that audiences are already familiar with and have them be widely accepted? It probably helped, some, that Cravalho was already a beloved Disney voice, having brought the character of Moana to life, and that Shaggy and Queen Latifah are both well-known talents with established fan bases and mainstream recognition. The production was broadcast live, intersplicing the animated film with staged musical numbers before a live audience, and without much comment—neither a full step in a new direction nor a stubborn adherence to what once was. The changes that had been happening in the years before did not lead to a radical reimagining of this narrative space. *The Little Mermaid* starring Halle Bailey premiered in 2023 and was a step further in the process. It was refreshing to see a move toward more deliberate reimagining, but, still, the dual attempt to expand the Disney fairy-tale mode while still holding on to the original Disney version of the story caused a tension that could not quite be resolved. The addition of specific historical and geographic elements caused more questions to be asked when the real historical contexts clashed with the logic of the fairy-tale world, and, as with the world building deployed in the live-action *Aladdin*, the most earnest performances on behalf of the cast could not in the end overcome the implicit racialized politics of a specific time and geography. When difference becomes hyperspecific in terms of how historical details are deployed to make a Disney world more *believable*, the cracks in the Disney fairy-tale mode become the most apparent. It is not a narrative mode that was developed to deal with the real, because as a narrative mode, it seeks to compress, to obfuscate, to make fit. If Disney truly wants to reach for equitable, multivocal, and pluralistic inclusion, it will have to grapple with how its fairy-tale mode is built into the structural DNA of the company on an ongoing basis.

Since 1989 the corporation has certainly seen a degree of change as it has expanded globally, both in terms of its cultural capital and in terms of the narratives it tells and then decides are "classics." In some ways, this feels like a reheralding of another cycle of "multiculturalism." There was a return to a key fairy-tale narrative, diversified in its casting and presented anew, with audiences also well aware that even more different-but-similar productions are yet to come from Disney. Such productions included the 2023 live-action and CGI theatrical remediation of *The Little Mermaid*, the allegedly more culturally authentic *Mulan* (2020), Pixar's *Soul* (2020), the Southeast Asia–inspired *Raya and the Last Dragon* (2021), and even 2023's *Wish*, which is a potential backstory for the Fairy Godmother of *Cinderella* fame (with intertextual dialogues also implied to exist with the Blue Fairy from *Pinocchio*, given an end credit scene featuring the "When You Wish Upon a Star" melody). Given Disney's penchant for not only recursive cycles but mining its previous work to branch out in new or different directions, it is not really surprising that there is a consistent pattern of reiteration of classic films alongside new productions.

This is a pattern that both fans and scholars should most likely expect to continue, with Disney reaching both further into its vault for reiteration inspiration and more broadly across the globe as it looks to incorporate "new" things into its construct of the Magic Kingdom. Disney plays with the construct of its own version of the fairy-tale genre or modality of telling global fairy tales. Simultaneously the corporation replicates a "stages historicism of European modernity . . . where the genre of the 'fairy tale' is still generally understood as European and North American [and] the Middle East constructed as the Orient has produced . . . wonder tales that have become identified with exotic magic and fantasy" (Bacchilega, *Fairy Tales Transformed*, 21). In this construct, "most of the rest of the world has or had 'folktales' that can become 'fairy tales,' but are not yet" (21). In this book I have examined in part where Disney engages in the act of transforming various legends or folklore into its own brand of fairy-tale narrative. However, as the corporation continues to widen the world it creates in its idealizing image, viewers, critics, and creatives alike will need to be more conscious about questioning Disney's supremacy as *the* storyteller and become more aware of the paratexts of culturally specific criticisms that can no longer be ignored.

Disney is firmly positioned as a powerful stakeholder within the hegemonic mediasphere perpetuated especially by WENA countries, but that does not mean that the films it produces are as easily positioned or interpreted within a wider, global cultural context. Disney's films since 1989 have gradually shifted the perception of what a Disney narrative could be in terms of types of narrative arcs represented and, more important, who is granted what kind of agency within those narratives. This shift occurred alongside the expansion of access to the democratizing space of the internet, and such films have also over time come under more forceful and open scrutiny. Evaluating what might be positive or negative in such films varies based on the positionality of who is doing the evaluation. Extradiegetic materials, such as original contexts of the stories, other iterations of the narratives, the positionality of the producers and artists who create the filmic adaptations, and the various reactions and criticisms of the films by other viewers, add to a paratext that in turn adds to how audiences can position and understand the films in different contexts and construct meaning. What we can learn from a discrete, historical study that juxtaposes parallel elements of the films and from various academic and cultural criticisms of the films, so that both change and the lack thereof are more visible with time, is that Disney's relationship with authentic cross-cultural storytelling is, at best, complicated.

In this work I have explored how diverse representation in Disney fairy-tale and folkloresque films shifted from the Disney Renaissance beginning 1989 to the present, using the construct of the Disney fairy-tale mode to describe how the company solidified its narrative norms and what happens when those norms collide with narrative conventions that cause them to fracture, or break. In Chapter 1 I explored the solidification or formation of the Disney fairy-tale mode and how it becomes more visible based on what happens when it breaks to fit other cultures or representations than what had already been established as its "classic" narrative base. The Disney fairy-tale mode becomes important to how we see Blackness or Black identities represented in Disney fairy-tale and folkloresque spaces, as seen in Chapters 2 and 3. If the core of the mode relies on an aesthetic of canonical whiteness, then what we see in relation to that is that there are two ways that Blackness or representation of Black identities actually ends up breaking that fairy-tale mode. First, there is this idea of Blackness in absentia, where the corporation represents recognizable hallmarks of a culture without the politics of putting Black bodies in white spaces. The other way involves inserting Black bodies into fairy-tale narratives but complicating the resolution in terms of what limits are placed on the potentials for the realization of fairy-tale wonder or magic for people of certain identities. All of this becomes a problem, because both the absence and the presence of these bodies in the white space that is Disney makes visible the systems or habits of whiteness that are normalized. Whether Blackness in absentia or Blackness with narrative limitations, the narrative disruption or pattern disruption causes audiences to question why these narratives might be different. The implicit comparison point makes it difficult to retain the invisibility of whiteness at the center of the corporation's aesthetic.

In Chapter 4 I considered Disney as a projector of orientalism, but by teasing out Sara Ahmed's idea of orientation in the construction of orientalism. As such, I examined how and where Disney is oriented in relation to what it deems Other, even as it tries to fold that difference into the scope of the Disney fairy-tale mode, and how that negotiation of position also has an effect on the realization of different narratives. Essentially, Chapter 4 lets us consider not only how and where Disney is oriented but also how and where the Disney fairy-tale mode writes from and to whom. This sets up the consideration in Chapter 5 of how audience position has shifted in relation to the corporation and how Disney in its remake and remediation era can no longer pretend to be the sole arbiter of race, culture, and difference as it continues to "make race" on a global stage. All the problems that had before only raised their heads significantly in relation to Black representation are now also visible in the spaces of creating other cultures or representing complications. Culture-clash narratives or colonial or imperial narratives also lead us as viewers back to narratives that center whiteness. The use of magical creatures as Indigenous stand-ins while simultaneously re-creating the hallmarks of medievalist worlds, or placing Agrabah into a sense of the medievalesque through the invocation of a Silk Road setting, leads to many questions about having to deal with the complications of the intrusions of real histories and contexts. We can better question what it means to put things in relation when there is very real history as well as other points of view from which to orient the power and place of these narratives.

Thus one effect of the Disney fairy-tale mode is not just to show how Disney bends things to fit but to make visible Disney's habits of whiteness, much in the way Kimberly Lau's work makes visible the systems of whiteness that underpin European fairy tales. This thus starts to break apart the idea that it is possible to just transplant narratives into different contexts, because there is always that effect of glocality, that dialogue between the global and the local that always exists and that always exists on multiple planes of realization. It is just a matter of whose voices are being heard in terms of asserting where the difference works or does not work in different ways.

Disney fairy-tale and folkloresque narratives are, for better or worse, a global phenomenon. As the world becomes both bigger and smaller in modernity, it remains necessary to keep asking who is granted access to this Magic Kingdom and for whom access comes with caveats of being changed or rewritten by the corporation. What I hope I have begun to reveal through analysis of the corporation's most recent decades of productions is that Disney's strategy for diversity on a global and glocal stage relies on unapologetically deploying tokenism from a conservative

WENA hegemonic worldview marketed heavily as benign offerings of equity, which crumbles under scrutiny. This is important in the context of an evolving children's and family mediasphere that is working to diversify in the current climate, in terms of learning to identify quality and equitable representation when one corporation can flood the market with quantity that is difficult for other producers to keep up with. Viewers, fans, and critics can recognize growth and still demand better from a company that helps shape and reaffirm the worldviews of billions globally through its fantasyscapes.

What has changed in this time is that criticisms of Disney are now far more accessible publicly, which arguably marks a transition in the balance of power between Disney as the monolithic media producer and various sociocultural groups that would levy criticism against the company's productions. Disney's assertion of "believability" not "realism" can be more directly and forcefully called into question. It is also arguable that the shift from sending a production team on a research trip and engaging consultants as needed to deliberately involving people who are of and invested in a particular culture to be part of the adaptation and storytelling process marks a significant change in how Disney has approached telling stories from other cultures. This latter move, involving cultural partners, is, at face value, one in the direction of collaboration, as the studio begins a necessary process of potentially moving away from appropriating and transforming cultural property in decontextualized ways and perpetuating harmful, often colonializing, stereotypes. In truth, true multivocal, pluralistic depictions of diversity would necessarily require the dismantling of Disney's core aesthetic, and therefore Disney's core audience, which has been built on representing or speaking primarily to an American, conservative, white, cisgender, heteronormative, ableist, and patriarchal audience. It is impossible to say or project whether such a thing could ever be possible, but the current trajectory in the context of the contemporary social and political moment is something that bears watching, as whatever direction Disney moves in is sure to have a ripple effect (and almost certainly its own backlash effect) on children's and family media at large.

That being said, this transition in production processes is only the first step in moving away from stereotypical, flat representations of "diversity" or "diverse identities" that are concerned primarily with the level of the image rather than with the problematic constructions at the narrative level and toward authentic multicultural or transcultural storytelling, and this move needs to be viewed as such. Although more authentic, ethical depictions of difference may well begin to speak back to institutionally and culturally embedded biases and inequalities, these cannot function as such if the ethics and contexts of the production processes are not thoroughly examined. For example, it would be worth probing, in the future, how and why Disney insists on representing its so-called diverse characters only outside the context of the United States (barring Tiana) and only from distinct historical or semimythical periods of time. By problematizing further how the divide between cultures is maintained through various elements of film production, a better picture of how difference—not necessarily diversity—becomes encoded socially through such representations is possible. In essence, it is necessary for future research to probe how the separation between "normal" and Other is maintained through casting, construction of setting, use or disregard of historical contexts of various ethnic and cultural diaspora, and many other facets of cultural erasure and inequality within even just the socio-historical-cultural context of the United States. There will always be tension between the corporation's mandate to protect and increase its profit margins and the assertions of the marginalized to their right to accurate and ethical representation.

Coloniality is a system of economic and cultural exchange that reinforces current hegemonic power structures, and Disney's depictions of otherness simultaneously support that structure while also claiming to disrupt it through diversifying the kinds of stories adapted. How coloniality remains embedded in Disney's particular narrative structure needs further examination to better understand how, beyond the intentions of any production team, the films can still encode negative representations of other ethnicities or contribute to harmful stereotypes. Encoding that sense of otherness while also incorporating transcultural narratives under the Disney umbrella limits the opportunity for authentic representations of diversity in Disney animated films; viewers are invited into a narrative but are constantly reminded of all the potential barriers between them and the source material and thereby the source culture. Anamik Saha's conception of how media and culture industries "make race" becomes a useful tool in disentangling and reading how

Disney's world creation is in dialogue with our real conceptions of racialized identities. A better understanding of the coloniality embedded in the production and presentation of Disney films—as the company's oeuvre continues to deal in adaptations of its own multicultural material, especially as navigated through Sara Ahmed's conception of orientation, where the corporation stands when creating its cultural products with their implicit norms—may lead to a better understanding of how to tell more authentic stories without compromising the integrity of the culture being borrowed from.

To put it simply, despite the incorporation of "the world" into Disney, Disney is not, in fact, the world, despite its best efforts to maintain that illusion. The adage of "nothing about us without us" (*nihil de nobis, sine nobis*) seems to be one that Disney as a corporation needs to better understand—and the steps taken with films such as *Frozen II* show potential for measures that might prove fruitful if collaborative practices and treaties or contracts specifying cultural ownership become not only normative but an industry standard. Rather than the Disney habit of imposing its own take on appropriated narratives under the patina of research, the creative process was disrupted on a structural level. Cultural stakeholders were recognized as having the primary right to decide how they were represented; thus the way to make structure changes with lasting, recognizable effects is to change the structure. One such potential structural change was the appointment of Latondra Newton to the position of senior vice president and chief diversity officer of the Walt Disney Corporation in February 2017; in terms of timeline, this appointment coincided with the change in corporate tactics used to interact with cultural stakeholders and the marked shift in open statements against racism followed by a pledge of $5 million to social justice causes after the murder of George Floyd by police sparked global protests. Despite the consistent periods of anti-Black violence and subsequent public outrage since the founding of the Black Lives Matter movement in 2013 following the murder of Trayvon Martin by an armed vigilante in 2012, this is the first such statement made by the corporation, not only through internal communications to "cast members," but also through posts across its social media outlets (T. Bell; S. Robinson; "Walt Disney Company Pledges"; @S_Mittermeier). Of course, this line of reasoning can only be speculation, and looking back from 2024 on that period, there are many more things to critique structurally about where Disney puts its actual money in comparison with the social justice lip service it pays to project an inclusive and aware image, but it does also indicate that the ties between individuals who determine the corporate structure and public social impact bear further scrutiny.

But do small individual actions from actors with power ultimately cement institutional change? That is the question that will likely be answered or come closer to being answered over the next couple of decades. One of the roadblocks to having concrete answers to the question of has Disney changed (or is Disney changing) in a fundamental way when it comes to questions of multicultural or diverse representation is that the company is incredibly vast and incredibly compartmentalized across divisions and internal brands, and, perhaps most important, the production timelines on things such as theatrically released feature films can be several years long. These timelines and such compartmentalization might well account for what has looked like, across this book's scope, a process of progress and regression. Nevertheless, this does not mean that there should be a complacency when it comes to analyzing the corporation's efforts, statements, and, most important, varied impacts when it comes to considered progressive growth.

But as noted, change and progress are often met with resistance, especially with a brand that is so rooted in a particular kind of nostalgia. For some viewers—and critics—there might be a reactionary need to call small incremental changes signs of significant change for the better. But I would assert again that such a mind-set ignores the feelings of those who are never fully seen and furthermore centers whiteness at the heart of a project ostensibly about diversification and better multicultural, more globalized, more pluralistic representation. Should there be the ability to continue to push for deeper representations by Disney, perhaps the wish expressed by Kheli R. Willetts will become fulfilled, and fulfilled for people from a multitude of backgrounds and positionalities without reliance on stereotype, caricature, or shallow misunderstood pastiche that leads to effacement:

> I still search for images of myself, and now, my daughter, in Disney; I still long to see diverse representations of diverse people. I imagine a blockbuster film featuring everyday people—Latinas

without sass, Asians without choppy English, and Africans without rhythm or rage. This is my *Fantasia*, perfectly suitable for animation, with villains and heroines characterized by their character and not misrepresented by caricatures, color or culture. Perhaps, one day, Disney will make new magic, complete with enough sparkle for everyone, and finally fulfill my wish for images that look, and feel, familiar and beautiful. (Willetts, 20)

Like Willetts, I too still wait for this. I wait for the day when the fairy tale I see on screen, see brought to life across other Disney media outlets, might also be one where I might enter the Magic Kingdom myself and not just watch from the outside. And that will be again, perhaps, where this story, and the Magic Kingdom waiting to be fully realized, finally begins.

And yet there are still steps being taken—not toward more fully realized and inclusive fairy tales, necessarily, but arguably, to the idea of a different "fairy tale" altogether. If part of fairy-tale narratives is about reimagining the world as it might be, then there is a different kind of reimagining happening in another way in newer films that engage with fairy-tale or folkloresque elements. Films such as *Onward* (2020), *Encanto* (2021), *Luca* (2021), and *Turning Red* (2022) are all driven by magical elements, but the narratives and the resolution center more on family relationships than on fairy-tale or quest narratives. Taken individually, these narratives are all quite different: *Onward* is a quest story about two brothers in a world where people have chosen the convenience of technology over magic, but magic might yet reunite them with their dead father; *Luca* is about a young sea monster fascinated with the world on land; *Encanto* is about Mirabel finding her place within her family as the only member without a magical gift; and *Turning Red* follows the adolescent Mei as she learns about her family's secret ability to transform into red pandas. But taken together, another pattern appears. In each of these narratives, the magic is incidental to the emotional arc of the story. Instead, the potentials for transformation come from intergenerational and cross-boundary communication and better understanding between members of families and between individuals and wider communities—a new "fairy tale" told through the hallmarks of the old, but leading to far more fulfilling narrative closures with more resonances for wider audiences. And in a time when intergenerational discourses are fraught,[1] positive modeling of intergenerational communication on a global level is not a small thing.

In this conclusion I would like to point to the possible solidification of a new "fairy tale" or "fantasy" at the center of the Disney mediascape and how this intersects with deployment of the folkloresque while centering family narratives and stories about intergenerational relationships. Films such as those just mentioned highlight a move to narratives that use the folkloresque to communicate narratives that coalesce around solidarity and communication, new family forms, and, even specifically, intergenerational relationships in racialized or culturally specific spaces. In all these films, there is a "fairy tale" of families or communities addressing and acknowledging specific traumas and having open dialogues that resolve and renew family connections while leaving room for growth for all. Whether looking at grief following the loss of a parent and renewed bonds between siblings the way that *Onward* does; or grappling in some ways with inherited culture and environmental culture as a child of immigrants, as *Turning Red* does; or dealing with a fear of outsiders but also the fear of letting go of one's child into a new world and also childhood abandonment, as in *Luca*; or dealing with the legacies of inherited trauma and violence, as in *Encanto*, the focus on the narrative of family relationships has given rise to another level of magically inflected wish-fulfillment narratives. The fairy-tale mode remains present through narrative arcs and the presence of magic and fairy-tale symbols, the idea that at the end there will be a certain kind of resolution. But at the same time, by letting the stories breathe into the space of the fantastic, by loosening the adherence to the fairy-tale mode—the idea that there have to be set mythic, legendary, folkloresque, or cultural narratives that are then reformed to fit Disney's patterns of storytelling—we simultaneously see a process of not incorporation but writing new kinds of families and relationships into the mainstream. And to be clear, when I am talking about intergenerational communication as a new fairy-tale

1   See the European Research Council–funded *Constructing Age for Young Readers* project. Disclosure: I was recruited for this project for a six-month postdoctoral research fellowship from September 2021 through February 2022 and retained my affiliation with the University of Antwerp through January 2025.

narrative mode for Disney, I am not identifying intergenerational communication and understanding as unlikely. Instead, I am rather identifying it as a model through which salient, accessible transformations can occur for individuals, families, and wider communities.

Now, all these films except for *Encanto* are technically Pixar films, which might speak to some of the narrative flexibility. But given that Pixar is no longer as distinct an entity within the Disney corporation, there does seem to still be a larger lesson for Disney here. And even *Encanto*, which is at its heart culturally and temporally specific in terms of landscape and other details, by not making it an adaptation of a specific tale but rather a tale with magic reflecting people of a specific culture, the focus became shifted to the characters rather than adhering to a formula. There is something interesting brought to the fore when comparing even briefly *Encanto* with the live-action and CGI remediation of *The Little Mermaid*. Although efforts were made to orient the remediation in a specific historical and cultural context while retaining the emphasis on the mermaid magic, the net effect from Eric's added backstory to speeches about a tension between the land beings and the sea beings and to details about Caribbean trade (which raises questions about where the Caribbean slave trade is in all this) is that the story becomes weighed down. The fairy-tale narrative that Bacchilega and Greenhill note "has given solace and joy to those who imagine or seek alternative embodiments, including queer and transgender folks" and that also "suggest[s] a desirably disabled world" (Bacchilega and Greenhill, 4) becomes twisted in an attempt to become everything to every kind of audience while still holding its original shape. But *Encanto*, as an original production, does not carry the same nostalgic baggage. What this means, ultimately, is that both the conflict and the resolution could follow their own paths and emotional trajectories without being confined by a superimposed fairy-tale narrative. Thus, what could have been a story solely about Mirabel saving the magic through some specific quest or about Mirabel earning her own powers instead becomes a story about intergenerational communication. The magic is saved not through magic but through communication, reflection on wrongdoing, and acceptance of people for who they are and not what they can do or what value they add. And importantly, this is not one-directional. The resolution does not come just because Alma, the family matriarch, apologizes for how she has treated her family but instead comes only after Mirabel sees the pain and grief and trauma Alma suffered when her children were infants.

Importantly too, the resolution of *Encanto* sees the moment that *Frozen II* backed away from come to fruition: The house of the family Madrigal, Casita, is literally torn down when the problems within the family come to a head. It is rebuilt from the ground up, accompanied by lyrics that talk about needing a new foundation after Alma and Mirabel reconcile and Alma apologizes to the rest of her children and grandchildren. Where Elsa saves Arendelle from the wave that would have wiped out the kingdom, quite literally the consequences of her ancestor's actions, Casita must fall first and be rebuilt. By doing this, the "fairy tale" at the heart of *Encanto* is not that magic exists and can make life easier but rather that with communication families can build themselves into something stronger, even if that process involves tearing down the old and the bad first.

There is much more that can be said about these films and the new families they write into the mainstream, how they push back against Disney's own norms and visual orthodoxies, but I also want to note that the existence of these films pushes against another Disney norm: that its core brand needs to be continually defined through nostalgic repetition or the adherence to a specific type of narrative or aesthetic to be successful as a media corporation. Instead of changing the world to become incorporated into its boundaries, Disney can and needs to change. If the fairy-tale mode cannot really accommodate stories that do not fit its narrow source remit, such as a narrow geographic bound of fairy tales and Anglophone children's classics, perhaps then it needs to be abandoned. Something new needs to come up in its place to tell stories to a broadening world. But that only happens if Disney as a corporation can let go, slightly, of its own myth making and self-mythologizing and of a particular audience's nostalgia for a "classic" Disney where most everyone else was Other, absent, or otherwise represented in inhumane and stereotypical ways.

WORKS CITED

@KarlreMarks. "I will no longer use the term 'the West.' From now on it's WENA for Western Europe and North America. Pun possibly intended." Twitter post, 19 April 2016, 1:39 p.m. twitter.com/KarlreMarks/status/722404296785072128 (accessed 5 July 2020).

@S_Mittermeier. "I had truly not expected this, but this is what every official Disney account looks like right now." Twitter post, 1 June 2020, 10:01 a.m. twitter.com/S_Mittermeier/status/1267380759909851137 (accessed 18 June 2020).

Ahmed, Sara. *On Being Included: Racism and Diversity in Institutional Life*. Duke UP, 2012.

———. *Queer Phenomenology*. Duke UP, 2006.

Aladdin. Directed by Ron Clements and John Musker. Performances by Scott Weinger, Robin Williams, and Linda Larkin. Walt Disney Animation Studios, 1992.

Aladdin. Directed by Guy Ritchie. Performances by Will Smith, Mena Massoud, and Naomi Scott. Walt Disney Pictures, 2019.

Amatangelo, Amy. "Disney+'s Gender-Flipped *Sneakerella* Has the Dance Moves but the Story Drags." *Paste Magazine*, 9 May 2022. www.pastemagazine.com/movies/disney-plus/sneakerella-review (accessed 4 July 2023).

Anderson, Elijah. "The White Space." *Sociology of Race and Ethnicity*, 2015, vol. 1, no. 1, pp. 10–21. doi: 10.1177/2332649214561306.

"Animal Transformations and Dehumanization." *Writing with Color*, 24 November 2014. writingwithcolor.tumblr.com/post/103503165606/ive-seen-a-lot-of-rhetoric-pointing-out-how (accessed 30 May 2020).

Anjirbag, Michelle A. "Enter the Castle: Reiterating Medievalism in the Framing of Disney's Fantasyscapes." *Children's Literature Association Quarterly*, 2020, vol. 45, no. 4, pp. 346–63. doi: 10.1353/chq.2020.0043.

———. "*Maleficent: Mistress of Evil* (Joachim Rønning, 2019) and the Construction of Fantasy Spaces." *Fantasy/Animation* (blog), 7 February 2020. https://www.fantasy-animation.org/current-posts/maleficent-mistress-of-evil-joachim-rnning-2019-and-the-construction-of-fantasy-spaces?rq=anjirbag (accessed 10 June 2020).

———. "Mulan and Moana: Embedded Coloniality and the Search for Authenticity in Disney Animated Film." *Social Sciences*, 2018, vol. 7, no. 11, p. 230. doi: 10.3390/socsci7110230.

———. "New Agrabah, Same Old Disney Orientalism: Commodity Racism and Western Effacement of the 'Middle East.'" In *The Oxford Handbook of the Disney Musical*. Edited by Dominic Broomfield-McHugh and Colleen Mongomery. Oxford UP, 2025, pp. 101–24.

———. "Pumpkin-Carriage Palimpsests: Disney's Cinderellas and the Disney Fairy-Tale Mode." *Journal of American Culture*, 2024, vol. 47, no. 2, pp. 97–104.

———. "Reforming Borders of the Imagination: Diversity, Adaptation, Transmediation, and Incorporation in the Global Disney Film Landscape." *Jeunesse: Young People, Texts, Cultures*, 2019, vol. 11, no. 2, pp. 151–76. https://utppublishing.com/doi/10.3138/jeunesse.11.2.151.

Anjirbag, Michelle A., Bertha Chin, and Jingan Young. "Panel Discussion: The Live-Action *Mulan* (2020) and Disney's Approach to Racial Diversity." In *Fan Phenomena: Disney*. Edited by Sabrina Mittermeier. Intellect Books, 2022, pp. 62–74.

Anjirbag, Michelle, and Madeleine Hunter. "A Twist in or out of Time? Adapting the Disney Classic for a YA Audience." In *Adaptation in Young Adult Novels: Critically Engaging Past and Present*. Edited by Dana Lawrence and Amy L. Montz. Bloomsbury Academic, 2020, pp. 139–52.

Atlantis: The Lost Empire. Directed by Gary Trousdale and Kirk Wise. Performances by Michael J. Fox, Jim Varney, and Corey Burton. Walt Disney Animation Studios, 2001.

Atlantis: Milo's Return. Directed by Victor A. Cook, Toby Shelton, and Tad Stones. Performances by James Taylor, Cree Summer, and John Mahoney. Disney Television Animation, 2003.

Attebery, Brian. "Affordances of Fantasy." *Genre*, 2024, vol. 57, no. 1, pp. 1–23.

———. *Fantasy: How It Works*. Oxford UP, 2022.

Ayres, Brenda, ed. *The Emperor's Old Groove: Decolonizing Disney's Magic Kingdom*. Peter Lang, 2003.

Bacchilega, Cristina. *Fairy Tales Transformed? Twenty-First-Century Adaptations and the Politics of Wonder.* Wayne State UP, 2013.

———. *Postmodern Fairy Tales: Gender and Narrative Strategies.* U of Pennsylvania P, 1997.

Bacchilega, Cristina, and Pauline Greenhill. "Fairytale Reanimation and Wonder Wanted for a Better Future." *Imagining the Impossible: International Journal for the Fantastic in Contemporary Media,* 2022, vol. 1, no. 1, pp. 1–23.

Banh, Jenny. "Moana: Daughter of the Chief and Polynesian (In)Visibility." In *Recasting the Disney Princess in an Era of New Media and Social Movements.* Edited by Shearon Roberts. Lexington Books, 2020, pp. 129–46.

Barber, Rebekah. "How the Civil Rights Movement Opened the Door to Immigrants of Color." *Facing South: A Voice for a Changing South,* Institute for Southern Studies, 3 February 2017. www.facingsouth.org/2017/02/how-civil-rights-movement-opened-door-immigrants-color (accessed 30 June 2020).

Baudrillard, Jean. *Simulacra and Simulation.* Trans. Sheila Faria Glaser. U of Michigan P, 1994.

Bayless, Martha. "Disney's Castles and the Work of the Medieval in the Magic Kingdom." In *The Disney Middle Ages: A Fairy Tale and Fantasy Past.* Edited by Tison Pugh and Susan Aronstein. Palgrave Macmillan, 2012, pp. 39–56.

Beauty and the Beast. Directed by Bill Condon. Performances by Emma Watson, Dan Stevens, and Luke Evans. Walt Disney Pictures, 2017.

Beauty and the Beast. Directed by Gary Trousdale and Kirk Wise. Performances by Paige O'Hara, Robby Benson, and Jesse Corti. Walt Disney Animation Studios, 1991.

Beauty and the Beast: A 30th Celebration. Directed by Hamish Hamilton. Performances by H.E.R., Josh Groban, Joshua Henry, and Rita Moreno. Walt Disney Television, 2022.

Bell, Christopher E., ed. *Disney Channel Tween Programming: Essays on Shows from "Lizzie McGuire" to "Andi Mack."* McFarland, 2020.

Bell, Christopher E., Marissa Lammon, Angela M. Guido, and Julie Estlick. "Introduction: A Road Map to the Disney Channel Universe." In *Disney Channel Tween Programming: Essays on Shows from "Lizzie McGuire" to "Andi Mack."* Edited by Christopher E. Bell. McFarland, 2020, pp. 1–27.

Bell, Elizabeth, Lynda Haas, and Laura Sells, eds. *From Mouse to Mermaid: The Politics of Film, Gender, and Culture.* Indiana UP, 1995.

Bell, Tom. "Disney Executives Address 'Time of Unrest' in a Message to Cast Members." *Disney Information Station,* Werner Technologies, 31 May 2020.

www.wdwinfo.com/news-stories/disney-executives-address-time-of-unrest
-in-a-message-to-cast-members/ (accessed 18 June 2020).

Benson, Stephen, ed. *Contemporary Fiction and the Fairy Tale*. Wayne State UP, 2008.

Beyoncé and various artists. *The Lion King: The Gift*. Parkwood Entertainment and Columbia Records, 2019.

"Big Changes." *Into the Unknown: Making Disney "Frozen II,"* season 1, episode 4, *DisneyPlus*. Disney, 2020. www.disneyplus.com/video/789ad3c5-d782-4814-94fa-4b9667fa44b0.

Bishop, Rudine Sims. "Mirrors, Windows, and Sliding Glass Doors." *Perspectives: Choosing and Using Books for the Classroom*, 1990, vol. 6, no. 3, pp. ix–xi.

—— (as Rudine Sims). "What Has Happened to the 'All-White' World of Children's Books?" *The Phi Delta Kappan*, 1983, vol. 64, no. 9, pp. 650–53. www.jstor.org/stable/20386841.

Black Is King. Directed by Beyoncé Knowles-Carter, Emmanuel Adjei, and Blitz Bazawule. Performances by Beyoncé Knowles-Carter, Folajomi Akinmurele, and Connie Chiume. Walt Disney Pictures and Parkwood Entertainment, 2020.

Bodenner, Chris. "Does Disney's Pocahontas Do More Harm Than Good? Your Thoughts." *The Atlantic*, 30 June 2015. www.theatlantic.com/entertainment/archive/2015/06/pocahontas-feminism/397190/ (accessed 13 May 2020).

Bonilla-Silva, Eduardo. "The Structure of Racism in Color-Blind, 'Post-Racial' America." *American Behavioral Scientist*, 2015, vol. 59, no. 11, pp. 1358–76.

Bonomolo, Cameron. "*The Little Mermaid*'s Daveed Diggs Was Uneasy About Voicing Sebastian in Disney's Live-Action Remake." Comicbook.com, 30 January 2021. comicbook.com/movies/news/the-little-mermaids-daveed-diggs-uneasy-voicing-sebastian-the-crab-accent/ (accessed 27 June 2023).

Bradford, Clare. *Unsettling Narratives: Postcolonial Readings of Children's Literature*. Wilfrid Laurier UP, 2007.

Brave. Directed by Mark Andrews, Brenda Chapman, and Steve Purcell. Performances by Kelly Macdonald, Billy Connolly, and Emma Thompson. Walt Disney Pictures, Pixar Animation Studios, 2012.

Breaux, Richard M. "After 75 Years of Magic: Disney Answers Its Critics, Rewrites African American History, and Cashes In on Its Racist Past." *Journal of African American Studies*, 2010, vol. 14, no. 4, pp. 398–416.

Brode, Douglas T. *Multiculturalism and the Mouse*. U of Texas P, 2005.

Brother Bear. Directed by Aaron Blaise and Robert Walker. Performances by Joaquin Phoenix, Jeremy Suarez, and Jason Raize. Walt Disney Animation Studios, 2003.

Brother Bear 2. Directed by Ben Gluck. Performances by Patrick Dempsey, Mandy Moore, and Jeremy Suarez. Disneytoon Studios, 2006.

Browne, David. "'The Lion Sleeps Tonight': The Ongoing Saga of Pop's Most Contentious Song." *Rolling Stone*, 7 November 2019. www.rollingstone .com/music/music-features/lion-sleeps-tonight-lion-king-update-879663/ (accessed 4 June 2020).

Bruckner, Rebekah. "Tony Bancroft Brings APU Animation Program to Life." Azusa Pacific University, 21 March 2018. www.apu.edu/articles/disney -animator-tony-bancroft/ (accessed 21 April 2020).

Brunner, Raven. "Awkwafina's Awkward 'Little Mermaid' Rap 'The Scuttlebutt' Shows She's Learned Nothing from 'Blaccent' Backlash." *Decider*, 23 May 2023. decider.com/2023/05/23/awkwafina-awkward-little-mermaid-rap-the -scuttlebutt-blaccent-backlash/ (accessed 28 June 2023).

Bryant, Taylor. "Why 'Hercules' Has the Best Disney Soundtrack of All Time." *Nylon*, 23 June 2017. www.nylon.com/articles/hercules-movie-soundtrack -anniversary (accessed 28 March 2025).

Bryman, Alan. *The Disneyization of Society*. SAGE, 2004.

Budd, Mike, and Max H. Kirsch, eds. *Rethinking Disney: Private Control, Public Dimensions*. Wesleyan UP, 2005.

Buhler, Stephen M. "Shakespeare and Company: *The Lion King* and the Disneyfication of *Hamlet*." In *The Emperor's Old Groove: Decolonizing Disney's Magic Kingdom*. Edited by Brenda Ayres. Peter Lang, 2013 [2003], pp. 117–29.

Byrne, Eleanor, and Martin McQuillan. *Deconstructing Disney*. Pluto Press, 1999.

Cai, Mingshui. *Multicultural Literature for Children and Young Adults: Reflections on Critical Issues*. Greenwood Press, 2002.

Cao, Steffi. "Awkwafina's Statement Finally Addressing 'Blaccent' Contro-versy Is Drawing More Backlash." Buzzfeed News, 6 February 2022. www .buzzfeednews.com/article/stefficao/awkwafina-blaccent-appropriation -backlash (accessed 27 June 2023).

Carrieasagiri. "#kristoff is a sami." *Misete anata no sugata wo*, 17 March 2014. carrieasagiri.tumblr.com/post/79919789155/i-took-these-pictures-from-my -printed-copy-of (accessed 13 June 2020).

Cecire, Maria Sachiko. *Re-Enchanted: The Rise of Children's Fantasy Literature in the Twentieth Century*. U of Minnesota P, 2019.

Centre for Literacy in Primary Education (CLPE). *Reflecting Realities: Survey of Ethnic Representation Within UK Children's Literature 2018*. CLPE, 19 September 2019. clpe.org.uk/RR.

The Cheetah Girls. Directed by Oz Scott. Performances by Raven-Symoné, Adrienne Houghton, and Kiely Williams. Disney Channel, 2003.

Cheu, Johnson, ed. *Diversity in Disney Films: Critical Essays on Race, Ethnicity, Gender, Sexuality, and Disability*. McFarland, 2013.

Chief Roy Crazy Horse. "The One Called Pocahontas." www.powhatan.org/play.html (archived 27 March 1997). Archived at web.archive.org/web/19970327025049/http:/www.powhatan.org/play.html (accessed 16 May 2020).

———. "Pocahontas Myth." www.powhatan.org/pocc.html (archived 27 March 1997). Archived at web.archive.org/web/19970327024425/http:/www.powhatan.org/pocc.html (accessed 16 May 2020).

"Cinderella." In *The Oxford Companion to Fairy Tales*. Edited by Jack Zipes. Oxford UP, 2000, pp. 95–97.

Cinderella. Directed by Kenneth Branagh. Performances by Lily James and Cate Blanchette. Walt Disney Pictures, 2015.

Cinderella. Directed by Clyde Geronimi, Wilfred Jackson, and Hamilton Luske. Performances by Ilene Woods, Eleanor Audley, and Verna Felton. Walt Disney Animation Studios, 1950.

Clark, Nicole. "*Raya and the Last Dragon*: Creating Disney's First Southeast Asian–Centered Movie." IGN, 26 January 2021. www.ign.com/articles/raya-and-the-last-dragon-creating-disneys-first-southeast-asian-centered-movie (accessed 25 September 2023).

Coco. Directed by Lee Unkrich. Performances by Anthony Gonzalez, Gael García Bernal, and Benjamin Bratt. Walt Disney Pictures and Pixar Animation Studios, 2017.

Descendants: The Rise of Red. Directed by Jennifer Phang. Performances by Kylie Cantrall, Nalia Baker, and Dara Reneé. Disney Channel, 2024.

Diaz, Vicente M. "Don't Swallow (or Be Swallowed by) Disney's 'Culturally Authenticated Moana.'" *Indian Country Today*, 13 November 2016. https://ictnews.org/archive/dont-swallow-or-be-swallowed-by-disneys-culturally-authenticated-moana/ (accessed 21 April 2020).

"Disney First: Black Princess in Animated Film." MSNBC.com, 9 March 2007. www.today.com/popculture/disney-first-black-princess-animated-film-wbna17524865 (accessed 13 March 2020).

"Disney Magazine: Cast and Crew Interviews." Archived from *Disney Adventures Magazine*, 31 July 1995, at The Waterfalls: A Pocahontas Site. cbl.orcein.net/pocahontas/misc/interviews.htm#russellmeans (accessed 10 May 2020).

"Disney Millennium Celebration Super Bowl XXXIV Halftime Show." YouTube, uploaded by Oh My Churro, 4 February 2013. www.youtube.com/watch?v=6dWxq1D-B9s.

"Disney's Aladdin: 'World of Aladdin' Special Look." YouTube, uploaded by Walt Disney Studios, 16 May 2019. www.youtube.com/watch?v=-GUrDu_duuE.

Dong, Lan. *Mulan's Legend and Legacy in China and the United States*. Temple UP, 2011.

Do Rozario, Rebecca-Anne C. "The Princess and the Magic Kingdom: Beyond Nostalgia, the Function of the Disney Princess." *Women's Studies in Communication*, 2004, vol. 21, no. 1, pp. 34–59.

Dudley, Sean. "Paths of Discover: The Making of Brother Bear (Full Documentary)." YouTube, 15 May 2018. www.youtube.com/watch?v=vv1B39OSeCg (accessed 16 May 2020).

Dumbo. Directed by Sam Armstrong, Norman Ferguson, Wilfred Jackson, Jack Kinney, Bill Roberts, and Ben Sharpsteen. Performances by Edward Brophy, Sterling Holloway, and Verna Felton. Walt Disney Animation Studios, 1941.

Dundes, Lauren, and Madeline Streiff. "Reel Royal Diversity? The Glass Ceiling in Disney's *Mulan* and *Princess and the Frog*." *Societies*, 2016, vol. 6, no. 4. dx.doi.org/10.3390/soc6040035.

Dunne, Cindy. "Reservations About Films: Disney's Pocahontas." *Lakota Children's Enrichment*, 11 September 2015. lakotachildren.org/2015/09/reservations-about-films-disneys-pocahontas/ (accessed 14 May 2020).

Dutka, Elaine. "The Angriest Actor: Native American Activist Russell Means Focused His Fierce Will at Wounded Knee. Can a Revolutionary Co-Exist with 'Pocahontas'?" *Los Angeles Times*, 11 June 1995. www.latimes.com/archives/la-xpm-1995-06-11-ca-11761-story.html (accessed 14 May 2020).

Ebert, Roger. "Jolly 'Little Mermaid' Will Delight Everyone." *Chicago Sun Times*, 17 November 1989. www.rogerebert.com/reviews/the-little-mermaid-1989.

Elliott, Kamilla. "Tie-Intertextuality, or, Intertextuality as Incorporation in the Tie-In Merchandise to Disney's *Alice in Wonderland* (2010)." *Adaptation*, 2014, vol. 7, no. 2, pp. 191–211. doi: 10.1093/adaptation/apu007.

Elliott-Groves, Emma, and Stephanie A. Fryberg. "'A Future Denied' for Young Indigenous People: From Social Disruption to Possible Futures." In *Handbook of Indigenous Education*. Edited by Elizabeth Ann McKinley and Linda Tuhiwai Smith. Springer, 2017, pp. 1–19. doi: 10.1007/978-981-10-1839-8_50-1.

"Elton John: 'Circle of Life' (From 'The Lion King'/Official Video)." YouTube, uploaded by DisneyMusicVEVO, 4 November 2017. www.youtube.com/watch?v=lwH9YvhPN7c.

The Emperor's New Groove. Directed by Mark Dindal. Performances by David Spade, John Goodman, and Eartha Kitt. Walt Disney Animation Studios, 2000.

Encanto. Directed by Jared Bush and Byron Howard. Performances by Stephanie Beatriz, María Cecilia Botero, and John Leguizamo. Walt Disney Pictures, 2021.

Epstein, Jeffrey. "'Dream Big, Princess' Inspires Girls and Kids of All Ages to Realize Their Ambitions." *Disney Parks Blog*, 12 February 2016. disneyparks.disney.go.com/blog/2016/02/dream-big-princess-inspires-girls-and-kids-of-all-ages-to-realize-their-ambitions/ (accessed 7 April 2020).

Fantasia. Directed by James Algar, Samuel Armstrong, Ford Beebe Jr., Norman Ferguson, David Hand, Jim Handley, T. Hee, Wilfred Jackson, Hamilton Luske, Bill Roberts, Paul Satterfield, and Ben Sharpsteen. Performances by Deems Taylor, Leopold Stokowski, and the Philadelphia Orchestra. Walt Disney Animation Studios, 1940.

Fantasia 2000. Directed by James Algar, Gaëtan Brizzi, Paul Brizzi, Hendel Butoy, Francis Glebas, Eric Goldberg, Don Hahn, and Pixote Hunt. Performances by Steve Martin, Itzhak Perlman, and Quincy Jones. Walt Disney Animation Studios, 1999.

Flores, Terry. "(Sort of) True Tales of the South Pacific." *Variety Magazine*, 22 November 2016, pp. 121–22.

Foster, Michael Dylan. "Introduction: The Challenge of the Folkloresque." In *The Folkloresque: Reframing Folklore in a Popular Culture World*. Edited by Michael Dylan Foster and Jeffrey A. Tolbert. Utah State UP, 2016, pp. 3–33.

Foster, Michael Dylan, and Jeffry A. Tolbert, eds. *The Folkloresque: Reframing Folklore in a Popular Culture World*. Utah State UP, 2016.

Frozen. Directed by Chris Buck and Jennifer Lee. Performances by Kristen Bell, Idina Menzel, and Jonathan Groff. Walt Disney Animation Studios, 2013.

Frozen II. Directed by Chris Buck and Jennifer Lee. Performances by Kristen Bell, Idina Menzel, and Josh Gad. Walt Disney Animation Studios, 2019.

Garber, Marjorie. *Quotation Marks*. Routledge, 2003.

Gilbert, Sophie. "Revisiting *Pocahontas* at 20." *The Atlantic*, 23 June 2015. www.theatlantic.com/entertainment/archive/2015/06/revisiting-pocahontas/396626/ (accessed 1 September 2023). Archived at web.archive.org/web/20151107082857/https://www.theatlantic.com/entertainment/archive/2015/06/revisiting-pocahontas/396626/.

Gilio-Whitaker, Dina. "Disney Refines Its Cultural Competence in *Moana*, but Bigger Questions Remain." *Indian Country Today*, 9 November 2016. https://ictnews.org/archive/disney-refines-its-cultural-competence-in-moana-but-bigger-questions-remain/ (accessed 21 April 2020).

———. "The Problem with the Ecological Indian Stereotype." KCET.org, 7 February 2017. www.kcet.org/shows/tending-the-wild/the-problem-with-the-ecological-indian-stereotype (accessed 2 June 2020).

Giorgis, Hannah. "The Blind Spot of Beyoncé's *Lion King* Soundtrack." *The Atlantic*, 19 July 2019. www.theatlantic.com/entertainment/archive/2019/07/disney-beyonce-lion-king-soundtrack-incomplete/594139/ (accessed 5 June 2020).

Giroux, Henry A., and Grace Pollock. *The Mouse That Roared: Disney and the End of Innocence*, 2nd ed. Rowman & Littlefield, 2010.

Glenn, Cerise L., and Landra J. Cunningham. "The Power of Black Magic: The Magical Negro and White Salvation in Film." *Journal of Black Studies*, 2009, vol. 40, no. 2, pp. 135–52. www.jstor.org/stable/40282626.

Goldsmith, Jerry. "*Mulan*" (review). *Jerry Goldsmith Online*. www.jerrygoldsmithonline.com/mulan_review.htm (accessed 11 May 2020).

Greenhill, Pauline, and Sidney Eve Matrix. "Introduction: Envisioning Ambiguity—Fairy Tale Films." In *Fairy Tale Films: Visions of Ambiguity*. Edited by Pauline Greenhill and Sidney Eve Matrix. Utah State UP, 2010, pp. 1–22.

Gregory, Sarita McCoy. "Disney's Second Line: New Orleans, Racial Masquerade, and the Reproduction of Whiteness in 'The Princess and the Frog.'" *Journal of African American Studies*, 2010, vol. 14, no. 4, pp. 432–49.

Grossman, Barbara Wallace. "*The Lion King*: A 'Blockbuster Feline' on Broadway and Beyond." In *The Disney Musical on Stage and Screen: Critical*

Approaches from "Snow White" to "Frozen." Edited by George Rodosthenous. Bloomsbury Methuen Drama, 2017, pp. 117–31.

Gutierrez, Anna Katrina. *Mixed Magic: Global-Local Dialogues in Fairy Tales for Young Readers.* John Benjamins, 2017.

Haase, Donald. "Hypertextual Gutenberg: The Textual and Hypertextual Life of Folktales and Fairy Tales in English-Language Popular Print Editions." *Fabula*, 2006, vol. 47, nos. 3–4, pp. 222–30. doi: doi.org/10.1515/FABL.2006.024.

Hawk, Hunter. "The Waiapi Tribe: The Protectors of the Amazon Rainforest." *Harvard International Review*, 26 October 2019. hir.harvard.edu/the-waiapi -tribe-the-protectors-of-the-amazon-rainforest/#:~:text=Indigenous %20Tribe%20Lands%20in%20the,it%20for%20generations%20to%20come (accessed 22 October 2024).

Haydel, Sheryl Kennedy. "#NolaBorn: Tiana and the Road Home for New Orleans Residents." In *Recasting the Disney Princess in an Era of New Media and Social Movements.* Edited by Shearon Roberts. Lexington Books, 2020, pp. 117–27.

Hennard Dutheil de la Rochère, Martine, Gillian Lathey, and Monika Woźniak. *Cinderella Across Cultures: New Directions and Interdisciplinary Perspectives.* Wayne State UP, 2016.

Hercules. Directed by Ron Clements and John Musker. Performances by Tate Donovan, Susan Egan, and James Woods. Walt Disney Animation Studios, 1997.

Herman, Doug. "How the Story of 'Moana' and Maui Holds Up Against Cultural Truths." *Smithsonian Magazine*, 2 December 2016. www .smithsonianmag.com/smithsonian-institution/how-story-moana-and -maui-holds-against-cultural-truths-180961258/ (accessed 21 April 2020).

Herreria, Carla. "Disney Pulled That Offensive 'Moana' Costume: Here's Why It Matters." *Huffington Post*, 21 September 2016. www.huffpost.com/entry/ disney-maui-costume-brownface_n_57e0c4cde4b08cb14097b892 (accessed 10 October 2019).

hooks, bell. "Eating the Other: Desire and Resistance." In *Black Looks: Race and Representation*, by bell hooks. South End Press, 1992, pp. 21–39.

Hopkinson, Nalo. "Maybe They're Phasing Us In: Re-Mapping Fantasy Tropes in the Face of Gender, Race, and Sexuality." *Journal of the Fantastic in the Arts*, 2007, vol. 18, no. 1, pp. 99–107.

Horton, Helena. "Disney Redraws First Black Princess After Anti-Racism Campaigners Claim Her Skin Is 'Too White.'" *The Telegraph*, 23 September 2018.

www.telegraph.co.uk/news/2018/09/23/disney-redraws-first-black-princess-anti-racism-campaigners/ (accessed 13 March 2020).

Howard. Directed by Don Hahn. Stone Circle Pictures, Disney+, 2018.

Howard, Courtney. "'Sneakerella' Review: Disney+ Innovative, Imperfect Cinderella Story Has Lots of Heart and Sole." *Variety*, 9 May 2022. variety.com/2022/film/reviews/sneakerella-review-1235261750/ (accessed 4 July 2023).

Huggan, Graham. *The Postcolonial Exotic: Marketing the Margins*. Routledge, 2001.

The Hunchback of Notre Dame. Directed by Gary Trousdale and Kirk Wise. Performances by Demi Moore, Jason Alexander, and Mary Kay Bergman. Walt Disney Animation Studios, 1996.

Hurley, Dorothy L. "Seeing White: Children of Color and the Disney Fairy Tale Princess." *Journal of Negro Education*, 2005, vol. 74, no. 3, pp. 221–32. www.jstor.com/stable/40027429.

Hutcheon, Linda, with Siobhan O'Flynn. *A Theory of Adaptation*, 2nd ed. Routledge, 2013.

Huykc, David, and Sarah Park Dahlen. *Diversity in Children's Books 2018*. sarahpark.com (blog), 19 June 2019. readingspark.wordpress.com/2019/06/19/picture-this-diversity-in-childrens-books-2018-infographic.

The Incredibles. Directed by Brad Bird. Performances by Craig T. Nelson, Holly Hunter, and Samuel L. Jackson. Pixar Animation Studios and Walt Disney Pictures, 2004.

Jackson, Angelique. "Daveed Diggs Is No Imitation Crab: How the Tony Winner Found His Version of Sebastian in 'The Little Mermaid.'" *Variety*, 26 May 2023. variety.com/2023/film/features/daveed-diggs-sebastian-the-little-mermaid-1235620934/ (accessed 28 June 2023).

Jackson, Lauren Michele. "Who Really Owns the 'Blaccent'?" *Vulture*, 24 August 2018. www.vulture.com/2018/08/awkwafina-blaccent-cultural-appropriation.html (accessed 27 June 2023).

James, Kendra. "It's Possible: An Oral History of 1997's 'Cinderella.'" *Shondaland*, 2 November 2017. https://web.archive.org/web/20210212030025/https://www.shondaland.com/inspire/a13138172/brandy-whitney-houston-oral-history-cinderella/ (accessed 5 September 2022).

Jenkins, Henry. *Convergence Culture: Where Old and New Media Collide*. New York UP, 2006.

Jhappan, Radha, and Daiva Stasiulis. "Anglophilia and the Discreet Charm of the English Voice in Disney's *Pocahontas* Films." In *Rethinking Disney:*

Private Control, Public Dimensions. Edited by Mike Budd and Max H. Kirsch. Wesleyan UP, 2005, pp. 151–77.

Joubin, Alexa Alice. "Others Within: Ethics in the Age of Global Shakespeare." In *The Routledge Handbook of Shakespeare and Global Appropriation*. Edited by Christy Desmet, Sujata Iyengar, and Miriam Jacobson. Routledge, 2020, pp. 25–36.

The Jungle Book. Directed by Wolfgang Reitherman, James Algar, and Jack Kinney. Performances by Phil Harris, Sebastian Cabot, and Bruce Reitherman. Walt Disney Animation Studios, 1967.

Kaʻili, Tēvita O. "Goddess Hina: The Missing Heroine from Disney's Moana." *HuffPost*, 6 December 2016. www.huffpost.com/entry/goddess-hina-the-missing-heroine-from-disney%CA%BCs-moana_b_5839f343e4b0a79f7433b6e5?utm_source=reddit.com (accessed 5 April 2025).

Keene, Adrienne. "Dear JK Rowling, I'm Concerned About the American Wizarding School." *Native Appropriations*, 9 June 2016. nativeappropriations.com/2015/06/dear-jk-rowling-im-concerned-about-the-american-wizarding-school.html (accessed 3 June 2020).

———. "'Magic in North America': The Harry Potter Franchise Veers Too Close to Home." *Native Appropriations*, 7 March 2016. nativeappropriations.com/2016/03/magic-in-north-america-the-harry-potter-franchise-veers-too-close-to-home.html (accessed 3 June 2020).

Kelly, Mary Louise. "'Magical Negro' Carries the Weight of History." NPR, 11 February 2019. www.npr.org/2019/02/11/693587521/magical-negro-carries-the-weight-of-history (accessed 7 July 2020).

King, C. Richard, Carmen R. Lugo-Lugo, and Mary K. Bloodsworth-Lugo. *Animating Difference: Race, Gender, and Sexuality in Contemporary Films for Children*. Rowman & Littlefield, 2010.

King, Jason. "Toni Braxton, Disney, and Thermodynamics." *Drama Review*, 2002, vol. 46, no. 3, pp. 54–81.

King, Susan. "Q & A with 'Princess and the Frog' Animators." *Los Angeles Times*, 22 November 2009. www.latimes.com/archives/la-xpm-2009-nov-22-la-ca-princess22-2009nov22-story.html (accessed 5 April 2025).

Korkis, Jim. "Lost 'Fantasia': The Disappearance of Sunflower." *Cartoon Research*, 27 March 2020. cartoonresearch.com/index.php/lost-fantasia-the-disappearance-of-sunflower/. (accessed 11 May 2020).

Kunze, Peter C. *Staging a Comeback: Broadway, Hollywood, and the Disney Renaissance*. Rutgers UP, 2023.

———. "Why Belle Loves Books: Industrial Approaches to Children's Culture." Centre for Research in Children's Literature at Cambridge, lecture given at the University of Cambridge, 27 May 2020.

Lacroix, Celeste. "The Images of Animated Others: The Orientalization of Disney's Cartoon Heroines from *The Little Mermaid* to *The Hunchback of Notre Dame*." *Popular Communication*, 2004, vol. 2, no. 4, pp. 213–29. doi: 10.1207/s15405710pco0204_2.

Larrick, Nancy. "The All-White World of Children's Books." *Saturday Review*, 11 September 1965, pp. 63–65, 84–85.

Lau, Kimberley. *Specters of the Marvelous: Race and the Development of the European Fairy Tale*. Wayne State UP, 2024.

Lee-Oliver, Leece. "Pocahontas: Digital Coloniality, Coercive Fiction, and 'Renewing' Western Hegemonic Power." In *Recasting the Disney Princess in an Era of New Media and Social Movements*. Edited by Shearon Roberts. Lexington Books, 2020, pp. 163–80.

Leon-Boys, Diana, and Angharad N. Valdivia. "The Location of US Latinidad: *Stuck in the Middle*, Disney, and the In-Between Ethnicity." *Journal of Children and Media*, 2020, vol. 15, no. 2, pp. 218–32. doi: 10.1080/17482798.2020.1753790 (accessed 26 April 2020).

Lindahl, Carl. "Definition and History of Fairy Tales." In *The Routledge Companion to Media and Fairy-Tale Cultures*. Edited by Pauline Greenhill, Jill Terry Rudy, Naomi Hamer, and Lauren Bosc. Routledge, 2018, pp. 11–19.

The Lion King. Book by Roger Allers and Irene Mecchi. Music by Elton John. Lyrics by Tim Rice. Directed by Julie Taymor. Original cast performances by Jason Raize, Scott Irby-Ranniar, and John Vickery. New Amsterdam Theater, New York, opened 13 November 1997.

The Lion King. Directed by Roger Allers and Rob Minkoff. Performances by Matthew Broderick, Jeremy Irons, and James Earl Jones. Walt Disney Animation Studios, 1994.

The Lion King. Directed by Jon Favreau. Performances by Donald Glover, Seth Rogen, and Beyoncé Knowles-Carter. Walt Disney Pictures, 2019.

The Lion King II: Simba's Pride. Directed by Darrell Rooney and Rob LaDuca. Performances by Matthew Broderick, Neve Campbell, and Andy Dick. Walt Disney Animation Australia, 1998.

The Little Mermaid. Directed by Ron Clements and John Musker. Performances by Jodi Benson, Samuel E. Wright, and Rene Auberjonois. Walt Disney Animation Studios, 1989.

The Little Mermaid. Directed by Rob Marshall. Performances by Halle Bailey, Jonah Hauer-King, and Daveed Diggs. Walt Disney Pictures, 2023.

The Little Mermaid Live! Directed by Hamish Hamilton, Ron Clements, and John Musker. Performances by Auli'i Cravalho, Shaggy, and Graham Phillips. ABC, 2019.

Luca. Directed by Enrico Casarosa. Performances by Jacob Tremblay, Jack Dylan Grazer, and Emma Berman. Walt Disney Pictures and Pixar Animation Studios, 2021.

Macleod, Dianne Sachko. "The Politics of Vision: Disney, *Aladdin*, and the Gulf War." In *The Emperor's Old Groove: Decolonizing Disney's Magic Kingdom*. Edited by Brenda Ayres. Peter Lang, 2013 [2003], pp. 179–92.

Magoon, Kekla. "Our Modern Minstrelsy." *The Horn Book*, 5 June 2020. www.hbook.com/?detailStory=our-modern-minstrelsy (accessed 5 June 2020).

Makalintal, Bettina. "Awkwafina's Past Makes Her a Complicated Icon of Asian American Representation." *VICE*, 24 January 2020. www.vice.com/en/article/pkeg9g/awkwafinas-past-makes-her-a-complicated-icon-of-asian-american-representation (accessed 27 June 2023).

Maleficent. Directed by Robert Stromberg. Performances by Angelina Jolie, Elle Fanning, and Sharlto Copley. Walt Disney Pictures, 2014.

Maleficent: Mistress of Evil. Directed by Joachim Rønning. Performances by Angelina Jolie, Elle Fanning, and Chiwetel Ejiofor. Walt Disney Pictures, 2019.

Mansky, Jackie. "The True Story of Pocahontas." *Smithsonian Magazine*, 23 March 2017. www.smithsonianmag.com/history/true-story-pocahontas-180962649/ (accessed 14 May 2020).

Maslin, Janet. "Disney's 'Beauty and the Beast' Updated in Form and Content." *New York Times*, 13 November 1991. Archived at web.archive.org/web/20170305002730/https://www.nytimes.com/1991/11/13/movies/review-film-disney-s-beauty-and-the-beast-updated-in-form-and-content.html.

Mendelson, Scott. "What the Disney-Fox Deal Means for 'Avatar' and 'Star Wars.'" *Forbes*, 30 July 2018. www.forbes.com/sites/scottmendelson/2018/07/30/what-the-disney-fox-deal-means-for-avatar-and-star-wars/ (accessed 21 May 2020).

Menon, Radhika. "Stream It or Skip It: 'Sneakerella' on Disney+, a Gender-Swapped Take on 'Cinderella.'" *Decider*, 13 May 2022. decider.com/2022/05/13/sneakerella-disney-plus-review/ (accessed 4 July 2023).

Milligan, Mercedes. "'Frozen 2' Will Get Sámi Language Version." *Animation Magazine*, 19 July 2019. www.animationmagazine.net/features/frozen-2-will -get-sami-language-version/ (accessed 11 June 2020).

Mittermeier, Sabrina. *A Cultural History of the Disneyland Theme Parks: Middle Class Kingdoms*. Intellect, 2021.

Moana. Directed by Ron Clements and John Musker. Performances by Auli'i Cravalho, Dwayne Johnson, and Rachel House. Walt Disney Animation Studios, 2016.

Moon, Kat. "*Raya and the Last Dragon* Introduces Disney's First Southeast Asian Princess. Advocates Say Hollywood Representation Shouldn't Stop There." *Time*, 5 March 2021. time.com/5944583/raya-and-the-last-dragon -southeast-asia/ (accessed 28 June 2023).

Mulan. Directed by Tony Bancroft and Barry Cook. Performances by Ming-Na Wen, Eddie Murphy, and B. D. Wong. Walt Disney Feature Animation, 1998.

Mulan. Directed by Niki Caro. Performances by Yifei Liu, Donnie Yen, and Tzi Ma. Walt Disney Pictures, 2020.

Murphy, Patrick D. "'The Whole Wide World Was Scrubbed Clean': The Androcentric Animation of Denatured Disney." In *From Mouse to Mermaid: The Politics of Film, Gender, and Culture*. Edited by Elizabeth Bell, Lynda Haas, and Laura Sells. Indiana UP, 1995, pp. 125–36.

Myers, Christopher. "Young Dreamers." *The Horn Book*, 6 August 2013. www .hbook.com/?detailStory=young-dreamers (accessed 24 July 2020).

Nagle, Rebecca. "Research Reveals Media Role in Stereotypes About Native Americans." *Women's Media Center*, 18 July 2018. www.womensmediacenter .com/news-features/research-reveals-media-role-in-stereotypes-about -native-americans (accessed 3 June 2020).

Ngata, Tina. "For Whom the Taika Roars (An Open Letter to Taika Waititi)." *The Non-Plastic Maori*, 24 October 2014. https://web.archive.org/web/2017 0412193110/https://thenonplasticmaori.wordpress.com/2014/10/24/for-whom -the-taika-roars-an-open-letter-to-taika-waititi/ (accessed 21 April 2020).

Ngata, Tina, and Anne Keala Kelly. "Reclaiming Mana Moana: Dialogue." *Tangata Whenua*, 9 October 2016, syndicated 16 January 2020. ewirelessnews .com/reclaiming-mana-moana-tangatawhenua-com/ (accessed 21 April 2020; URL unavailable).

Nicklas, Pascal, and Oliver Lindner. "Adaptation and Cultural Appropriation." In *Adaptation and Cultural Appropriation: Literature, Film, and the Arts*. Edited by Pascal Nicklas and Oliver Lindner. De Gruyter, 2012, pp. 1–13.

Nsofor, Ifeanyi, and Esther Ngumbi. "Opinion: We Are Africans. Here's Our View of Beyoncé's 'Black Is King.'" NPR, 7 August 2020. www.npr.org/sections/goatsandsoda/2020/08/07/899421948/opinion-we-are-africans-heres-our-view-of-beyonc-s-black-is-king (accessed 28 June 2023).

OED Online, s.v. "authenticity." Oxford UP, March 2020. www.oed.com/view/Entry/13325.

Once Upon a Time. Created by Adam Horowitz and Edward Kitsis. Performances by Ginnifer Goodwin, Jennifer Morrison, and Lana Parrilla. ABC Studios, 2011–2018.

Onward. Directed by Dan Scanlon. Performances by Tom Holland, Chris Pratt, and Julia Louis-Dreyfus. Walt Disney Pictures and Pixar Animation Studios, 2020.

Orr, Raymond, Katelyn Sharratt, and Muhammad Iqbal. "American Indian Erasure and the Logic of Elimination: An Experimental Study of Depiction and Support for Resources and Rights for Tribes." *Journal of Ethnic Migration Studies*, 2019, vol. 45, no. 11, pp. 2078–99. doi: 10.1080/1369183X.2017.1421061.

O'Sullivan, Emer, and Andrea Immel. "Sameness and Difference in Children's Literature: An Introduction." In *Imagining Sameness and Difference in Children's Literature: From the Enlightenment to the Present Day*. Edited by Emer O'Sullivan and Andrea Immel. Palgrave Macmillan, 2017, pp. 1–25.

Pallant, Chris. *Demystifying Disney: A History of Disney Feature Animation*. Bloomsbury Academic, 2011.

Paquette, Danielle. "Beyoncé Released a Video Celebrating 'African Tradition.' Then Came the Backlash." *Washington Post*, 9 July 2020. www.washingtonpost.com/world/africa/beyonce-black-is-king-africa-backlash/2020/07/08/cfaa2dd2-c079-11ea-864a-0dd31b9d6917_story.html (accessed 28 June 2023).

Parasher, Prajna. "Mapping the Imaginary: The Neverland of Disney Indians." In *Diversity in Disney Films: Critical Essays on Race, Ethnicity, Gender, Sexuality, and Disability*. Edited by Johnson Cheu. McFarland, 2013, pp. 38–49.

Parekh, Pushpa Naidu. "*Pocahontas*: The Disney Imaginary." In *The Emperor's Old Groove: Decolonizing Disney's Magic Kingdom*. Edited by Brenda Ayres. Peter Lang, 2013 [2003], pp. 167–78.

Parody, Clare. "Franchising/Adaptation." *Adaptation*, 2011, vol. 4, no. 2, pp. 210–18. doi: 10.1093/adaptation.apr008.

Peter Pan. Directed by Clyde Geronimi, Wilfred Jackson, Hamilton Luske, and Jack Kinney. Performances by Bobby Driscoll, Kathryn Beaumont, and Hans Conried. Walt Disney Animation Studios, 1953.

Phillips, Maya. "'Hamilton,' 'The Simpsons,' and the Problem with Colorblind Casting." *New York Times*, 8 July 2020. www.nytimes.com/2020/07/08/arts/television/hamilton-colorblind-casting.html (accessed 12 July 2020).

Pinocchio. Directed by Ben Sharpsteen and Hamilton Luske. Performances by Cliff Edwards, Dickie Jones, and Christian Rub. Walt Disney Animation Studios, 1940.

Pocahontas. Directed by Mike Gabriel and Eric Goldberg. Performances by Mel Gibson, Linda Hunt, and Christian Bale. Walt Disney Animation Studios, 1995.

Pocahontas II: Journey to a New World. Directed by Tom Ellery and Bradley Raymond. Performances by Irene Bedard, Billy Zane, and Jim Cummings. Walt Disney Video Premiere and Walt Disney Television Animation, 1998.

Potter, Anna. "It's a Small World After All: New Media Constellations and Disney's Rising Star—The Global Success of *High School Musical*." *International Journal of Cultural Studies*, 2011, vol. 15, no. 2, pp. 117–30.

The Princess and the Frog. Directed by Ron Clements and John Musker. Performances by Anika Noni Rose, Keith David, and Bruno Campos. Walt Disney Animation Studios, 2009.

Purdum, Todd S. "The Slipper Still Fits, Though the Style Is New." *New York Times*, 2 November 1997. www.nytimes.com/1997/11/02/arts/television-the-slipper-still-fits-though-the-style-is-new.html (accessed 13 March 2020).

Putnam, Amanda. "Mean Ladies: Transgendered Villains in Disney Films." In *Diversity in Disney Films: Critical Essays on Race, Ethnicity, Gender, Sexuality, and Disability.* Edited by Johnson Cheu. McFarland, 2013, pp. 147–62.

Ralph Breaks the Internet. Directed by Phil Johnston and Rich Moore. Performances by John C. Reilly, Sarah Silverman, and Gal Godot. Walt Disney Animation Studios, 2018.

Raya and the Last Dragon. Directed by Don Hall and Carlos López Estrada. Performances by Kelly Marie Tran, Awkwafina, and Izaac Wang. Walt Disney Pictures and Walt Disney Animation Studios, 2021.

The Rescuers Down Under. Directed by Hendel Butoy and Mike Gabriel. Performances by Bob Newhart, Eva Gabor, and John Candy. Walt Disney Feature Animation, 1990.

Rivas, Jorge. "Russell Means Voiced the Most Powerful Scene of Disney's ' Pocahontas.'" *Colorlines*, 22 October 2012. www.colorlines.com/articles /russell-means-voiced-most-powerful-scene-disneys-pocahontas (accessed 11 May 2020).

Roberts, Shearon. "Recasting the Disney Princess in an Era of New Media and Social Movements." In *Recasting the Disney Princess in an Era of New Media and Social Movements*. Edited by Shearon Roberts. Lexington Books, 2020, pp. 3–19.

——, ed. *Recasting the Disney Princess in an Era of New Media and Social Movements*. Lexington Books, 2020.

Robinson, Joanna. "How Pacific Islanders Helped Disney's *Moana* Find Its Way." *Vanity Fair*, 16 November 2016. www.vanityfair.com/hollywood/2016/ 11/moana-oceanic-trust-disney-controversy-pacific-islanders-polynesia (accessed 21 April 2020).

Robinson, Sheila. "Latondra Newton: Chief Diversity Officer, The Walt Disney Company." 2020 Inclusion Innovation Leadership Summit. www .diversitywoman.com/innovation/portfolio_page/latondra-newton/ (accessed 18 June 2020; URL unavailable).

Rogers, Patrick. "A True Legend." *People*, 10 July 1995. people.com/ archive/a-true-legend-vol-44-no-2/. Archived at web.archive.org/web/ 20180309134623/https://people.com/archive/a-true-legend-vol-44-no-2/ (accessed 15 May 2020).

Saha, Anamik. *Race and the Culture Industries*. Polity, 2018.

Saïd, Edward. *Orientalism*. Penguin, 2003.

Sanders, Julie. *Adaptation and Appropriation*, 2nd ed. Routledge, 2016 [2006].

Sandlin, Jennifer A., and Julie C. Garlen, eds. *Disney, Culture, and Curriculum*. Routledge, 2016.

Schickel, Richard. *The Disney Version: The Life, Times, Art, and Commerce of Walt Disney*, 3rd ed. Simon & Schuster Paperbacks, 2019 [1968].

Schilling, Vincent. "The Rock's Husky Polynesian God from Disney's *Moana* Gets Mixed Reviews." *Indian Country Today*, 7 July 2016. https://ictnews .org/archive/the-rocks-husky-polynesian-god-from-disneys-moana-gets -mixed-reviews/ (accessed 21 April 2020).

Schneider, Michael. "'Heartstopper' Leads All Winners at 1st Annual Children's & Family Emmys (Full List)." *Variety*, 11 December 2022. variety.com/2022/ tv/news/childrens-family-emmys-winners-list-2023-1235456208/ (accessed 4 July 2023).

Sciretta, Peter. "Interview: *The Princess and the Frog* Directors Jon Musker and Ron Clements." *Film: Blogging the Reel World*, 21 October 2009. www .slashfilm.com/interview-the-princess-and-the-frog-directors-jon-musker -and-ron-clements/ (accessed 13 March 2020).

"She Is of a Mythical Race." *Writing with Color*, 31 December 2014. writingwithcolor.tumblr.com/post/106727327207/out-of-curiosity-do-you -consider-kida (accessed 30 May 2020).

Short, Sue. *Fairy Tale and Film: Old Tales with a New Spin*. Palgrave Macmillan, 2015.

Shotwell, Alyssa. "Awkwafina May Have Forgotten Her 'Blaccent,' but We Didn't and She Was Finally Confronted on It." *The Mary Sue*, 22 September 2021. www.themarysue.com/awkwafina-blaccent-aave/ (accessed 27 June 2023).

Simonpillai, Radheyan. "Disney Signed a Contract with Indigenous People Before Making *Frozen II*." *Now Toronto*, 19 November 2019. nowtoronto .com/movies/features/disney-frozen-2-indigenous-culture-sami/ (accessed 10 June 2020).

Sinha-Roy, Piya. "How Agrabah Was Brought to Life in Disney's Live-Action *Aladdin*." *Entertainment Weekly*, 16 May 2019. ew.com/movies/2019/05/16/ aladdin-production-design-agrabah/ (accessed 9 June 2020).

———. "How Disney Handled the Casting and Cultural Authenticity of Live-Action *Aladdin*." *Entertainment Weekly*, 21 December 2018. ew.com/movies/ 2018/12/21/disney-aladdin-cultural-authenticity/ (accessed 8 June 2020).

Sito, Tom. "Fight to the Death, but Don't Hurt Anybody! Memories of Political Correctness." *Animation World Magazine*, 1996, vol. 1, no. 7. www.awn.com/ mag/issue1.7/articles/sito1.7.html (accessed 12 May 2020).

Sleeping Beauty. Directed by Clyde Geronimi. Performances by Mary Costa, Bill Shirley, and Eleanor Audley. Walt Disney Animation Studios, 1959.

Smith, Thomas. "Celebrating 100 Years of Disney and the Wonder of Mickey and Minnie." *DisneyParks* blog, 4 January 2023. disneyparks.disney.go.com/ blog/2023/01/celebrating-100-years-of-disney-and-the-wonder-of-mickey -and-minnie/#:~:text=2023%20marks%20the%20100th%20anniversary ,hearts%20throughout%20the%20past%20century (accessed 10 July 2023).

Sneakerella. Directed by Elizabeth Allen Rosenbaum. Performances by Chosen Jacobs and Lexi Underwood. Disney Channel, 2022.

Snetiker, Marc. "Alan Menken Tells Stories Behind 7 Classic Disney Songs." *Entertainment Weekly*, 22 January 2015. ew.com/article/2015/01/22/alan -menken-disney-songs/ (accessed 28 March 2025).

Snow White and the Seven Dwarfs. Directed by William Cottrell, David Hand, Wilfred Jackson, Larry Morey, Perce Pearce, and Ben Sharpsteen. Performances by Adriana Caselotti, Lucille La Verne, and Stuart Buchanan. Walt Disney Animation Studios, 1937.

Sonoda-Pale, M. Healani. "Disney's Commodification of Hawaiians." *Honolulu Civic Beat*, 7 October 2016. www.civilbeat.org/2016/10/disneys -commodification-of-hawaiians (accessed 21 April 2020).

Soo Hoo, Fawnia. "How the 'Beauty and the Beast' Costume Designer Worked with Emma Watson to Bring a 'Modern, Emancipated' Belle to Life." Fashionista.com, 13 March 2017. fashionista.com/2017/03/beauty-and-the-beast -2017-dress-costumes (accessed 6 March 2020).

Soul. Directed by Pete Docter. Performances by Jamie Foxx, Tina Fey, and Graham Norton. Walt Disney Pictures and Pixar Animation Studios, 2020.

Stripes, James. "A Strategy of Resistance: The 'Actorvism' of Russell Means from Plymouth Rock to the Disney Studios." *Wicazo Sa Review*, 1999, vol. 14, no. 1, pp. 87–101. www.jstor.org/stable/1409517 (accessed 10 May 2020).

Tangled. Directed by Nathan Greno and Byron Howard. Performances by Mandy Moore, Zachary Levi, and Donna Murphy. Walt Disney Animation Studios, 2010.

Tarzan. Directed by Chris Buck and Kevin Lima. Performances by Tony Goldwyn, Minnie Driver, and Brian Blessed. Walt Disney Animation Studios, 1999.

Tatar, Maria, ed. *The Classic Fairy Tales*, 2nd ed. Norton, 2016 [1999].

Teverson, Andrew. *Fairy Tale.* Routledge, 2013.

Thomas, Ebony Elizabeth. *The Dark Fantastic: Race and the Imagination from "Harry Potter" to the "Hunger Games."* New York UP, 2019.

Thompson, Sydnee. "So Much Modern Slang Is AAVE: Here's How Language Appropriation Erases the Influence of Black Culture." Buzzfeed News, 7 September 2021. www.buzzfeednews.com/article/sydneethompson/aave -language-appropriation (accessed 27 June 2023).

Thuraisingam Robbins, Hannah. "Nostalgia and Escapism in *The Princess and the Frog.*" Paper presented at "StageStruck! 5: Nostalgia and the Hollywood Musical," Hybrid Conference, Carmel, IN, 16 May 2024.

Tiffin, Jessica. *Marvelous Geometry: Narrative and Metafiction in Modern Fairy Tale.* Wayne State UP, 2009.

Treasure Planet. Directed by Ron Clements and John Musker. Performances by Joseph Gordon-Levitt, Emma Thompson, and Martin Short. Walt Disney Animation Studios, 2002.

Tulk, Janice Esther. "An Aesthetic of Ambiguity: Musical Representation of Indigenous Peoples in Disney's *Brother Bear*." In *Drawn to Sound: Animation Film Music and Sonicity*. Edited by Rebecca Coyle. Equinox, 2010, pp. 120–37.

Turner, Sarah E. "Blackness, Bayous, and Gumbo: Encoding and Decoding Race in a Colorblind World." In *Diversity in Disney Films: Critical Essays on Race, Ethnicity, Gender, Sexuality, and Disability*. Edited by Johnson Cheu. McFarland, 2013, pp. 83–98.

Turning Red. Directed by Domee Shi. Performances by Rosalie Chiang, Sandra Oh, and Ava Morse. Walt Disney Pictures, 2022.

Valdivia, Angharad N. "Mixed Race on the Disney Channel: From *Johnnie Tsunami* [sic] Through *Lizzie McGuire* and Ending with *The Cheetah Girls*." In *Mixed Race Hollywood*. Edited by Mary Bettrán and Camilla Fojas. New York UP, 2008, pp. 269–89.

VanDerWerff, Emily. "Here's What Disney Owns After the Massive Disney/Fox Merger." *Vox*, 20 March 2019. www.vox.com/culture/2019/3/20/18273477/disney-fox-merger-deal-details-marvel-x-men (accessed 22 May 2020).

van Ginneken, Jaap. *Screening Difference: How Hollywood's Blockbuster Films Imagine Race, Ethnicity, and Culture*. Rowman & Littlefield, 2007.

Wabuke, Hope. "Do Black Lives Matter to *Westworld*? On TV Fantasies of Racial Violence." *Los Angeles Review of Books*, 4 June 2020. lareviewofbooks.org/article/black-lives-matter-westworld-tv-fantasies-racial-violence/ (accessed 5 June 2020).

Waking Sleeping Beauty. Directed by Don Hahn. Walt Disney Motion Pictures, 2009.

"The Walt Disney Company Pledges $5 Million to Support Nonprofit Organizations That Advance Social Justice." Walt Disney Company, 3 June 2020. thewaltdisneycompany.com/the-walt-disney-company-pledges-5-million-to-support-nonprofit-organizations-that-advance-social-justice-2/?fbclid=IwAR1Hi1nSeb5XpMKFPx4oeyGOyWsg-rnAtktWBCtCjmolKYl1CNYMg5RtMmg (accessed 17 June 2020).

Ward, Annalee R. *Mouse Morality: The Rhetoric of Disney Animated Film*. U of Texas P, 2002.

Warner, Kristen. "In the Time of Plastic Representation." *Film Quarterly*, 2017, vol. 17, no. 2, pp. 32–37.

Warner, Marina. *Once Upon a Time: A Short History of Fairy Tale*. Oxford UP, 2014.

———. *Stranger Magic: Charmed States and the "Arabian Nights."* Vintage Books, 2012.

———. *Wonder Tales: Six Stories of Enchantment.* Chatto & Windus, 1994.

Wasko, Janet. *Understanding Disney: The Manufacture of Fantasy.* Polity, 2001.

Wells, Paul. *Animation and America.* Edinburgh UP, 2002.

Whitley, David. *The Idea of Nature in Disney Animation: From "Snow White" to "WALL-E,"* 2nd ed. Ashgate, 2012 [2008].

Whitten, Sarah. "Disney Bought Marvel for $4 Billion in 2009; a Decade Later It's Made More Than $18 Billion at the Global Box Office." CNBC, 22 July 2019. www.cnbc.com/2019/07/21/disney-has-made-more-than-18-billion -from-marvel-films-since-2012.html (accessed 22 May 2020).

Wickstrom, Maurya. "*The Lion King*, Mimesis, and Disney's Magical Capitalism." In *Rethinking Disney: Private Control, Public Dimensions.* Edited by Mike Budd and Max H. Kirsch. Wesleyan UP, 2005, pp. 99–121.

Willetts, Kheli R. "Cannibals and Coons: Blackness in the Early Days of Walt Disney." In *Diversity in Disney Films: Critical Essays on Race, Ethnicity, Gender, Sexuality, and Disability.* Edited by Johnson Cheu. McFarland, 2013, pp. 9–22.

Wise, Christopher. "Notes from the *Aladdin* Industry: Or, Middle Eastern Folklore in the Era of Multinational Capitalism." In *The Emperor's Old Groove: Decolonizing Disney's Magic Kingdom.* Edited by Brenda Ayres. Peter Lang, 2013 [2003], pp. 105–14.

Wish. Directed by Chris Buck and Fawn Veerasunthorn. Performances by Ariana DeBose, Chris Pine, and Alan Tudyk. Walt Disney Pictures, 2023.

Wolfe, Patrick. *Settler Colonialism and the Transformation of Anthropology: The Politics and Poetics of an Ethnographic Event.* Cassell, 1999.

Woltmann, Suzy. *Woke Cinderella: Twenty-First-Century Adaptations.* Lexington Books, 2020.

The Wonderful World of Disney and Whitney Houston Present Rodgers and Hammerstein's Cinderella. Directed by Robert Iscove. Performances by Brandy, Whitney Houston, and Whoopi Goldberg. ABC, 1997.

Yin, Jing. "Popular Culture and Public Imaginary: Disney vs. Chinese Stories of Mulan." In *The Global Intercultural Communication Reader.* Edited by Molefi Kete Asante, Yoshitaka Miike, and Jing Yin. Routledge, 2014, pp. 285–304.

Yoshinaga, Ida. "Disney's *Moana*, the Colonial Screenplay, and Indigenous Labor Extraction in Hollywood Fantasy Films." *Narrative Culture*, 2019, vol. 6, no. 2, pp. 188–215.

Young, Helen. *Race and Popular Fantasy Literature: Habits of Whiteness*. Routledge, 2016.

Zambelich, Ariel, and Cassi Alexandra. "In Their Own Words: The 'Water Protectors' of Standing Rock." NPR, 11 December 2016. www.npr.org/2016/12/11/505147166/in-their-own-words-the-water-protectors-of-standing-rock (accessed 22 October 2024).

Zipes, Jack. "Americanization of the Grimms' Folk and Fairy Tales: Twists and Turns of History." In *Grimm Legacies: The Magic Spell of the Grimms' Folk and Fairy Tales*. By Jack Zipes. Princeton UP, 2015, pp. 78–108.

———. "Breaking the Disney Spell." In *From Mouse to Mermaid: The Politics of Film, Gender, and Culture*. Edited by Elizabeth Bell, Lynda Haas, and Laura Sells. Indiana UP, 1995, pp. 21–42.

———. *Fairy Tales and the Art of Subversion*. Routledge Classics, 2012.

———. *The Irresistible Fairy Tale: The Cultural and Social History of a Genre*. Princeton UP, 2012.

———. "Media-Hyping of Fairy Tales." In *The Cambridge Companion to Fairy Tale*. Edited by Maria Tatar. Cambridge UP, 2015, pp. 202–19.

———. *Relentless Progress*. Routledge, 2009.

<h1 style="text-align:center">INDEX</h1>